PAULINE BOTY

For Bridget Boty, who saved the paintings.

MARC KRISTAL

PAULINE BOTY

British Pop Art's Sole Sister

FRANCES LINCOLN

CONTENTS

Opposite The artist before her famous collage wall (seen in full on p.2), September 1963.

INTRODUCTION

There are no easy answers to the question of how you live in a world you want to change radically.
  – Sheila Rowbotham, *Promise of a Dream*

In October 2013, I visited an exhibition at Christie's in London called *When Britain Went Pop – British Pop Art: The Early Years.* My attendance was accidental: motivated by the rain that began to fall as I passed Christie's posh King Street venue; surprise that an auction house had mounted a show that seemingly didn't involve selling; and by the fellow stationed beside the reception desk, who when I opened the door and took a speculative look in, enjoined me to *Enter!* with the high-key gusto of a carnival barker.

When enter I did, the impact was arresting. Here were 142 artworks, created between 1948 and the end of the 1960s, by the legends of British Pop – the names I knew included Peter Blake, Richard Hamilton, Allen Jones and R B Kitaj – colourful and exuberant, sexually provocative, politically engaged and, not least, transformative. My familiarity with the period was limited. But despite my ignorance, and the passage of time, the shock of the new still thwacked its arrow home.

So lively was the environment that I initially had trouble finding my focus. Two pictures, however, drew me to a stop – both, as it happened, for the same reason. The first was David Hockney's 1962 *Cleaning Teeth, Early Evening (10pm) W11*: two abstract male figures in classic '69' position, each with a red tube of Colgate in place of a phallus, spurting writhing ribbons of toothpaste into one another's mouths.

The other sent a different sort of message. A mixed-media canvas from 1964, measuring about four-by-five feet, its midsection was consumed by a grid of male stars – Elvis, Proust, Fellini and Mastroianni, John and Ringo, Muhammad Ali – plus a matador, a Native American chief and a classical Greek head: a glam hall of fame punctuated by a luscious, unmistakably metaphoric rose. This collage was rendered with a fan's exuberance. Yet the picture's upper and lower zones arrested one's pleasure. Above, a soaring American Air Force fighter jet, opposite a helmeted pilot. Below – flanked by images of Einstein and Lenin, the irrefutable forces of physics and history – the fatal frame from Abraham Zapruder's Kennedy assassination film.

I looked at the title: *It's a Man's World I.*

Indeed. Glamour, celebrity and power, sandwiched between images of dealing, and receiving, death. What struck me in particular about the presentation of this world's double-edged nature was its answering duality: on the one hand celebratory and uncritical, on the other cold-eyed in its judgment – a work at once light-hearted and pitiless.

What both *Cleaning Teeth* and *It's a Man's World* had in common – what had commanded my attention – was the powerful presence of each artist's nature. Though nearly opposite in content and character, the two pictures were, in a sense, self-portraits – each, in its way, said *Here I am*. The difference was that David Hockney is not only world-famous as an artist, but a well-known personality, a condition that coloured my experience of his painting. Whereas the maker of *It's a Man's World I* – whose name I read off the card on the wall – was completely unknown to me: Pauline Boty.

The opportunity to come to an artist without any preconceptions is a gift: you discover the work with nothing to influence your response beyond that which you behold. Yet precisely because I'd felt such a strong sense of Boty's personality, I was curious to know more about her. So I did some research. What I discovered was remarkable.

She had been, in her day, the It Girl of Swinging London: a charter member of the British Pop Art movement and one of its very few females. After graduating in 1958 from the Wimbledon School of Art – where her beauty, allure and independence earned the title 'the Wimbledon Bardot' – Boty attended London's Royal College of Art during its fervent postwar years, going on to produce a small but indelible group of collages and paintings.

Boty was also, in that gaudy age, a particularly vivid presence. She appeared with the painters Peter Blake, Derek Boshier and Peter Phillips in Ken Russell's BBC documentary *Pop Goes the Easel;* was a dancer on the rock'n'roll television programme *Ready Steady Go!*; and worked on stage, notably at the Royal Court Theatre, and in film and television, as an actress, including a piquant appearance opposite Michael Caine in *Alfie.* Living and working in a pre-posh Notting Hill bedsit, Boty modelled for London's premier photographers, including David Bailey, Roger Mayne and Lewis Morley; her style influenced the free-spirited character of Liz, played by Julie Christie in her breakout role in *Billy Liar* (a part for which Boty herself screen-tested with its star, Tom Courtenay).

A feminist *avant la lettre*, Boty also became a social commentator, delivering incisive monologues on the BBC radio programme *The Public Ear.* 'A revolution is on the way,' the artist declared in one memorable broadcast. 'All over the country, young girls are sprouting, shouting and shaking, and if they terrify you, they mean to.' Certainly, she practised what she preached. A sophisticated artist with a nuanced understanding of sexual politics, Boty was also an unapologetic 'dolly bird' who remained uninhibited about her desires (and their fulfilment) and cheerfully posed naked with her own paintings. Derek Boshier was continually shocked by how 'upfront' she was regarding sex, which was 'so unusual at the time – blokes would be really taken aback'.

But what truly made Boty distinctive was the character of her work. In the painter's *oeuvre*, observed the art historian Sue Tate, 'a celebration of pleasure and a critical awareness of the construction of that pleasure are not mutually exclusive ... she refused to accept the apparently irreconcilable oppositions between sexual woman and serious artist, between celebration and critique, between high and low culture'. Boty's 'double vision' was decades ahead of its time and prefigured a diversity of creators, among them Caroline Coon, Tracey Emin and Madonna.

In 1965, married to the literary agent Clive Goodwin (ten days after meeting him) and finding herself unexpectedly pregnant, Boty discovered she had cancer; told that effective treatment would require an abortion, the artist chose instead to postpone therapy to save the baby, and died at age 28, four months after the birth of a daughter. As the life went, so too did the art. The bulk of Boty's *oeuvre* vanished – stashed away, first in the attic of her parents' suburban home, then a room on her brother's farm in Kent. For decades, few of her pictures were exhibited, and the artist was largely forgotten.

And then, the miracle. The art historian and curator David Alan Mellor, planning his 1993 exhibition *The Sixties Art Scene in London* at the Barbican Centre, was taken to Kent by Boty's then 26-year-old daughter, where he discovered, he said, 'this thing of massive cultural importance – suddenly the whole history of British Pop Art was different'. Whether or not this was infatuation-driven hyperbole (Mellor's crush on Boty dated from his teens), the inclusion of a handful of the artist's canvases in the Barbican show saw the rough beast of her reputation rise from obscurity and slouch towards renown: from a presentation at London's Mayor Gallery (contemporaneous with the Barbican's) to a substantive joint exhibition, at the Whitford Fine Art and Mayor galleries, five years later, to a comprehensive museum show, in Wolverhampton, in 2013. Finally, in a kind of apotheosis, Boty herself features in Ali Smith's novel *Autumn,* which was shortlisted for the Man Booker Prize in 2017.

Though the impulse to privilege Boty's story over her work was perhaps irresistible (*The Independent* titled a 1993 article, by Sabine Durrant, 'The Darling of Her Generation'), the critical response to the artist's re-emergence proved both serious and perceptive. 'London Calling', Thomas Crow's overview of the Barbican show in *Artforum*, took up Boty's cause in the second paragraph, noting that 'works like Peter Blake's *Girlie Door,* 1959, and Allen Jones' *La Sheer,* 1968, face quiet demolition at the hands of Boty's adjacent *It's a Man's World II,* 1963–65 ...

The layering of illicit vernacular with high-art references, the simultaneity of different visual codes within one canvas, and Boty's plainspoken technique predict the tactics adopted by David Salle more than ten years later.'

The artist William Packer, reviewing the 1998 Whitford-Mayor exhibition in the *Financial Times*, observed that 'the first surprise is the variety of the work, or rather the breadth of its reference, from Abstraction to photography and collage ... [S]he asserts her independence with a gently-stated but positive proto-feminism that keeps her closer to the socio-political position of older artists, such as [John] Heartfield and [Richard] Hamilton, than to the formal hedonism of her more immediate contemporaries.' Writing of the 2013 Wolverhampton show in *The Independent,* Adrian Hamilton spoke of 'works of astonishing freshness and warmth', and grasped an essential difference between the artist and other Pop painters: 'You always feel in their work a standing back by the artist from the work while he considers its composition and effect. With Boty you feel the artist herself in her emotions.'

Whatever their particular take, all recognized a creator of consequence. 'What is now clear is that the central position Pauline Boty once held within British Pop-Art ... was not simply the due deference owed to beauty and personality,' Packer declared. '[H]ers ... was a contribution quite distinctive, as much in its form as in its content.' He concluded, 'We have her work again, and it is the work that counts.' To which – 15 years later – Hamilton aptly appended: '[I]t is simply incredible that it has taken so long.'

It can be difficult to pinpoint why one chooses to write about a particular subject. While I'd like to say that my interest in Boty was entirely academic or art historical – that I wished only to relate how she evolved into the artist I so admired (an admiration that increased as I experienced more of her work) – it is also the case that, as a novelist and screenwriter, I know a good story when I hear one. Thus I saw in Boty's saga what that legendary maker of colossal Hollywood epics, Cecil B DeMille, might have described as an intimate personal story set against a backdrop of great events: a social history of broad and compelling appeal, with a singular figure – glamorous, protean and iconic – at its centre.

Yet there was, admittedly, another aspect to my interest. It had to do with the peculiar, poignant circumstances of Boty's death in 1966, her decision to postpone cancer treatment – to, in effect, privilege the life of her unborn child over her own. In the course of research, I spoke with many of the artist's friends about her choice, but it was an individual who'd never met her that came closest to providing a cogent explanation: Tariq Ali, the activist, author and filmmaker whose career Clive Goodwin supported, both as an agent and as co-founder, with Ali, of the left-wing broadsheet *The Black Dwarf*. Goodwin remained famously close-mouthed about what had happened to his wife. Yet Ali once asked him the essential question: why hadn't Clive compelled Pauline to have an abortion?

And he said, 'It was her choice, really, Tariq. It was her decision, she had to make it.' And then he said to me once, when we returned to the subject, as we did at various times, 'Suppose she'd aborted the baby, and they still hadn't been able to treat her?' It was quite primitive, in those days, treatment of leukaemia. Not too many people survived. And Clive said that that's why Pauline took the decision. That she felt, 'At least there will be something left of me, for you and others to remember when I'm gone.'

Boty's words chill the heart – for not only the artist, but her husband and daughter, too, died young and tragically. Yet her stated desire also provokes a fundamental question. None of us knows how, in a crucible in which no choice comes without heartbreak, we might react. Boty's well-documented response to learning of her pregnancy, moreover, was one of unmixed joy. And yet: why would a woman as broadly accomplished as *Pauline Boty* think she needed an heir to keep her memory alive – think it so strongly that she was prepared to produce a child who might well be motherless? Could Boty have believed that she had nothing of significance to show for her 28 years – that those many accomplishments, in so many arenas, didn't matter?

It is a question that, like the artist herself, compels us to consider how much, and how little, things have changed. Like someone removed from suspended animation, Pauline Boty has begun to emerge from the glacial ice of history into a world transformed, a world more ready to receive her message than the one in which she lived. Her story is rich in relevance: to art and politics, sex and free expression, celebrity and popular culture, the possibilities and limitations of mass media, and to the struggle to be a fully actualized woman in societies still suffering from sexual stereotyping and gender inequality.

At the same time, Boty's life, as will be seen, stands as a cautionary tale. The artist is widely regarded today as a proto-feminist, and in many ways, to be sure, she was. But her story can also be understood from an opposing perspective: as that of a woman preternaturally disposed to revolution yet undermined, not only by the culture without but, more fatally, the culture within her, the man's world she skewered so thoroughly yet had nonetheless internalized. Boty's 'double vision', her desire to embrace contradiction and contain multitudes, offers an admirable example. But no less crucial to contemplate is the double vision of a supremely confident woman who, in some small measure, may have sided against her self-belief.

Boty's story is not a usual one, and I have chosen to tell it in an unusual way: by entwining a straightforward narrative with a 'collage' of voices, drawn from conversations with the artist's family and friends; the Pop painters and Wimbledon and RCA schoolmates who were her colleagues and contemporaries; and figures from the lively and plastic arts whose lives she touched. There is also Boty's own voice, taken from a trove of writings, interviews and public statements – frank, funny and perceptive, often sharp but never strident. And, too, an array of supporting materials – book, newspaper and magazine excerpts, TV and radio transcripts, personal letters – that illuminate the artist's experience, the ways in which she was perceived (and perceived herself) and the character of the times.

To be sure: what follows is an interpretation, my own particular view of the trajectory of this singular life. I remain very well aware that mine is an interpretation that some will dispute. To those who might argue that I have compromised the artist's significance as a culture figure and creative spirit, however, I would suggest the opposite: that a critical consideration of Boty's experience reminds us of how even the strongest, most heroic individual can be buffeted by the conditions, both obvious and unconscious, of the place and time in which she finds herself.

'It cannot be repeated too often that in Art the biography should never get in the way of the work,' William Packer noted in his 1998 review of Boty's exhibition. 'But then again it sometimes happens that without the special pleading of life and circumstance to keep memory alive, the work would be forgotten altogether. And if from this it follows that the work is suddenly and comprehensively brought back to light, then biography clearly has its uses.'

What follows is not the first recounting of Pauline Boty's story, nor will it be the last. But it is my most sincere hope that this book, in this moment, has its use.

PAULINE BOTY
from *The Public Ear*, 9 February 1964

Well mums, daughters and females everywhere, have you taken a good look at yourselves recently – at the clothes in your wardrobe? Have a good look at yourself now and the other females in the room, and I bet most of you over the age of 25 somehow fade into it, somehow you're lost in your surroundings. The blend look; the 'I'm no one' look, the 'don't whatever you do look at me' look.

When you buy your clothes, what's the idea of you you have in mind? Who, if anyone, do you base yourself on? Why, oh why is it good to be so unobtrusive? Clothes should be assets to show off and enhance you, to enjoy and be enjoyed, not just something warm, comfortable and dull. But what else can we expect? One of the most photographed women in England sets standards for us all, which are, in a word, hideous. And what about those dreary, dreary country girls, who are always celebrating their engagement to some colonel's or stockbroker's son in the pages of our national magazines?

Got your shapeless sweater on? Your sat-out tweed skirt, your horsy school-girl manner and ugly, raw, upper-class voice? So this is the example of the rich who can afford really beautiful clothes. Poor retiring English females, so unsure of their sexuality, their femininity – walking around with cold folded arms like horsy, diffident men, never, never like a woman, painfully shy, incredibly unrelaxed. Your men are the ones who talk, who act, who do. You're only their wives, a nondescript appendage, a second-class citizen. You haven't even got a name of your own and at parties how apparent all this is. If the conversation turns to anything interesting at all, it's the men who are talking. The little woman won't be heard. We'll never know what she thinks and it's assumed she doesn't.

But things are beginning to change, thank goodness. Some women just don't want to be a female nonentity and it's the younger girls who are showing the way. They're not going to be squashed and certainly don't intend to be wallflowers. A revolution is on the way and it's partly because we no longer take our standards from the tweedy top. All over the country young girls are sprouting, shouting and shaking, and if they terrify you, they mean to and they're beginning to impress the world. This is what John Crosby, a well-travelled columnist of the *New York Herald Tribune* wrote the other day, about British girls: 'Take a look at these girls, striding along in their black leather boots, their capes, their fur hats, their black stockings with wild designs. They look like something out of Alexander Dumas with that challenging walk and those challenging clothes. All they need is a sword, these girls. They look like they're looking for trouble, with a "look at me" cockiness that is a thorough menace to male drivers.'

This is the image of the future, and it might frighten you but at least it is different. And anything would be a change from that cold, cardigan-clad, sexless ghost traditionally known to the world as the English woman.

Pauline, in full cry, in Ken Russell's 1962 documentary **Pop Goes the Easel**.

1

SUBURBAN

GIRL

1938–1954

'Pauline was a force of nature,' recalls the film producer Tony Garnett. 'With talent pouring out of her. And she just appeared in London, and everybody seemed to fall in love with her. She had a joy in her, a love of life. And she wasn't inhibited, she'd just fucking tell it like she thought it was, cheekily. And a self-confidence, which for a respectable middle-class suburban girl, brought up in the fifties – you don't remember the fifties, I do, and it was a fuckin' awful decade, I'll tell you – you don't know where that came from. It was only just the beginning, really, of that second feminist movement. Women had not been brought up to be assertive, or to be themselves, or to be sexual beings. Or to be free. So how she just burst open and became all those things, I don't know.'

On the night in November 1995 that she died, at the age of 29, Pauline's daughter, Boty Goodwin, read an account of her childhood to an audience of fellow students and faculty at the California Institute of the Arts. Boty began with a description of her maternal grandmother.

I remember you and your fruit cakes, thick, dense and sticky once you had cut through the icing. You were proud of them and of your appearance, and that all three of your sons had been virgins when they got married, even John, who didn't get married until he was 28. You secretly wished that he had become a priest, if only to put in a good word for the rest of the family to God or Our Lady.

You weren't interested in socializing or society. You were happy in your own world of Ian Fleming novels, Milton's Paradise Lost *and* Woman's Hour *on the BBC.*

In the evenings you would pour yourself a very large sherry and cook some of the best meals I have ever tasted in my life while listening to Maria Callas on the record player. You barely saw your husband. You always seemed to switch on the television or turn up the radio when he came in. You had had every conversation you were ever going to have with each other. The bitterness toward your own father for not allowing you to attend the Slade School of Art, because women simply didn't do that kind of thing, had long fermented into despising your husband and the more than comfortable life he had provided. But it wasn't just his conventions you were trapped in, it was your own. Which was ironic because you had always pictured yourself as elegant and elusive, almost eccentric, which you probably were in the tight affluent suburban world you inhabited.

It is a portrait of the end of possibility, of resignation. Which returns us to

Tony Garnett's conundrum: where did that 'force of nature' come from?

Pauline Veronica Boty was born at home on 6 March 1938, in the London suburb of Croydon. Her father, Albert, was a chartered accountant and, by all accounts, a caricature of a certain sort of Englishman: enamoured of sport and gardening, of Sunday roasts, port and gin, a self-made burgher with a domineering streak and, while helpless without his wife's ministrations, the absolute ruler of the suburban roost.

'When I was a child I didn't realize that the routines within my grandparents' house were any different from anybody else's,' Boty Goodwin wrote. 'It was only when friends would remark about how they loved coming to our house because we did all the things that English people "did in books" did I really think about it. Now I remember my grandfather pedantically teaching me how to make a real cup of tea, carefully mixing equal amounts of the best Earl Grey and Ceylon tea together, gently warming the tea pot before adding the tea leaves and boiling water ... When I was four years old, he sat me on his knee and said: "If you want to get on in this world you have to know the rules of cricket," which I learnt and would solemnly recite.'

'Very like the actor Bob Hoskins, if you can imagine that sort of short, round, swarthy, got all his grey matter working very well, thank you very much,' says Boty's schoolmate, Kate Terence. 'He'd definitely adopted the way of being British.' Terence's note about adoption hints at something unexpected: Albert was not, in fact, of English origin. He had been born in 1907 in Bushehr, a port in today's Iran. His father, Charles, was the Belgian captain of a merchant ship, and Albert's mother, Regina Chaia, was Persian.

'I felt quite sorry for Granddad,' says Pauline's sister-in-law, Bridget. 'His father was pirated in the Persian Gulf and then died of yellow fever, and his mother married the partner in the business. And the two boys, Granddad and his brother, were farmed off. They went to a Catholic school up in the Himalayas. I took him on the QE2 up to Norway once – he kept getting lost, and we'd hear, *Would either Bridget or Arthur Boty come to the purser's office* – and he said it reminded him of his childhood, the glaciers up there.

'When he got to about 12, 13, he was farmed off to a relation over here, him and his brother. They went to a very smart school up in Harrogate [Pannal Ash], and when he came out, the money that had been put aside for him had all gone. He had to start to do the work he was going to do, because he had to earn his living.'

Without means, abandoned by his mother in a foreign land – he never saw her again – Albert spent the next half-dozen years studying accountancy and apprenticing in the City, to which he commuted from his relation's home in Lewisham, in London's southeast. According to Adam Smith, Pauline's first

Clockwise from top left
Pauline's paternal
grandparents on
their wedding day.
Pauline's father
in Bushehr, Iran.
Following his
emigration, Albert
became a chartered
accountant and
exchanged his Belgian-
Persian origins
for an impregnable
English identity.

biographer, Albert got to know the Stewart family in his middle-teens, developing an attraction to daughter Veronica. Whether by necessity or design, he passed their house each day, in a morning suit, on the way to the train. One wonders how the Belgian-Persian immigrant, sweating to find his place, felt about Veronica's response to his peacocking. 'He used to dress up very smart – "the Accountant" – and she used to laugh at him, going down the street,' says Bridget.

Even so, it worked: they were married in 1932. Albert was 24; Veronica, 20. Arthur, Bridget's future husband, arrived before Christmas, and identical twins John and Albert Jr appeared two years later. In 1937, Albert established his own practice in nearby Croydon, and the family of five was able to move out of the Stewart home and set up on their own, at 12 Dingwall Avenue, where Pauline's appearance served as a one-day-late sixth anniversary present.

As for Albert's wife, Veronica – Nana, as she was called – 'I think "delicate" sums her up quite well,' Bridget says. 'Very Irish, red hair, with the Irish colouring. Pale skin. And she always looked smart. A real lady.' In the great *Rashomon* that is a family's history, Bridget's view of the marriage aligns imprecisely with Boty's.

'They were very happily married. I'm quite a good judge of that now, and I take my hat off to them. In those days, you were looked after by your man, weren't you? I think Nana would have liked to have done something else. But she'd come from a much poorer family, and they'd become kind of upper middle class by the end. And she quite liked that.'

Pauline had this side to her as well. More than one of her contemporaries has observed that, among British Pop artists of the period, she was one of the few who were not working class. Nor did Pauline attempt to conceal her origins, according to the television director Philip Saville, who was her lover: 'She seemed to know about the good things in life. And she liked the good things. She came from this very ordinary family, and was very proud of that.'

No surprise: her family – her father – had given her something essential. Observing Albert in the fullness of his success, it would have been easy to make assumptions about his embrace of conformity. That, surely, was how he wanted it: Albert's identity constituted an extraordinary triumph – he had fought to achieve it and, perhaps, to believe in it, to inhabit it authentically after a quarter-century of loss, displacement and uncertainty. In the catalogue for her 2013 exhibition *Pauline Boty: Pop Artist and Woman,* at the Wolverhampton Art Gallery, Sue Tate notes that Pauline 'flauntingly challenged' her 'anti-woman' father; 'she would take him on before breakfast,' her brothers remembered, resulting in 'terrible rows'. Whatever the goad, surely the urge to bait the bear arose, in part, from rage: Pauline's frustration at not being seen, by her father, for what she was. Albert's sons, virgins on their wedding nights, were not the inheritors of his narrative – that of breaking in, demanding and getting a place at the table – or, for that matter, his character. Both were claimed by his daughter.

Yet if we can see in Pauline that part of her father that was determined to be formidable in a milieu that might be disinclined to accept him – the DNA that enabled her to become one of the only female artists in a movement, not only dominated by men, but devoted to a male ethos of pinups, pop stars and wrestling – another part of her nature owed itself to fortune. 'I like chaos in a way,' Pauline would admit to the writer Nell Dunn. As well she should have: it was liberating. Chaos entered her life within a week of its beginning, in the form of the *Anschluss,* Hitler's annexation of Austria, on 12 March 1938.

'During the war years, it was bleak, really, quite bleak,' says the fashion designer Stella Penrose. 'To be a child wasn't very nice. In that, when I would call for my friends, I was never invited in the house. I was kept on the step, 'cause everybody had rations, so they didn't offer you any food.'

Two years younger than Pauline, Penrose occupies an unusual position in the artist's story. Their personal encounters were few. Yet Penrose and Pauline grew up within miles of each other, attended the same grammar school, and both went on to the Wimbledon School of Art *and* the Royal College of Art. How interested Pauline was in Penrose is unknown, but the latter remained a fascinated observer of the older girl. They also shared overlapping experiences: of the random depredations of wartime, and also a kind of obtuseness, on the part of grown-ups in those years, regarding the lived experience of children.

'We'd be out all day, and knock on doors and say, "Can we have some water?" And they'd give us a drink,' Penrose remembers. 'I mean, you wouldn't allow a child to live like that now. But there was no danger anywhere. We just felt utterly safe. But you had to go out and play away from adults. My mother had a rule, no talking at the table. Well, that's where you have a chat, having a meal! But we weren't allowed to speak at the table.'

One wonders if this state of affairs suited Pauline. Like Penrose, a free spirit with a strong will, she would have angled for a minimum of adult interference. And if peacetime might have brought supervision's return, chaos once again intervened in her favour. In 1948, Veronica was diagnosed with tuberculosis, which cost her a lung, and eighteen months: six in South Croydon Hospital, the remainder in quarantine in Pauline's bedroom, 'with a glass drain protruding from her left side', writes Adam Smith. In her 1965 book, *Talking to Women*, Nell Dunn recorded the effect on Veronica's daughter.

Pauline: *There are certain conventions that of course I'm not bound by that my father tried to vaguely impose because he had a lot of Victorian ideas. He didn't even want me to work when I left school but when I was eleven my mother got TB and the whole family became chaotic and we really had a fantastic amount of freedom, in fact we were left completely to ourselves, except that I was expected to be mum immediately and take over and cook and do stupid things, and so I haven't had a very conventional sort of life although my parents are fairly conventional. I mean compared with my brothers, my life became unconventional much earlier than theirs.*

Albert left '14-year-old John to run the household, including cooking the ceremonial Sunday lunch', Smith notes. Pauline was elsewhere. 'You were bedridden, while your teenage daughter enjoyed a freedom few girls had ever had,' Boty Goodwin wrote. 'She jived through the fifties in jazz clubs with her brothers while you convalesced at home, pale, thin, only half alive, but still with that ever present cigarette dangling from your manicured hands. When you finally recovered, so many years later, your daughter was someone you barely recognized. She had dyed blonde back-combed hair, thick black eyeliner across her eyelids and wore skirts above the knee. To her contemporaries she looked beautiful and hip, while to you she looked like a prostitute.'

Pauline wasn't quite a teenager when Veronica took sick, and it wasn't

'She jived through the fifties in jazz clubs,' wrote Boty Goodwin of her mother (far right).

'so many years' before she returned to everyday life. Yet Boty's sketch is largely accurate. What she omits is her mother's formative relationship with Albert Jr and John, who called their podgy sister 'Porky Pauline'.

Pauline: *My brothers always tortured me fantastically and in some ways probably – I mean they probably helped to make me what I am an awful lot but they used to torture me 'til I was in such a rage that I would pick up anything to kill them, you know, and this was their whole point of doing it, you see, to get me to this point where I was just a screaming maniac.*

'Arthur always used to say he had to defend Pauline against the twins,' Bridget recalls. 'They ganged up on her.' 'She felt bullied by them, that was the impression I got,' says the fashion designer Celia Birtwell, for a time Pauline's flatmate. 'She was quite brave and quite game to stand up to them, and I think that came through in her nature. Pauline was very defiant. That might have been why.' Adds the painter Caroline Coon: 'It's exhausting, though, darling. And heartbreaking. And traumatic.'

The extent of that trauma figured in the chat with Dunn. That interview, the first of nine in the book, is today largely remembered for a single passage.

Pauline: *I used to think that I had an ugly cunt you see. I don't now …
It has a very good basis you see, because when I was very little surrounded by my*

brothers and everything, who kept yelling 'Shut up, you're only a girl.' I wanted to be a boy. I used to pull – you know that sort of skin you have – I used to pull it you see and I slightly deformed it to make it sort of longer and so I used to spend all my time when I went to bed with someone thinking 'They'll find out.' But now I've got sort of free and easy about it.

To Dunn, Pauline also admitted something else: though her seizing of independence and combative defiance forged her character, there was an emotional flip side to the constructive chaos of Veronica's TB.

Pauline: *I began getting terrible depressions really after my mother, I mean I began to get these ridiculous depressions without good reason ... I might be thinking this wrongly but it seems to me that – I think that up to then my life had been fairly sort of happy in one way ... I'm sure I didn't get big weepy depressions until I was about eleven. But I got all sort of things, I got a terrible stammer.*

In a July 1962 profile in the *Daily Herald*, 'Pauline Talked Her Way to the Top', occasioned by her first dramatic role on television, Pauline's impediment forms the purplish lede. 'The shy little girl found shopping a nightmare – for she was painfully conscious of her stammer. She would hand in her mother's shopping list, her big blue eyes full of tears in case somebody spoke to her.' 'Sometimes when I saw that glassy, embarrassed look creep into people's eyes as I struggled to get my words out, I was tempted to give up,' our heroine admits. 'But,' we are assured, 'Pauline Boty had courage.'

The tabloid melodrama cannot suppress a truth: that soldiering on in the face of childhood trauma – the loss (even temporary) of a parent or parents, the shattering of a sense of security and subsequent destabilization – demands resilience and, indeed, courage. But as Pauline's revelations remind us, such occurrences leave a mark. They did so on Albert, then his daughter; and in the end, they did so on Boty.

In 1949, the year following the onset of Veronica's illness, Pauline began her first term at Wallington County School for Girls. The family had moved twice since setting up on Dingwall Avenue, initially to a place near the Croydon airfield (counterintuitive, as it was a Luftwaffe target), then to a four-bedroom semi-detached residence at 108 Beddington Gardens in Carshalton, four miles from Croydon and a short walk from school.

'I started there in 1950,' Penrose remembers. 'It was such a shock to me after junior school – it was enormous, it had something like 600 children, and long marble corridors. I was terrified of the place. We'd move from class to class, and you weren't allowed to speak in the corridor. So I spent a great deal of time sitting in the entrance hall because I'd been naughty and spoken. I was a kind of awkward child who was always in trouble.'

Not so Pauline. 'She was the wild one,' Penrose says. 'She had this huge pile of blonde hair, and she was utterly outrageous. She found everything terribly funny, she spent a lot of time laughing. Thought it was all ridiculous, which it was, all those little rules at school were just ridiculous. She'd have an insolent stare about her. She just wasn't going to bow down to any of their rules, or do anything they said.

'I was a tomboy, so my wildness was about climbing trees. I didn't have any wildness of a sexual nature. Which she had. In abundance. She just oozed sexuality. And people would talk about her. Everybody would always talk about what *Pauline Boty* was up to. The first thing I can remember, it must have been when I was about 16 – I think it was '55 or '56 – my friend had seen her at Carshalton Public Hall on New Year's Eve, and she'd worn *black stockings*! Well, no one wore black stockings, so it was, "Ahhh, Pauline Boty was in black stockings!"'

Pauline began her studies at Wimbledon in 1954, so by the time she was thrilling the Carshalton locals with her hosiery, she'd moved on as an artist and individual. But while at Wallington, Pauline appeared in a production of Sheridan's 18th-century comedy *The School for Scandal,* and Penrose's memory of her performance 'as some kind of tart' remains her most vivid. 'She was brilliant, absolutely brilliant,' she says. 'She burst out of her body, she burst out of whatever she was. She kind of overflowed, the life poured out of her. I wonder now if she knew she hadn't got long to live. Do you know? Because she had that incredible electricity, and life in her. And onstage it just came right across. It was marvellous. But also shocking. Because she was so uninhibited, and so alive.'

It is indeed shocking to bear witness to an uninhibited display of the life force, especially when it comes from a suburban accountant's daughter in her middle teens. Yet it offers an answer to Tony Garnett's question. *Pauline Boty* arose from a highly particular fusion of character and circumstance: a personality naturally inclined towards indomitability, freed from the constraints of convention, then steel-tempered by sibling combat so extreme that she resorted to genital self-mutilation rather than accept that she could be in any way traduced. The electricity and lack of inhibition witnessed by Penrose in the most mundane of contexts – a grammar-school play – was, too, a harbinger of things to come: Pauline's willingness to risk misunderstanding or ridicule, her desire to be taken on her own terms no matter the set-up. Manifest in her stammer was the spectre of depression; whether or not, in the end, the condition defeated her depends on how one interprets this story. Yet on her ruthless independence – even facing her own mortality – Pauline never reneged. As yet it was latent. But on the cusp of entering Wimbledon, it was all there.

Pauline: *I think of the present. Not much about the future. Well only in terms of sort of like I found myself sort of living my life as though I'd probably only got a few more years left to live – because the bomb was going to drop and I found this terribly exciting – not the bomb but living for today.*

'What had gone so wrong?' wrote Boty Goodwin. 'You had tried to mold my mother so perfectly, giving her paints and pencils, encouraging her to draw ... You had envisaged her attending art school to paint perfectly rendered portraits and still lives, then marrying someone sensible and solid, but she had very different ideas ... '

Pauline's objective was postgraduate study at London's Royal College of Art; aware that Wallington would not help her cause, she submitted a portfolio of artworks to Wimbledon School of Art and received a scholarship. 'Her father would have preferred her to sit her A-levels and embark on some more solid profession,' Smith writes, 'but was always putty in Pauline's hands.'

It is unlikely that Pauline's desire to go to Wimbledon was the exclusive outcome of her mother's ambitions. Equally improbable is the notion that Albert's acquiescing to his daughter's desires brought him joy. Did Nana twist Granddad's arm into letting Pauline go to art school? 'Very much so,' says Bridget. 'Pauline got on well with Nana, whereas she really had to fight Granddad. But once Pauline got Nana on her side, Granddad was done for. Nana knew exactly how to get round him.'

'She was going to art school,' Boty wrote. 'She was going to do the things that your father hadn't allowed you to do.'

Yet as her daughter's memoir observes – and though Pauline did produce artworks in various genres, among the most evocative of which is a self-portrait painted at about 16 – Pauline's objective, to the extent that she had thought it through, was not the sort of artistic career Veronica had in mind. In the summer of 1954, mother and daughter travelled on the *Queen Mary* to the United States, for an extended visit with Veronica's brother and his family in Ohio (plausibly making Pauline, in Adam Smith's estimation, the first British Pop artist to visit Pop's mecca, America). Following their return, Pauline began her Intermediate studies, and with them came a change of nickname: from 'Porky Pauline' to 'the Wimbledon Bardot'.

A pen-and-ink self-portrait, from a 1955 sketchbook (**above**), reveals a more assured and serious Pauline than the dowdy, tentative teen who sailed to America on the **Queen Mary** the previous year (**right**).

2

WIMBLEDON
BARDOT

1954–1958

A founding member of the Temperance Seven, the Royal College of Art's 'trad jazz' house band, the production designer Philip Harrison enrolled at Chelsea School of Art in 1952. 'In those days there was a wonderful system in England of art schools,' he recalls. 'Quite often, people really were useless for anything else, had probably been totally un-academic, failed as pupils on normal schooling, but had a modicum of talent. Every town, even quite small market-size towns, had their own art schools, so it gave people space, time, to find out if they could do anything. There were no fees. We were taught by practising artists. We didn't know how lucky we were.'

For Stella Penrose, the appeal was simpler: 'It was a whole other world. Doors opened for me and I loved it.' Penrose, who entered Wimbledon three years after Pauline, precisely fits Harrison's profile: she'd been struggling to find her métier. What she discovered, at the campus on Merton Hall Road, was a kind of fever dream, of freedom, camaraderie and creativity.

'I'd always been considered odd, and even people who liked me thought I was strange,' she says. 'But directly I got to art school, there were people who were just like me. I remember my friend Sue at dinner. We were eating, and she said, "God, I'm so *greedy*." And I looked at her, my eyes opened wide. That she could *admit* to being greedy and it was fun and all right!

'Oh, and we had this man model. And he was *so fit*. He would hold the most difficult poses for us. He only read one book. He said, "I don't need any other book, Emerson is all I need." There were lots of strange people like that. People who didn't want to fit in with a job and offices and things. But found a way of earning a living, like this man did.'

'We were doing Anatomy, Life Drawing, Composition,' recalls the graphic designer Richard Hollis, who began at Wimbledon in 1955. 'You had to do Lettering. You learned how printing worked, you prepared the lithographic plate or stone. The whole process of making was quite important.'

If the curriculum remained comprehensive, the atmosphere was laissez-faire. 'We'd have specific classes, but if you were working on something, you didn't have to go,' Penrose relates. 'No one was really hard on us. And hardly anybody taught us, you just got on with it yourself. At break time, you'd sit on the lockers and talk. In a sort of angst. Where it feels like the very air is tickling your skin, do you know? That sort of incredible ennui that kind of catches teenagers. Where they're kind of thinking, and kind of miserable, and it's delicious. It was paradise. Just paradise.'

Opposite Pauline at art school, circa 1958.

And, too, a moment of tension, a sea change. In many schools, as Adam Smith observes, 'The younger staff were just starting to upset the old order,' but the operative word is *just*: if Penrose found Wimbledon a liberation, the more experienced students discovered only the freedom to look back. 'I was there for 18 months – I left because I wasn't learning anything,' says Hollis, who'd completed a year at Chelsea and two years' National Service prior to enrolling. 'The atmosphere was very old-fashioned, extremely bourgeois in general attitude. The principal, Gerald Cooper, was this person who, really, painted like the 17th-century Dutch painters. What I remember most about him was that he made a painting for an advertisement for a room deodorant called Airwick. He painted this, well, it was like a Dutch still life with flowers. And in front of it was this Airwick bottle painted in by a commercial artist.'

Yet there was one department at Wimbledon – thanks to the individual at the head of it – in which the New was ascendant. 'The course to get the National Diploma in Design [NDD] was four years,' Hollis explains. 'The first two years you were working towards something called the Intermediate examination in Arts and Crafts. Then after the Intermediate exam, you specialized. And Pauline and my friend Gillian Wise, they went into Stained Glass, simply because it seemed to be curious, that being a very antique medium, it had in fact the most modern outlook, because of Charles Carey. People were in awe of him. They found him so much a breath of fresh air.'

Charles de Vic Carey arrived at Wimbledon in 1955, taking the reins of the Stained Glass department from the more traditional tutor Barry Wilkinson and transforming its character, thanks to his view of art and teaching and, no less significantly, his persona. 'Virtually all the other staff were "prewar", if you know what I mean,' says the stained-glass artist Ray Bradley, who began his studies in 1953. 'Older. Mature. Solid. Charles didn't seem like a tutor at all. He was like one of us.'

'I suppose that's how people did relate to me,' Carey acknowledges. 'What was I, 25, 26? A friend of mine said, "When I first saw you I thought you were one of the students."' 'Barry Wilkinson was very precise technically, which was a good thing, 'cause Charlie wasn't,' Bradley says. 'Charles was sort of, I won't say slaphappy, but he was cavalier about the technical side. When Charles came, he used to cook pies in the kiln.'

Carey's own artistic journey began in his teens, at London's short-lived Anglo-French Art Centre. 'A painter called Alfred Green, who was half-French, bought it as a studio for himself, but decided to use it as an art school,' Carey says. 'He had lots of contacts in Paris, for a whole load of artists. And every month he would invite a different one to come to the school, and wander amongst the students, talking to them, and have an exhibition. The first exhibition was these Picasso prints and Rouault and all that. Modern art was a discovery to me – yes, it was a revelation.'

Following his National Service, Carey's aesthetic *coup de foudre* led him to study at Wimbledon, then the Royal College of Art, where – finding the Stained Glass department's work more stimulating than that of the Painting school – he chose to pursue the former. This was followed by a French government scholarship to Paris, and an apprenticeship with the influential etcher Johnny Friedlaender, whose studio mate, Edmond Desjobert, was the printer of choice for some of France's legendary artists. 'There were all these lithographic stones, and they had names on the back like Picasso, Matisse. You were a bit wary that when you were working, somebody might come looking over your shoulder and you might find it was Braque.' Carey's Continental sojourn came to more than good stories. Gwyneth Berman, who in 1978 made Pauline the subject of her MA dissertation at Sussex University, notes that Carey 'absorbed established European trends in art, and on his return to England they became an integral part of his course'.

'Charles came back to teach,' says Bradley. 'And we didn't want to follow the rather stolid and old members of staff anymore. Because we had this *young guy*.'

Pauline, whose Intermediate studies focused on Lithography, initially pursued a National Diploma in Painting, 'in a department', according to Berman, 'dominated by the Stanley Spencer vein of realism and flower painting, which she found boring and unimaginative'. But in Carey, Pauline recognized a compatriot: someone who followed, not a set path, but his nose. Certainly she wanted to paint. But at 18, Pauline had sufficient maturity to understand that, while learning the craft was important, no less so was learning how to lead an artist's life – the mentality, not the medium, was the message. Carey represented a piece of luck, and as was Pauline's wont, she grabbed it: switching, in 1956, from Painting to Stained Glass. It was, arguably, the most important choice of her creative life.

'They were doing semi-realist type pictures, totally using a medieval technique and that sort of thing,' Carey relates. 'And I thought, "This is too dull for words." On the first day, I said, "You're grown up now, you haven't got a lot of time to start producing something original." And that was really how it happened.'

Though Berman ascribes Carey's methods, in part, 'to the principles of the Bauhaus in which the interests of the students determined the direction' of the classwork, 'I had no formal system of teaching,' the tutor says. 'I just did what I'd had for myself, when I went to the Anglo-French. Just learning by talking and absorbing what people were thinking and exchanging ideas.' On Bradley, the effect was transformative: 'Charles was an amazingly good teacher, because he didn't teach. He *sowed seeds.* He would come along, and chat away, but not telling you what to do.

Opposite
Charles Carey's
influence is evident
in one of Pauline's
early stained-glass
efforts.

Right
**Untitled (Self-Portrait
with Cat)**, circa 1957,
lithograph,
26 × 36.8 cm

Below
**Untitled (Notre
Dame)**, circa 1957,
lithograph,
59.4 × 44.5 cm

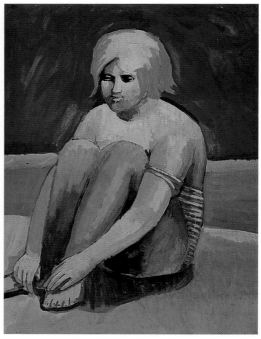

Clockwise from top left
Nude in Interior,
oil on hardboard,
60 × 50.2 cm

Untitled (Girl on the Beach),
circa 1958–59,
watercolour
on paper,
38.5 × 48.5 cm

Untitled (Still Life with Paint Brushes),
circa 1959–61,
watercolour with
gold and bronze
gilt paint,
50 × 40.2 cm

And then two or three weeks later, you'd say, "Charles, I had a good idea, I thought I would do" ... and he would just smile. Because that was the seed he'd sown.'

Though a modernist influence entered postwar stained glass in the form of abstraction, Carey viewed it as insufficiently radical. Instead, he sought to liberate his students' creativity by insisting they develop designs inspired by nontraditional sources. 'I gave them projects that were quite outside the things that glass was usually designed for,' Carey explains. 'I'd say, "Here's this very rich bloke and he's got a swimming pool, and he wants stained-glass windows round the edge." And I gave them the plan of the place and photographs or drawings.' Along with windows that drew on the *Illustrated London News* and *Punch*, the comic strips *Beano* and *Dandy*, and very vivid (and very Pop) advertising imagery, Carey encouraged more esoteric pursuits. According to Berman, 'They had to base a design on the poems of García Lorca in order to examine the connection between words and imagery.'

Perhaps the most potent – and, for Pauline, indelible and lasting – influence came from collage. 'One of the first things I did was to get them all to do work with collage materials that they had to find in the street,' Carey told Berman in 1978. 'There was a sort of rule that they could not choose it – it had to be found. When they had made their collages, I got photostats made six or seven feet high and then got them to work directly using the collage as the source, copying it as closely as they could so that they could not make stained-glass-type decisions that would prejudice or limit them.'

Pauline's interpretation of Bonnard's 1936 **Nude in the Bath: Untitled (Girl in Bath)**, circa 1957, watercolour on paper, 51.5 × 37 cm

Few of Pauline's Wimbledon efforts have survived (Carey had a portfolio of them, pinched from his office and never recovered). But she was a prolific collagist at the Royal College and afterwards, and the technique strongly influenced her approach to painting. Likely this arose from Carey's own leap of understanding: that converting an artwork from one medium to another could enrich, intensify or alter its impact and meaning.

'If you made a collage, and then turned it into stained glass, you got a very new and immediate sense of transformation,' Carey explains. 'Just as in a way medieval glass was talking in its own language of its time, and people all dressed in the clothes of the period, suddenly here was stained glass dressed in the clothes of *its* period. If you think about Pop artists, if you took their work, like Roy Lichtenstein, and turned it into stained glass, it would work very well. And that was the time when Pop Art was beginning to arrive. At the Royal College, I'd done windows influenced by Matisse, Chagall. Pauline was very responsive to that – that combination of French painting of the period, Pop Art and influences from what we use every day.'

'Artists like Matisse and Léger provided [Pauline] with the impetus for the technical side of her stained-glass work, particularly in the windows of Audincourt and Vence,' Berman observes. Similarly, 'It was during these years that she first became attracted to France and all things French – she smoked French cigarettes, saw French films, took French magazines like "PARIS MATCH" and became very involved with the French way of life,' which included frequent Parisian sojourns and, via Carey, an introduction to Friedlaender, with whom she studied etching.

'We all went together to exhibitions, travelled around the country looking at windows in cathedrals and things,' Carey recalls. 'We became a very close-knit group.' Energized by their tutor and one another, Wimbledon's five stained-glass students – the others were Tony Attenborough and Anna Lovell – were immensely prolific and, Berman reports, put together frequent in-school exhibitions. None of which precluded fun and games. In her 1993 article about Pauline in *The Independent*, Sabine Durrant writes that Carey 'remembers walking into the stained-glass room to find his students jiving to Buddy Holly and dressing up in each other's clothes. And the end of the term ... he found 20 individual shoes under the easels.' 'They were generally creative people,' Carey says. 'I was trying to teach them to be artists, and find their own way. I never imagined that any of them would stick with stained glass, really. Ray Bradley was one of the few.'

As well as the enormity of his impact, Bradley also remembers Carey's then-wife, Jennifer. 'They were a very fantastic couple, we just looked with open mouths,' he says. 'They lived in this house in Putney with a garden down to the river on the south side.'

'We did, that's right,' Carey says. 'Deodar Road. There was a woman there called Joan Howson, and she did lots of stained glass, especially restorations. Joan had two houses that she joined together, and she gave us a ground-floor flat.' Students were encouraged to join informal Sunday life-drawing classes where, Berman relates, they were introduced to the Pop artists Richard Smith, Robyn Denny, and the man who would become Pauline's friend, mentor and influence, Peter Blake.

'It was a nice place to live, and paint, and to have big parties,' Carey says. 'It was before the age of dope. When that suddenly hit, in about 1962, the art school, it was like going through a haze of dope. We had pre-dope parties. We used to buy terrible wine, that was the main ingredient. I don't know how we survived it.'

Pauline's work ethic was absolute. Yet she would not have become known as the Wimbledon Bardot if she'd confined herself to artistic practice – indeed, given her nature, it is unlikely that she could have.

Pauline: *I've been fairly lucky in that I'm pretty attractive to men because I have a – quite a sexual sort of quality but along with a thing that's kind of like, Oh a happy dumb blonde you see.*
Nell: *How do you have the happy dumb blonde part?*
Pauline: *But I do have a happy sort of thing and under certain circumstances I can be extraordinarily dumb!*

'She was a flibbertigibbet,' says Richard Hollis.
'The trouble with Pauline was, she was very good-looking,' Bradley recalls. 'Very good-natured, and had a lovely sort of little giggle. She used to sit on the very tall lockers we had down the corridors, and at the time, it was frilly skirts, and lots and lots of underskirts. She used to sit up there with all this frill and froth.' 'That changed into tight black trousers later on,' Hollis says. 'That was Pauline's style, that was her personality. She and Gillian came to my mother's home, and my mother was appalled by Pauline's silver shoes – a "good-time girl".

'Pauline was physically very attractive, though I found her over-lush, you could say,' Hollis adds. 'I don't know if you'd call it pushy, you can't say exactly frivolous, but she was one of those extreme extroverts. She needed an audience, really.'

His view is not unique. 'I remember some student being very cheeky with her and saying, "Why do you wear all that lipstick, Pauline?"' Carey says. 'And she said, "To kiss you with!" And he fled the canteen. She was flamboyant, baroque. Everybody would have known who she was.'

'I don't think she was ambitious,' Hollis concludes. 'She wanted to be arty.'

Yet behind this judgment lies an awareness that there was more to Pauline than frill and froth. Ironically, the vehicle for his insight was the person Hollis perceived as Pauline's opposite: her Stained Glass classmate, the future British Constructivist Gillian Wise. 'Gillian was the person who really was a much more particular friend of mine,' Hollis says. 'She was more restrained. And certainly more intellectual, more interested in ideas having to do with art. I went with her to visit people in Paris, concrete artists and that sort of thing, which was just not Pauline's cup of tea at all.'

Nonetheless, Hollis understood the basis of their kinship. 'You could say that it was feminist. There was a finishing-school element to art schools then. Many girls were just hanging around waiting to find the right man. If they came from middle-class families, and weren't academically very endowed, they would tend to take art school as the soft option. While Pauline and Gillian had boyfriends, they were very free-spirited, very liberal-minded. They had an outlook of being themselves.'

Though Pauline embraced her flibbertigibbet side, she remained well aware of its pitfalls, and leery of being misperceived as a kind of outsized parade float of flagrant eroticism. Sue Tate quotes Pauline's classmate Beryl Cotton: '[S]he always had a bit of a hang-up about the position of women, she felt women were badly treated by men ... women should fight back, should be more than just sex symbols, should be able to do more and achieve more.' And, according to Cotton, Pauline was 'very ambitious. Even at that age, she would say, "Look at all these other students, they are just here filling in time 'til they get married ... That's not what I want."'

Charles Carey concurs. 'She didn't feel she had to belong to somebody else. She could take her place equally in the world, as a person and a painter. She was quite strong on that.'

Richard Hollis picked up on this despite himself. After departing Wimbledon, he only saw Pauline once more; her work was not, as he himself might have put it, his cup of tea. Yet encountering it after the artist's death, Hollis grasped the essence. 'It's direct, energetic, and I think that's how she was,' he admits. 'In a way, she was what she painted: she expressed her personality in both herself in relation to other people, and in relation to the work. Most artists are extremely, how would you say? Are neurotic, divided personalities, haunted by self-criticism. Pauline was to a degree self-critical, but not to the extent that it would undermine her confidence. Her work looks quite confident, which is what irritates me about it.'

Pauline was open about her belief that women had been hard done by, she wasn't going to be distracted by boys less talented and original, who couldn't hold their own. But that didn't preclude the desire to be intimate with someone.

When asked why he thought Pauline had switched from Painting to Stained Glass, Carey's reply doesn't touch upon the difference between the departments. 'She probably liked the look of me,' he says. 'I liked the look of her, too. Yes, it was probably a combination of those things.'

'She was having an affair with the man who ran the Stained Glass department,' says Stella Penrose. 'There was a school next door, and we used to go into their playing fields and lie on the grass. And I can remember her lying on the grass, and necking with him. And he was *married*, so it was a really shocking thing for someone to do. I was very prudish. We were all aghast. And she just thought it was funny.'

'That's not true,' Carey counters. 'I knew that Pauline had plenty of affairs, she was very attractive, and all that. But I wasn't sufficiently attracted to push it in that direction. And anyway I was her teacher. Those relationships are always problematical.'

The facts will always remain in dispute. But perhaps the most profitable pursuit isn't The Truth, but rather a consideration of what such a liaison – so commonplace then, so condemned today – might have meant.

'So I am a student at Central School of Art,' remembers Caroline Coon, seven years Pauline's junior. 'I'm 20, I've sweated blood and tears to get to art school. I'm being brought up on Gombrich's *The Story of Art*, I have been taught for two years by male artists who've never mentioned a woman artist, except Angelica Kauffman [Swiss, 1741–1807], who is mentioned in the most poisonously derogatory terms. So [Pop artist] Derek Boshier is a teacher at Central who takes a shine to me. And I made the decision to become his lover. In a way, that was the only way I was going to be able to benefit from his experience and his intellectual interests. So it was wonderful for me.'

Teachers sleeping with students, especially in the arts, is an old story. Yet as Coon observes, and particularly in the years predating the feminist movement, such unequal relationships could be conduits to knowledge: erotic, but also creative and intellectual. The difference between what Coon describes and Pauline's situation is that women artists were *not* disparaged in Carey's department: the female Stained Glass students outnumbered the males, and Carey distributed his wisdom without favour. If an affair took place, perhaps Pauline benefitted, as did Coon, transactionally. But there was something else to be gained, and while some of that surely was lovemaking beyond the abilities of Wimbledon's pimply *vitelloni*, one suspects that the key to it was Charles's wife, Jennifer – 'the most important factor in Pauline's work', Peter Blake told Berman in 1978.

Jennifer was, at the time, producing collages 'strongly influenced by Schwitters', Berman relates, 'that used found materials, together with painted figures and letters', some of which she would 'transfer to a print form', prefiguring

Pauline's technique of combining actual and 'painted' *trompe l'oeil* collages within a single artwork. As would Pauline, Jennifer also worked in theatre – eventually at the National, where she created masks, costumes and sets for *The Tempest* (1974), *Bow Down* (1977) and *Animal Farm* (1984) – pursuits which Berman credits with sparking Pauline's interest in making dolls.

Moreover, '[Pauline] and Jennifer would sit in front of a mirror transforming their faces with make-up,' Charles Carey remembers, 'starting off with a completely white face, and then colouring it in.' This, too, played a role in Pauline's development. 'The significance of masks to disguise the face and its expressions proved to be a dominant theme in Boty's later work,' Berman observes, 'whether in the "mask" of sunglasses, or the "mask" of a public image or the "mask" of a separate identity. The understanding she has of how these different disguises operate stems largely from her own fascination with role playing, which she began to develop at this time.'

And at the macro level: if there is a tradition of teachers sleeping with students, there is another, just as long, of young people idealizing couples. Were not Charles and Jennifer – talented, encouraging, unconventional – a better example than Albert and Veronica? Tate quotes Jennifer as saying that Pauline was 're-establishing what kind of a woman one could be'. Might not the re-establishment of womanhood extend to reinventing the family? Especially as the Careys offered that most seductive of possibilities: freedom, coupled with stability – precisely the opposite of what she'd known at home.

Whatever the erotics, Pauline's involvement with the Careys fits with a Wimbledon experience that seems exceptionally fruitful. She spent her days among Stella Penrose's 'like-minded people', in an atmosphere devoted to creative and personal expression. Her drawings and paintings progressed from those of a conventionally minded, able beginner to colourful and expressionistic pictures influenced by Picasso, Bonnard and other of the moderns. Following Carey's lead, Pauline came to the recognition that stained glass, being a version of collage, could be applied to pop cultural subject matter, and to political, sexual and surreal abstractions like those of Schwitters and Max Ernst (both of whom became influences).

She thrived in an autonomous unit that promoted independent thought, cross-disciplinary study and the making of connections from which one's own voice might emerge. In her female-majority department, encouraged by a tutor who believed in gender equality, Pauline cemented her conviction that she had the right to do what she did. And her engagement with the Careys – separately and together – revealed that Pauline, having outflanked her father and outfought her brothers, was prepared to exchange convention for an intimate paradigm that fed her appetite for friendship and inspiration, as well as (perhaps) sex: an already well-developed instinct for what would give her strength, and a lack of compunction about pursuing it.

With Carey's encouragement, Pauline submitted work to the yearly Young Contemporaries exhibition, held at the Royal Society of British Artists (RBA) galleries in London; her painting, *Nude in Interior*, appeared in the 1957 show (in which Robyn Denny, Richard Smith and Bridget Riley also featured), reinforcing her confidence as she applied to the Royal College. 'Wimbledon was a strong RCA feeder, particularly for Stained Glass,' Adam Smith writes. 'In a sparsely populated subject, Carey's students stood out a mile and typically occupied two of the five places on offer each year.'

One of which went to Pauline. She was accepted at the Royal College of Art, her studies to begin in the autumn of 1958.

'Granddad did well,' says Bridget, who with her husband started a dairy farm in Kent. 'The accountancy made him money to look after his family, to the manner he wanted them to become accustomed. They had a boat up on the Norfolk Broads, and the family had a good life. Arthur was dyslexic but he got to grammar school by private tutoring. Granddad set everybody up. Arthur would say to you, "I worked on the dustbins to buy this farm." But it was all his father's money.'

Describing her father-in-law, Bridget's adjective is 'chauvinistic'. Predictably, 'Pauline and Granddad were at each other's throats most of the time. Granddad didn't approve of her going to art college. But when she wanted anything, he came up with the money. I expect Nana wouldn't have spoke to him if he hadn't a done it. Nana said, "That's what she wants, that's what she's going to do." He didn't understand, he didn't understand at all. But he gave Pauline the same as he gave the others.

'You can't put our way on other people. It's like when you go abroad and the animals are being abused. You can't blame the people that are abusing them, that's the way they do it. He didn't think it was right for Pauline to go to art college.'

3

AT THE ROYAL COLLEGE

OF ART

1958–1961

Part 1: 'The place'

'You're writing about a girl who grew up in the fifties and died in the sixties,' observes the political cartoonist Nicholas Garland. 'And life was *so different* then. London was such a different city. It's very hard to get across.' To poet Christopher Logue, the ravaged metropolis 'was sad. A place of war-damaged, unpainted houses, cellars filled with water, stairs and windows open to the sky ... weed-covered bomb sites, mean "caffs", miles apart from one another and almost always empty'. Yet for Garland, it was precisely this condition that set the stage for magic. 'When there *was* something that was bright and dashing and full of life, it stood out like anything – the impact was colossal,' he says. 'Those days when it was boring, the paradox was that it was so exciting.'

And inspiring. 'The Pop Art movement was a light-hearted response to this, which intended really to replace everything with something new,' notes the painter Gerald Laing. 'It must be very hard for you to understand in this day and age, but if you had been surrounded by peeling posters from 20 or 30 years before all your youth, and somebody puts up a new one that's brightly coloured and painted and not in any way damaged, and advertising something new and exciting, you respond rather well to it.'

'I don't think that anyone who wasn't there can understand how exciting that made life,' Garland says. 'London was very beautiful – it wasn't just being young, it actually was. And so was Pauline.'

Pop Art's impact can be as hard to imagine as the *jolie laide* London of the 1950s. Yet, as Laing suggests, the movement emerged as an unexpected antidote to the funk of postwar Britain. The style incubated, in large measure, at London's Royal College of Art – which, when Pauline began in the autumn of 1958, was in the fervid midst of a Golden Age.

'The Royal College had a revolutionary liveliness to it that I don't think other colleges had at that time,' says Pauline's Stained Glass classmate William Wilkins. 'Partly of course most of the students would have been postgraduate so more confident, with more developed ideas. I think it meant that the College was outstandingly creative at this point.' 'It was an incredible sort of open place where it was hard to distinguish between the artwork and other things that people were doing,' affirms Ken Baynes, also in Stained Glass. 'And I think, with great wisdom, Robin Darwin encouraged this atmosphere.'

The moustache that roared: RCA principal Robert Vere 'Robin' Darwin.

Great-grandson of the famous Charles, the painter Robert Vere Darwin – called Robin by one and all – was made principal in 1948 and, according to Neil Parkinson, the RCA's Archives and Collections Manager, 'was horrified by what he found when he came to the College. He thought it was just totally on its knees.'

'It was a shock to find stamped on the drawing desks the date 1870,' Darwin recounted in a lecture, 'to find only one sewing machine in the Dress Section, and much of the weaving equipment dating from the early 19th century ... There were virtually no records of any sort, no paintings or other works by former students, and barely any of those memorial accretions which dignify a college, even though they sometimes embarrass it.'

'And he thought, "If we want to be proving our worth in this postwar economy, we've got to be really serious,"' says Parkinson. 'Fashion, Industrial Design, Graphic Design, they were all part of Darwin's great vision of us being relevant to an economy that had been hammered.'

Darwin's impact on the RCA has been likened to a palace coup. Yet in many ways his reforms cashed a cheque that had been written in 1837, when it was established as the Government School of Design (changed in 1864 to the National Art Training School, after moving to a purpose-built structure behind the Victoria and Albert Museum, then to its present name in 1896). Darwin's ambitions, in fact, reflected the College's original mission: the training of designers and craftspeople who could make British industry internationally competitive. From day one until Darwin's arrival, successive regimes wrestled with this mandate, with varied, imperfect results.

One of the most lasting gambits proved to be an early 20th-century restructuring that separated the College into four schools: Mural and Decorative Painting, Sculpture and Modelling, Architecture, and Design. Aware that, in the aftermath of the war, the need to re-energize British industry was uppermost, Darwin left the study of painting, engraving, sculpture, and architecture more or less intact, and remade the rest. According to RCA historian Christopher Frayling, 'There were to be new Schools of Ceramics; Textiles; Typography and Design for Publicity [changed to Graphic Design]; Silversmithing, Metalwork, and Jewellery; Fashion Design; and Light Engineering and Furniture (later retitled Woods, Metals and Plastics).' 'Woods, Metals and Plastics very quickly began to seem like a not-very-good name for a discipline,' says Parkinson, 'so it split and we had Furniture Design and Industrial Design coming out of it.'

Darwin also, as Frayling writes, '"sold" the idea of the College to the captains of industry', reminding business leaders that 'if they wanted quality, then they should treat their young designers better; the College should become a "pilot plant", to develop new ideas and sometimes test them out'. By the time of Pauline's appearance, Darwin's gamble had largely paid off. 'Without that degree of specialization,' he believed, 'we could never have made so rapid an impression upon industry for we could not have hoped otherwise to have produced so many students acceptable to it.'

'That degree of specialization' equally impressed the students, in an opposite way: for Pauline and her circle, Darwin's palace coup provoked an intense cross-pollination. 'Had one relied on staff, you might have come up with much more traditional ideas,' observes Brian Newman, also with Pauline in Stained Glass. 'The value of the College was that it brought all of these students together, who had ideas which they exchanged.' 'We encouraged each other,' says Derek Boshier, who entered Painting in 1959. 'In a way, if you like, there was a coterie.'

The multidisciplinary artist Geoffrey Reeve remembers it vividly. 'You'd be sitting round the canteen and bouncing things off each other. And somebody might say something – "If you want to do that, you've got to do so and so and so." Or, "Why don't you do this? Let's make some photographs." It was very ad hoc. If somebody wanted to get up and act the fool, they could.' 'We hung out as a group from different departments,' says Boshier. 'There were furniture designers, fine art people, painters, ceramicists. Ridley Scott was in the film school, which had just started. The graphic designers who worked on *ARK*, the famous Royal College magazine, went on to change the whole magazine design industry.'

The artist Allen Jones was dazzled by the breadth of opportunity. 'I remember

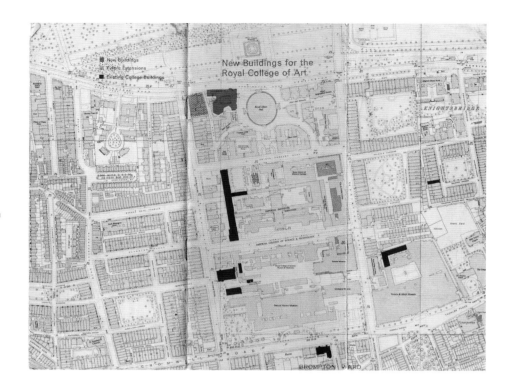

A 1959 map reveals the scattered buildings, indicated in blue, that comprised the Royal College of Art campus in Pauline's day.

Charles Eames giving a lecture, using a multi-screen presentation – I'd never seen anything like that. The General Studies courses, outside the practice of art class, were very good. We were given Plato and Aristotle to read, I was introduced to Russian literature – it was unbelievably positive as far as I was concerned. I mean one was just hungry for it.'

'We would party together, holiday together, we were in and out of each other's flats,' remembers fashion designer Sally Tuffin. 'Friendships were made, and they weren't made over a board meeting. It wasn't networking then. You just met people and liked them.' 'Ambitious as we all were, it was just incredible to be in a place of such activity. I thought I'd died and gone to heaven,' Jones affirms – 'the College was *the* place.' 'It is a moment in time, and it could never happen again,' says Baynes. 'But for a while, it was just – you might say anarchy – but from it came everything that the Royal College is remembered for from that period.'

The word 'anarchy' and its variants turn up frequently in the recollections of Pauline's College confrères, reflective of a hands-off attitude on the part of staff that seemed at times to border on indifference, as her Stained Glass classmates attest. 'We were on our own,' says Ray Bradley. '[Department head] Lawrence Lee didn't really teach, he sort of sat in his room and, I presume, administered. Keith was the one who met and mixed with the students when he wasn't with one of the girls.' 'Keith New was a visiting tutor,' Newman explains. 'But I only recall one tutorial.' According to fellow student Gerald Nason, 'Brian Newman taught me more about stained glass than the instructors did.'

This, too, was not without precedent. For decades prior to Darwin's tenure, there was a sense, at the RCA, that instruction in the rudiments of this or that art or craft should have taken place prior to a student's arrival – that 'basic training' was not what the College was for. 'According to the *Students' Magazine*, "The provinces" could deal quite adequately with that side of things,' Frayling reports. 'The College's primary function was to provide "your artistic suckling" with a stimulating environment – made up of museums, galleries and lively teachers – which would also allow him to have a good time.' This approach 'gave a lot of time to "individual idiosyncrasies", encouraged the students to develop an image of themselves as potential geniuses (or at least market leaders), and hoped that "the average student" would go elsewhere'.

Thus what Bradley, Nason and Newman perceived as fecklessness was a years-in-the-gestating philosophy of letting the lunatics run the asylum. Darwin effectively saw it as his task. 'He needed both to recruit staff who were artists or designers or craftspeople in their own right,' says Baynes. 'Not theorists, but people who did things. And then they needed to work with a light touch with their students. And let them get on with it, really.'

And so they did. 'I did Textiles as a way into the College, but you could go anywhere,' Reeve recalls. 'I did bookbinding, I did painting. Most of the time I was painting or collage-ing. Some of it was turned into fabrics – I was trying to produce big-scale things, like murals. Nobody censored me for that. Though I got reprimanded for always being in other departments.'

Part of the wanderlust derived from the school's physical reality. Today the RCA revolves around a trio of campuses, in South Kensington, Battersea and White City. But when Pauline and her classmates arrived in the late 1950s, they found a College scattered among the mansions, sheds and cultural institutions around Cromwell Road, the result of what Frayling calls the RCA's 'never-ending struggle to re-house and expand'. Inevitably, the structures varied in quality and character. The 1864 building, an L-shaped two-storey structure designed by a Royal Engineer, Captain Francis Fowke, featured large windows and an open plan. Yet the studios, set above museum galleries, a military barracks and a kitchen, were subjected to relentless noise and foul odours as well as the usual overcrowding, and within 20 years the building, off Exhibition Road, was considered entirely inadequate. Still, as the province of Graphic Design, Film and Television Set Design (eventually), and the Painting school, it remained a popular destination. 'I went out with a painter, so I was in and out of there quite a lot,' says the artist Nicola Wood. 'I loved the smell of paint and turpentine and all that stuff.'

Below Left
The senior common room, at 21 Cromwell Road, was styled as a traditional gentlemen's club.

Below right
The junior common room, in the same building, was of a very different character.

Other departments were in the Western Galleries of the Imperial Institute, just north of the V&A across Exhibition Road. The late 19th-century building – subsequently demolished but for its landmark Anglo-Indian Queen's Tower – featured long wings, one of which hosted the Textile department, in rooms above the aeronautical collection. 'You'd walk in and there were all these airplanes and stuff, and then we were upstairs,' Wood recalls. 'The Prints school was the first bit, and then the Weaving school was the second bit.'

Ceramics was located in one of a cluster of corrugated iron huts, west of Exhibition Road on Queen's Gate. Resembling, according to Parkinson, 'mini-aircraft hangars', the structures had originally served as a training hospital for Crimean War doctors and remained, in Pauline's day, largely unchanged. Silver-smithing, Metalwork and Jewellery, Industrial Glass, and Sculpture shared another hut, the last having been in residence since the 19th century. According to Nason, 'The sculptors were the ruffians of the Royal College of Art. They were all huge, being sculptors. They all drank a lot. And we used to fall out with them quite often, though I got to be great friends with them on the drinking side.'

Fashion Design, the outlier, filled an Edwardian terraced house in Knightsbridge. 'It was a very beautiful building,' Tuffin remembers. 'On several floors, with very large windows. Very genteel, as it were. Big staircase. We got there just when things were quite formal still. You weren't allowed to wear trousers, if you were a woman. You had to wear a skirt with a kick pleat in the back. It was quite elitist.'

In 1949, the RCA arranged long-term leases on its southernmost buildings, a pair of side-by-side mansions at 21 and 23 Cromwell Road. Today the French consulate, in the 1950s number 21 held the senior and junior common rooms, which could not have been more different in appearance or intention. The senior version, the province of the (almost entirely male) staff, was styled as a gentlemen's

club and served, Parkinson observes, as a kind of stage set. 'I feel like there's an inferiority complex going on, in terms of Darwin just being sort of desperate to prove that we were to be taken seriously,' he says. 'And the way he went about that was by creating an old-school sort of Oxbridge College senior common room that looked like we had this long reverential tradition. And then,' Parkinson adds, 'we have some photos of the junior common room, which basically looks like a rowdy canteen.'

After his arrival, Darwin shuttered the much-loved junior common room – in a Queen's Gate hut since around 1900 – but made amends with a new one, featuring a multicolored ceiling and elegant wood floor, in a ballroom in the mansion's first-floor addition. 'You could get lunch there for 2 and 6, and it was a very nice lunch,' says Tuffin. 'Quite handy.' Ordinarily the space was filled with tables, which were cleared out for events such as the College's revues, as well as dances. As the RCA's house band, the Temperance Seven played the venue regularly. 'Quite a big room, and there was a stage area, and it was used for all of the administrative functions, celebrations, diploma-givings and such like, but also for dances,' says band member Philip Harrison. 'We'd rehearse up in the bar, which was big enough for us to sit around and talk and figure out how to do things. Same building, upstairs.'

The Lethaby
Lectures
Thursday 19 Nov
Tuesday 24 Nov
Tuesday 1 Dec
Will be given by

CHARLES EAMES

In the
Victoria and Albert
Museum Lecture
Theatre at 4.30 pm

A programme of shorts

Terminus John Schlesinger **A star in the night** Don Siegal
6 sided triangle Christopher Miles **Charlotte et son Jules** Jean-Luc Godard
Le gros et le maigre Roman Polanski **Opera Mouffe** Agnes Varda

26 November 7pm RCA Jay Mews

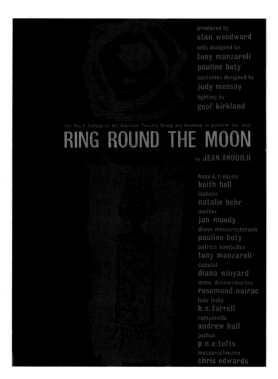

The film society also convened in the common room, where selections from the British Film Institute's collection were screened each Thursday. A primitive version of stadium seating was achieved by setting chairs atop the tables at the room's rear, with floor-level seats in front. 'The scene from Buñuel's *Un Chien Andalou* with the cutting of the eyeball caused everyone sitting in the raised seats to fall off in shock,' Reeve says. 'I tended to sit in the front row with my mates Tony Manzaroli, Mike Kidd and Terry Green, and [we] vied with each other to make the rudest comments during the showings.' 'And it wasn't just the film,' Boshier recalls. 'The posters that were made for it were amazing, and there were notes about it, and where it came from. Pauline, like many of us, was influenced by how good the society was. I think that her interest in the French and Italian films that she made a subject matter of came out of it. More than all the Pop artists, Pauline took from film.'

Pauline also participated in the theatre group, as both set designer and actress. After Darwin shuttered the Queen's Gate common room, where the Theatre Design school staged performances, the students re-launched the society on their own, with results not unrelated to their new venue. According to the cultural studies writer Alex Seago, 'The high quality, wit and originality of the College's theatrical productions were enhanced by the exceptional facilities of the new Students' Common Room at 21 Cromwell Road, which boasted a very large auditorium, professional light and sound equipment, and an elaborate movable stage.'

If Pauline's cultural life centred around number 21, her academic activities unfolded in the mansion's programmatically overstuffed next-door twin. In addition to the library, *ARK*'s editorial offices, and the Architecture, Interior Design and General Studies departments (and a bit of Silversmithing, Metalwork and Jewellery), 23 Cromwell Road was home to Stained Glass.

'It was a very small department,' Newman says. 'Pauline, myself and a guy called Brian Milne were the three people who came in at that one time – just three students.' According to William Wilkins, 'There was the main studio on the first floor, and then on the lower floor, there were the kilns and the leading benches. The big one was where you did design and also where you were mocking up the window with pieces of glass prior to leading them up. And then when you were satisfied with it, it would go down for making in the basement studio.' The conditions, Newman remembers, were less than ideal. 'One of the techniques used in stained glass is to etch it, so that you go through a layer of red glass, for instance, and white glass underneath or whatever. And that was done with hydrofluoric acid. So it wasn't doing us any good health-wise.' 'They were supposed to have ventilators to draw off the fumes, but didn't,' Nason adds. 'Most of the time, the ends of your fingers are all cut, from the lead and the glass. I don't think Pauline was terribly keen on it. Breathing these awful fumes all the time and cutting yourself.'

Opposite top left Posters advertising a lecture by Charles Eames and a presentation by the film society.

Opposite left Two theatre group offerings, to which Pauline contributed her acting and design abilities.

Despite their circumstances, the incoming Stained Glass students were initially optimistic regarding the medium's potential. In the postwar years, infiltrated by the movements that touched all of 20th-century art, stained glass had begun to shed its traditional character and inch towards the modern. The war's depredations created a demand for restoration work, primarily on the Continent but also in England, where Lawrence Lee, head of the RCA's Stained Glass department, collaborated on the windows for the reconstructed Coventry cathedral with former students Geoffrey Clarke and Keith New. On Ray Bradley, their impact was definitive. 'They made them in a big studio in the Victoria and Albert, and then six windows were exhibited in the sculpture hall,' he remembers. 'It was a holy sort of exhibition, all blacked out, and these big windows – seventy feet high – and appropriate music quietly playing in the background. I walked in, and I thought, "My God, this is monumental. Painting? Too small!"'

For most, however, the enthusiasm did not last. In part this had to do with a sense of unmet promise. 'Because of the Coventry windows, there was a lot of interest in stained glass,' Newman says. 'But by the time I got to the Royal College, interest was waning. There was quite a lot of interesting stuff being done on the Continent, but not here.' For others, stained glass had never been more than a Trojan Horse with which to gain admission to England's foremost postgraduate arts institution. Says the artist Paula Nightingale, 'It was bloody hard to get in as a painter. That's why Pauline and a lot of people went into Stained Glass – they didn't think they had a chance.'

However disillusioned the students, or disengaged the staff, one thing is certain: Pauline's commitment was unambiguous. 'She was no fly-by-night,' Reeve observes. 'She was ambitious. Determined. Focused. She was producing a huge amount of work. She was one of the boys, really. Because it was assumed that the chaps knew what they were doing. And she certainly knew what she was doing.' 'She was quite masculine in the way she behaved,' observes Celia Birtwell. 'Nothing cozy about Pauline. You *might* talk about your deep feelings. But I wouldn't describe her as *super*-worried about anybody else. She had that drive for herself. Although she looked incredibly pretty, Pauline was quite tough. I liked the way she was a female but very strong and one of the boys as well.'

Reeve got to know Pauline in 1958, the year she began at the RCA; Birtwell in 1961, when the two became housemates. Yet despite their different perspectives, both saw the artist the same way: as possessed of a 'masculine' ambition that came second to nothing, and no one.

Before and during Wimbledon, Pauline's single-mindedness emerged as an unwillingness to subdue any part of her nature. At the RCA, Pauline reinforced this, in a way suggested by Reeve's and Birtwell's characterization. Typically, when 'one of the boys' is applied to a woman, it is desexualizing: suggesting either someone who can hold her own with men in a typically male pursuit – drinking, for example – or else is more of a pal than an object of desire. In Pauline's case, however, 'one of the boys' has a different meaning. Though it refers in part to wanting to be taken seriously as an artist, not pigeonholed as a 'woman painter', it had also to do with a then- (and, surely, still-) prevailing double standard. Nicola Wood felt it acutely. 'Most women went through wanting to be dolly birds, because the men would whistle,' she acknowledges. 'But we wanted to be taken seriously. Men never had to dally with those two opposites. You know, they were just men, and they did whatever they wanted and it was right – for them. They didn't have this dual personality thing, which all women had at the time.'

All women – but not, it would seem, Pauline. She was determined to do whatever she wanted, and have it be right, and it is in this particular sense that Pauline was 'one of the boys'. Ironically, of course, even as she claimed 'masculine' prerogatives, she had to contend with that which everyone who remembers Pauline speaks of again and again: her extraordinary physical magnetism. To experience her times to the maximum, to enjoy them as participant, influence them as creator and critic, she had to ride the wild horse of her beauty rather than let it run away with her; turn the objectification to which she was subjected to her advantage; and find the vehicles that best suited how she wished to be seen and that enabled her to perfect the persona she perceived as genuine.

It proved a tall order – even for one of the boys.

4

AT THE ROYAL

COLLEGE

OF ART

1958–1961

Part 2: 'Technicolor'

At the Royal College, Pauline encountered a radical transformation of circumstances. She entered a dynamic institution that was in every way more challenging than the parochial place she'd been. Her fellow students were formidable, many upending the norms of art, design and culture even before collecting their diplomas. Stained glass, severed from Charles Carey, held diminished interest, and during her first year she lived at home, far from the action, in suburban Carshalton. Yet Pauline's effervescence and self-assurance immediately registered. Plus, no one could take their eyes off her, nor did she want them to. 'I suppose she was a show-off, wasn't she?' Celia Birtwell says. 'People who are beautiful like that, I think they enjoy it. And why not? It's great if you can enjoy it and spread it around.'

And she did. 'I was aware of her immediately,' Nason recalls. 'Like everybody else, I fell in love with her. She was a bit overwhelming, really.' 'She was quite overwhelming in many ways,' says Newman. 'Female art students in those days tended to be fairly understated as women. They tended not to wear makeup, they didn't wear flashy clothes, whereas Pauline was quite the opposite. She was Technicolor.'

'Just a really lively girl, singing, dancing,' remembers the textile designer Natalie Gibson, a close College friend. 'She was so vivacious, I mean, really.' 'Also a bit of a beatnik,' Birtwell adds. 'We dressed in Mary Quant clothes at the time, and that was a new step, with the music and everything that was going on. She was rather elegant, actually. Elegant in a modern way.' 'She was one of the first girls I knew that wore men's jeans,' says Peter Blake, 'because I remember taking delight in telling her one day that her flies were undone.'

To Newman, the seasoning she'd acquired at Wimbledon was evident. 'She was much more sophisticated than I was at the time,' he recalls. 'She'd been around more. She spoke French quite well. The three of us in our class went on a trip to Chartres to see the glass. And got there, and Pauline said, "Right. Let's have an ice cream." We'd actually sort of looked in the door, and it seemed overwhelmingly dull, so we spent our time having ice cream at this place that she knew. That was typical of her.'

Unexpectedly, beneath the dazzle lay warmth. 'She could have used the way she looked much more than she did, but I felt she was above that, somehow,' Tuffin remembers. 'There was something about her that was very touching. I couldn't describe her as a bitch or an opportunist or any of those things. I thought she was a very nice, genuine, sunny person.' 'She really was,' Nason believes. 'She was very kind, you see.'

Though not always. Not to everyone, and not, in particular, when it didn't suit her. Pauline could take advantage, play the queen and be, in moments of self-absorption, utterly thoughtless – in Birtwell's formulation, not 'super-worried about anybody else'. 'At the Royal College, they put on revues, and I thought I'd like to do that, too,' remembers Nicola Wood. 'I started thinking that my mother was wrong, that I wasn't undesirable. And I wanted to have fun, and do something different, that would give me more confidence. Pauline I guess became in charge of that, and when I went up and asked her, the answer was no. It wasn't a "who are you kidding", it was just, "there's no space for another girl" type of thing.'

Considering the 'come one, come all' recruitment policy of the revues, Pauline's refusal, contradicting Nason's assessment, was most unkind (if not quite bitchy). Yet it is fair to assume that, had she been a man dismissing a woman, none would have sat in judgment, or even noticed. Asserting her prerogatives, Pauline, as Wood herself might have put it, was doing as she pleased, and deeming it to be right. It is thus appropriate that the prerogative Pauline asserted in the most 'masculine' way, beginning at College and continuing thereafter, was sexual.

In this regard, Pauline was indeed, as Derek Boshier observed, one of the boys. 'She'd say that men were sexy, like film stars, talk about how sexy they were,' he remembers. 'At that time, she was one of the few women that talked about men that way.' In a letter, Pauline described the French film idol Jean-Paul Belmondo, splendidly, as 'the dish with the ravey navel', adding 'oh indescribable joy and lechery and slurp, slurp he's lovely just lovely … ' 'I remember her saying, "I really want to fuck John Lennon,"' says Gibson. 'I thought, "Wow! Okay, well, she probably will. He should be so lucky."'

Pauline did more than talk the talk. 'She had, you know, a pretty sixties attitude towards sex,' says Tariq Ali, the writer who entered Clive Goodwin's orbit after her death. 'She was usually the one, according to what I've heard, who took the initiative. Very strong woman like that – she knew what she wanted, and with who.'

A catalyst, as writer and producer, in the flowering of left-wing British television drama, Roger Smith met Pauline in 1963, following her marriage to Clive, who would become his literary agent. 'She suggested it one day, and took me to a hotel in London, and that was, you know,' he says. 'Wherever it was that we'd been to, she felt it was sort of a natural thing to happen. I didn't particularly want to betray Clive. She assured me that he'd never get to know about it.'

Which is not to say that Pauline was indiscriminate. Smith typified the men to whom Pauline, throughout her life, found her way: in search of a balance between sexual and romantic satisfaction, intellectual and emotional stimulation, and a formidability equal to her own. 'There was Derek Marlowe, the writer,' Boshier says, and 'the guy who took the famous photograph of Christine Keeler, Lewis Morley. She liked them because they were smart and clever.' Natalie Gibson remembers the photographer David Cripps: 'He was very good looking, so they looked gorgeous together, of course. I don't think it lasted very long. David Cripps was very glamorous, but quite shy. Suddenly she was with this guy called Philip Saville.' Described by Adam Smith as the 'dashing and successful director of ABC's *Armchair Theatre*', Saville received mixed notices from Pauline's pals. 'A bit of a smoothie,' Gibson offers. 'But clever and intelligent and intellectual. She did like to discuss things, and debate things. So I imagine that would turn her on.'

In fact, one of the most significant of Pauline's relationships was platonic, and exemplified the braiding, in her nature, of multiple strands: creative and intellectual avidity and alertness to opportunity, abiding self-interest and finely-tuned empathy, and callousness and generosity, of self and spirit both.

Pauline first met Peter Blake through Charles Carey – 'I remember seeing her with very long, curly hair, so looking very much like Brigitte Bardot,' says the painter. 'And just astonishingly beautiful' – and the two deepened their connection during her time at the Royal College and afterwards (until, in 1963, Pauline found Clive, and Blake married the California-born Pop artist Jann Haworth, with whom he co-created the famous cover of the Beatles' 1967 *Sgt. Pepper's Lonely Hearts Club Band*). Though often cited as Pauline's mentor – and unquestionably an influence – Blake soft-pedals his significance. 'I don't think I was ever critical, or offered technical advice,' he says. 'I just thought she was good.'

More significantly, Blake says, 'We were enormous friends. We were mates, we were pals. We were both painters, so we went out quite a lot. She was wonderful to go out with – imagine having her on your arm at a private view. I mean, she was sensational.' To his sorrow, Blake was smitten. 'I fell deeply in love with her, which wasn't reciprocated. She at one point made that classic statement, "I do love you, but not in that way." That real kind of movie statement. She was fond of me, I know that. And we were very good friends. But I suppose at that point it was a frustration for it not to be reciprocated.'

Blake's feelings were complicated by his past. 'When I was 17, I had a really nasty cycling accident, which smashed my face up. I knocked my teeth out and had a lot of stitches in my face, and I've still got scars from it. Psychologically that affected me enormously in relationships. In that I was clumsy. I didn't sleep with anyone 'til I was 29, I think. Because of all this stuff. So whatever that confusion was all about affected my relationship with Pauline as well.'

Surely, Pauline intuited the imbalance between them. One wonders if, consciously or otherwise, she twisted the knife, as when Blake arrived to take her to a Sarah Vaughan concert. 'I was meeting Pauline in a pub in Fulham,' he says. 'And when I got there, she was with a mutual friend of ours. David Cripps, one of her boyfriends. And chose not to come to the concert but to stay with David in the pub. And I went to the concert by myself to hear Sarah Vaughan, singing stuff like, "Every time we say goodbye I cry a little." You can imagine the pain of that.'

Yet if she meant to hurt, Pauline also offered tenderness – on one occasion in particular. 'Towards the end of our relationship, there was a scenario where we had a dinner party,' Blake remembers. 'She shared a flat at that point with – what was her name? Jane Percival. And [artist] Joe Tilson and Jane contrived a dinner party, and they went off, and left Pauline and I alone for the night. And when I look back, I realize, it probably was a set-up. And I was a mess. I mean, I was totally drunk. And I can just recall being in another room, and crying all night.

'They'd set it up as an arrangement. That Pauline must have been in on. And it was a situation that might have worked out. And it didn't.'

'Was she promiscuous? I don't think she was, really,' says Ray Bradley. 'Things were changing. So, okay, maybe people slept around more than they did earlier, there was a sort of nonchalance about things, but it was just life, wasn't it? The only people you didn't talk to about things was your parents.' Bradley's point reminds us that Pauline was, *enfin*, a product of her times. And while much has been made of her predation, it is worth remembering that, when she began at College, Pauline was scarcely out of her teens and more vulnerable to the vicissitudes of her world than might have been apparent, even to her.

Fortunately, she had an ally in Jane Percival, three years her senior, who'd been one of four women accepted into the RCA's Painting school in 1957. The two had met, by chance, in Paris at the Gare Saint-Lazare, during the summer before Pauline's final year at Wimbledon. Percival remembered spotting Pauline previously, at the Tate Gallery – she recognized the blonde hair – and introduced herself. The outcome was a day out of early Jean-Luc Godard, the women strolling down the Faubourg Saint-Honoré, laughing as Percival accidentally ruined her dress with a leaky bottle of black ink. Firm friends by nightfall, Pauline promised to visit her in London, where she was shortly to begin at College. 'When the new academic year began, Pauline was a regular guest at Percival's student digs in St James's Gardens, Holland Park,' writes Adam Smith, 'which Jane shared with Richard Bawden, son of the illustrator Edward.'

'Jane was the most supportive of Pauline's writing and thinking, and wanting to share lots of opinions,' explains the actor/artist Roddy Maude-Roxby. 'So many people were attracted to Pauline that she needed to talk to someone who wasn't interested in that side of her. Jane was strong and serious and good-humoured. She meant a lot to Pauline, because she could have the conversations she needed to have with another woman.' (As well, 'Pauline had a well-read serious side,'

'Imagine having her on your arm at a private view,' says Peter Blake (centre, **looking at the camera**) 'I mean, she was sensational.'

notes Smith, citing her mastery of Proust, 'and Jane is mainly why.')

Pauline moved in with Percival in her second College year, following a summer wander through Greece and Italy with a cavalcade that included Bawden, Patrick Caulfield, Jill Moore, Bridget McWilliam and Natalie Gibson. Recalls Bawden: 'Pauline was so beautiful everyone turned to stare, including some police in a Land Rover, who then bumped into the car in front!' (Two summers later, on a holiday in Spain, Sally Tuffin witnessed similar tumult. 'We were sitting in a square, and the people were flocking all over us. I said to Pauline, "Why are they looking at us, what's going on?" And she said, "Well, it's because I'm so beautiful."')

The Grecian odyssey proved anything but comic for the party's seventh member, Nicola Wood. 'When I was at Manchester Art School, I'd been dating a Greek guy,' she says. 'His family was quite well off. And I did get in touch with him, and he said, "You can come and stay at my mother's house in Athens." He met us off the train, and we all went to his mother's house, and spent the night there. And then we were all going off to Hydra, but I felt it was impolite of me to leave right away. Which was the biggest mistake of my life, because he raped me, and I got pregnant. I ran away from that to Hydra, looking for everybody. And they'd all gone to another island.'

She never caught up.

That autumn, Pauline and Percival, back from her own summer trip to Portugal, found a flat at 59-A Sutherland Place, in Notting Hill, scene of the notorious white-on-black Bramley Road race riots the year previous. Now posh in extremis, in 1959 the area offered a brute contrast to Carshalton: a world, in Adam Smith's formulation, of 'speakeasies, whores, gangs, slums, and heaps of rubbish'. 'It was a poor area, where you had to be careful walking down the road,' says the painter Paula Nightingale. 'I used to walk through Kensington Gardens to College in the morning. I remember there was a big lake. I remember the sea gulls over it in the winter.'

Nightingale was one of the other three women who'd entered the Painting school in Jane Percival's year. 'I'd wanted to live in London in that last year, because otherwise I was trudging up from South London,' she says. 'I found a room in some weird place, some funny old man was in the next room, and it was a bit horrid, actually. I mentioned this to Jane in passing, and she said, "Oh, Paula, no, there's a room in the flat Pauline and I have got, you can't be in some horrible place like that."

'The day I went to this weird place, I went into College, and they said to go to the secretary's office, and the secretary said that my mother had just phoned. And my mother said that all my paintings were on fire – she'd set fire to my paintings, in the garden. She was so upset me [leaving home]. So it was really nice that Jane and Pauline said, "Come and live here." I went and saw this little white room, a bit like a monk's cell. Jane had a room upstairs, and Pauline had another big room next door. I went down to Portobello Market and got a sort of funny bed. Just basically that. It was a very happy time, really, we were quite independent. She was a beautiful girl, Jane Percival, a really good, nice, deep person. I seem to remember her saying she'd been terribly depressed, I think she had something shattering happen before she came.' 'She'd been to Portugal,' says Nicola Wood, 'and she'd been raped in Portugal.'

To Nightingale, Pauline seemed 'a lovely girl, a great radiant sunshine. The way she had her room, the way she put things, little sketches and things. One of those great big mirrors that used to be taken out of hotels, with the gold round them. Things sort of stuck in it, all sorts of nice little bits and pieces, all the odd things that one collects as a creative person.'

An experiential difference was quickly revealed. 'I can't believe how naïve I was, in my little monk's room,' Nightingale says. 'I used to hear this sort of banging and bonking noise on the other side of the wall. I used to think, "What are they doing in there? Are they like kids jumping around on the bed?" No wonder they used to think I was funny, Jane and Pauline! I'd never even held hands with anyone.' And yet. 'She was kind of more vulnerable, really, underneath. I mean she was quite young, quite young, having to handle those things. Sad things.'

A particular 'sad thing' connects to the central conundrum of Pauline's story: why it was that, knowing she required an abortion to be properly treated for cancer, she chose to gamble – unsuccessfully, it turned out – with her life and see the pregnancy through. The theatre critic Kenneth Tynan's elder daughter, Tracy, who as a teen met the artist at her parents' London flat, thought Pauline's Catholicism might have been an influence: 'Maybe coming from the background she did, maybe that kicked in at a certain point, a rather traditional view.' The church's impact upon Pauline, however, seems overplayed, as Caroline Coon points out. 'People say, "Oh, she didn't have the abortion because she was Catholic." Not at any point up to 28 years have we seen any evidence that Pauline Boty had any inclinations to religion.'

More to the point: Nightingale relates that Pauline had an abortion while living with her and Percival. 'There was a guy called Nick we all called Knickers for some silly reason,' says Nightingale. 'Who was a stage manager at the Royal Court Theatre. He used to come round to see her, and she used to think he was lovely. The Knick was the big number at that point.'

'The person who introduced me was Roddy Maude-Roxby,' Nicholas Garland remembers. 'I knew Roddy from my art student days [at the Slade], but while I was at the Royal Court he was cast in a play that I was stage managing. One evening, Roddy said, "Come with me, there's someone you'll like to meet." I'd seen her in the revues at the Royal College, so I knew perfectly well who she was. I certainly did like to meet her.

'My memories of Pauline are of a straightforward, friendly, intelligent young woman, thinking, "What am I going to do, where am I going to go?" Because she was divided between the talents that she had. There was nothing sort of plodding or banal about her, rather the opposite – quick, a little bit magpie-like, to pick up ideas here and there and play with them. She was quite young of course, and feeling her way along, but she had a sort of strength as well, a bit of nerve to do things the way she thought she wanted to do them. All of that I found attractive.

'At the time we broke up, I was offered work. One [job] was to be an assistant artistic director of a repertory company in Gloucestershire, and the other was to join the BBC, which meant that you became a sort of civil servant. And I chose to take up the job at the Cheltenham Rep. And that meant leaving London, and leaving Pauline. I don't think she was broken-hearted. I was extremely fond of her, we were good friends, had a nice time, a short time together. And then I left.'

'And this lovely, radiant girl suddenly found out that she was pregnant, and she didn't know what to do about it,' Nightingale recalls. 'She said there was no way she could have told her family, no way. I remember her being so insistent about that. Jane told me that Pauline's family couldn't know, it would be absolutely devastating.'

Pauline: *One thinks of difficulties of having children without being married and unless you've got plenty of money it's a very nasty situation indeed, it can be*

absolutely awful ... Just the physical difficulties of finding a room and you know, when you've got a baby it's terribly difficult.

'We had no resources, as it were, to deal with it,' Garland admits. 'That required more money than either of us had. I borrowed it from a friend. The other thing was, I was working in Cheltenham by then. And – the thing is, I didn't go with her. I asked Roddy, "Will you go with her, she should have somebody with her," and he went with her. And I rang her. Over and over and over again. And she never picked up. I left messages, and she didn't call back. I thought, well, that's understandable, she's angry and hurt that I left her alone. It's one of the things in my life I feel bad about. I don't know why I didn't make more of an effort to go with her. I have a feeling I thought I wasn't welcome.'

Further complicating matters, abortion would not be made legal in England until 1967. 'She went to some expensive kind of place, where she could have it, and nobody would know,' Nightingale says. 'Jane and I went to see her there, and I can remember how shocking it was to see her in bed. I can remember her being so white, this poor girl on her own, and not able to tell her family. She was trying to be her jolly self. Not jolly, but just, as she'd decided to do that, she felt all right. You have to, I suppose.

Above
Paula Nightingale
(left, seated on the floor,
legs extended) and
Jane Percival (right)
were Pauline's
flatmates at
Sutherland Place.

'I connect it now with the tale that I heard later. She had to make that decision twice. She had to decide on the baby. Perhaps she felt she'd made the decision the first time, not having it, and the second time, she couldn't make that decision. So she went to have it. Tragic – so tragic. Life's a very weird business, isn't it?'

Reached in July 2020, Maude-Roxby affirmed that while he knew of Pauline's abortion, he was not the one who accompanied her.

The panting intrusions that, while on holiday, smothered Pauline at every step, the sexual violence visited upon Jane Percival and Nicola Wood; the mother who, unstrung by her daughter leaving home for an independent life, set fire to the agent of that independence; the prospect of having an illegal abortion, in secret, without the support of family or lover, to preserve one's freedom: these are pictures from an exhibition of womanhood prior to the onset of second-wave feminism. The woman who took a place in the RCA's Stained Glass department in 1958 established herself as a famous beauty and object of desire, reinforced by a comparably outsized personality, she was sexually liberated in word and deed, captivating in her nimble-minded intelligence, and remorseless in the pursuit of her interests. Yet Pauline was also young and vulnerable, and despite her advantages, she – and, indeed, her sisters – inhabited a world that objectified and trivialized women, and in every way held them back.

Gerald Laing and Nicholas Garland have spoken of how unimaginable life in postwar London must be to those without first-hand experience. Sally Alexander, author, educator and Women's Liberation Movement activist – she participated in the 'flour bombing' of the 1970 Miss World competition – is equally eloquent on how different was the existence of the female sex in Pauline's day. 'The situation with women now, where young women do have affairs all the time, they do gender fluidity, you just think, "In my time, it was another world,"' Alexander says. 'It was a world *demarcated* by sexual difference. How you dressed, how you looked, how you thought. Abortion wasn't legal. Divorce, you didn't have any rights as a wife. No equal pay. You didn't go to university. You didn't get trained to do anything. We didn't have a language, a way of talking about these things, at all. It *was* a man's world then. It really was. It's like, I could never feel terrible about equal pay in the 1980s and 1990s, because I just thought, "Oh, we're earning so much compared to what we used to be paid." I mean, my generation, we grew up with so little that it's very hard to describe what it was like.'

Nell Dunn elaborates: 'When I was young, men actually thought they were more important. I mean, it just amazes me, looking back on it now – the self-importance. Men were bored by women. Unless they were sleeping with them, they were bored. The idea of actually talking about your day, or what you felt, was just completely uninteresting to men. And yet a lot of women in their twenties, which was my age, were busy with children and friends and life. I would say it was true of all classes. You had to absolutely hide, if you'd spent your day looking after kids, you had to hide that. For fear that this would bore a man.'

As life went, so too did art. 'Women painters like myself felt very alienated,' Percival told Sabine Durrant. 'The full feminist movement hadn't come in and we worked in isolated pools, mostly of depression.' Art school was no better. According to Sue Tate, 'In 1958, when Boty was applying, only eight of the 32 final-year students in the School of Painting were women, and by the College's own standards of bestowing a First class qualification, they had to be better than the men to get in. Half of those eight women got Firsts, but only three of the 24 men ... Between 1948 and 1968, an average of 10 percent of the staff were women and there was no improvement during the "liberated" 1960s ... In 1963, when degree status was granted to the RCA diplomas, it was withheld from Fashion, the only school with a female professor and a majority of female students.'

It is a testament to the times that, given Darwin's mission to connect the College to commerce – and that fashion was a breakout industry in the 1960s – he would have viewed the school as, in Sally Tuffin's word, 'flippant'. Though her own post-College success, with partner and sister Fashion student Marion Foale, helped to upend the staid departmental sensibility, the attitude Tuffin encountered as an applicant was, compared to the RCA's overall vitality, antediluvian. 'We had to have gone to so many theatres, so many concerts – we had to prove that we did these things that we never did, as soon as we got there,' Tuffin remembers. 'You had to learn what to do at a cocktail party, and how to sit in a car. We all made sure that we had an umbrella, which was unheard-of at art school. You know, you wore jeans. But of course you weren't allowed to wear jeans at the Fashion school at all.'

The situation was no more enlightened elsewhere. Jann Haworth transferred to London's Slade School of Art, from the University of California Los Angeles, in 1961. 'When I wanted to start to get credit, I asked one of the tutors what I would have to do,' she explains. 'Did I have to submit a portfolio of work, to get my credits recognized if I went back to UCLA? And he said, "No, generally we don't look at the portfolios of the women students, we just need their photographs, 'cause they're here to keep the boys happy."'

Pauline suffered from the same mentality. An RCA boyfriend, Jim Donovan, was offered the editorship of the College's influential magazine *ARK* by Basil Taylor, head of the General Studies department. When he declined, and recommended Pauline instead, 'Taylor didn't even consider the idea for one moment,' Donovan told Sue Tate. '[W]hat he effectively said was that being a gorgeous young girl automatically disqualified her ... He almost snorted.'

To continue a leitmotif: just as it can be difficult to imagine the texture of

Opposite
Newsheet, the RCA's informal student-authored newsletter, ran a story on the election of the junior common room president. The responses to Pauline's candidacy reflect the ambivalent attitude toward women at the time.

postwar London, or a society utterly demarcated by sex, it is hard to wrap our 21st-century minds around the singularity of Pauline's response to her circumstances. Like all wartime children, she'd had to grow up quickly, the more so for the instability produced by her mother's TB; familial combat toughened her hide, and Wimbledon cemented her self-belief and proto-feminism. But some things lie beyond easy explanation, and one of them is what Pauline chose to do, in her years at the RCA, with the attention she got – given what she got it for, how she was perceived and how little the culture expected of her.

Pauline chose to celebrate herself – her beauty, sexuality and, as will be seen, her enthusiasm for pop culture. Being a woman of the left, she also allowed her attributes to be put in the service of causes in which she believed. Most unusually, Pauline used her image as a vehicle for personal expression: for comedy and self-parody to be sure, but also for a subtle feminist advocacy, a cultural critique.

Her beauty, declares Caroline Coon, 'wasn't that important to her. Can I say that? It's what she was born with. What was important to her was what she could do with her intellect, the challenge she could make on life. How important is David Hockney's beauty to *him*?'

AT THE ROYAL COLLEGE OF ART

1958–1961

Part 3: 'La Boty'

'Pauline was very interested in the presentation of new thoughts or ideas,' says Roddy Maude-Roxby, 'the idea that things were going to change, and would change up and down society.' 'She felt that she had a part to play,' adds Ken Baynes. 'Her paintings, of course, but I think she felt she could play a role.'

Caroline Coon's belief that the beauty Pauline was born with was of little importance, that what mattered was 'the challenge she could make on life,' bears consideration. But it is perhaps more accurate to say that her assets offered a way to clarify and direct that challenge. All of Pauline's contemporaries arrived at personal interpretations of Pop, using their particular arsenals of interests and abilities. But hers was in one respect unique: it involved the participation, not only of Pauline Boty, but of 'Pauline Boty'.

On the 17 November 1963 broadcast of *The Public Ear*, the BBC radio programme on which she appeared as a commentator (about which more to come), Pauline offered her perspective on the idea of fandom. Discussing the appeal of the actors James Dean and Jean-Paul Belmondo, Pauline observes that, when you connect with an idol, 'you know you're not alone anymore'. Dean, who belonged to an earlier moment, she describes as 'the hero teenage suffragette ... he says no to all the things you want to say no to'. Belmondo epitomizes the cultural jailbreak of the 1960s:

He lives carelessly, like young people of today, and according to his own morality. He is lawless, he creates about himself a feeling of anarchy ... He has no guilt, and I think this in particular is a contemporary feeling. His freedom makes him full of a marvellous kind of wild energy, and he belongs to here, and now.

One can understand her attraction, in particular to the absence of guilt and its facilitation of anarchic freedom. (To Nell Dunn, Pauline elaborated, equating a lack of 'vulnerability' – 'being completely open all the time and not being ashamed of anything' – with 'hipsterism'.) At the end of the broadcast, Pauline makes clear a hero's appeal.

I think that having any hero, or heroine, is like building an extension onto your own personality. You see, people aren't just made up of actions alone, everyone has dreams and fantasies and other lives going for them, as well as their everyday life, and one of the concrete aspects of this is revealed in our idols. Our fears, hopes, frustrations and dreams, we can pin them on a star who shows them to millions, and if you can do that, you're no longer alone.

This is revealing, for if many Pop artists wove images of idols into their work, she was perhaps the only one of her cohort who actually wished to *be* a star, of a sort. Pauline acted, as the saying goes, on stage, screen and television; many of her generation's foremost lensmen took her picture; and she posed with her own paintings, sometimes mimicking the gestures of a figure on the canvas, at other times making her feelings clear, as with her cheerfully provocative nudity – a 1960s take on François Boucher's 1751 *L'Odalisque blonde* – in front of *With Love to Jean-Paul Belmondo.*

Yet however much, as Richard Hollis believes, she needed an audience, Pauline wasn't interested in generic stardom. Rather, as people were already projecting their fantasies onto her, Pauline proposed to subvert that attention: to demonstrate to her admirers that they, too, were not alone – they were free to participate in a world in transformation, as both fans *and* heroes.

Pauline did so, as her time at the RCA got underway, with two major vehicles: Anti-Ugly Action, and the College revues.

Opposite (clockwise left to right)
Angela Heskett, as Integrity gone begging, 3 November 1959. Ken Baynes and Heskett in the **Evening Standard**. The Anti-Uglies depart 23 Cromwell Road for AUA Operation Four, 4 February 1959. The Anti-Ugly 'recommendation' card. Baynes costumed as a 17th-century architect in Kensington High Street.

Anti-Ugly Action, which the art critic Douglas Cooper called, at the time, 'the best thing that has happened in student movements in 30 years', was concerned with architecture. But its character derived from the presiding zeitgeist of postwar England – 'a feeling,' as Ken Baynes puts it, 'that the world was changing. Art was changing, architecture was changing. And there was a kind of fellow feeling between the different media, that they wanted to see this happen. We wanted to see our city, our country, get engaged with the future.'

The future with which Baynes and his comrades chose to engage involved the built environment. By the late 1950s, London's bombsites were being filled in at a brisk pace, and as is often the case – even when there hasn't been a war – redevelopment favoured money, not quality. 'The relaxation of building codes in the earlier half of the decade had paved the way for a building boom, principally in commercial property, under the Conservative government of Harold Macmillan,' notes the architectural historian Gavin Stamp in his 2015 essay about the movement. 'Anti-Ugly Action was in part a reaction to the sheer mediocrity of much of this speculative building, the work of a small group of property developers.'

Stained glass, with its connection to architectural practice, was a natural breeding ground for this form of protest. And because of the Royal College's anything-goes character, the students saw no reason why they shouldn't take it on. Indeed, observes Brian Newman, 'The interesting thing about Anti-Ugly is that it

Anti-Ugly

I recommend ....

....

for the Anti-Ugly Seal of disapproval.

New Architecture Group, 47, Westmoreland Terrace, London, S.W.1.

WEDNESDAY, MARCH 23, 1960

THE ANTI-UGLIES (NOT AT ALL ANGRY) CALL 'SAVE ST. MARTIN'S'

Evening Standard Reporter

A mass of coloured balloons bobbed about the Anti-Uglies as they demonstrated in the West End th:s after-noon.

Their hour-long walk in the sunshine from Russell Square to Marble Arch was in protest against the new building plan in the neighbourhood of St. Martin-in-the-Fields.

At the head of the procession were banners:

● *S O S St. Martin's.*

● *SAVE ST MARTIN'S FROM THE RIBA SHARKS.*

● *ENGLAND EXPECTS EVERY ARCHITECT TO USE HIS IMAGINATION.*

The marchers were a jolly bunch of 'teens and twenties in sweaters, duffel-coats and jeans —mostly students from the Royal College of Art, London University, the Architects Association and other colleges.

Howl

As they passed the basement offices of Sir Howard Robertson (designer of the St. Martin's building) a great howl of protest went up.

The procession, which grew to about 300 strong, reached Marble Arch where a great cloud of baloons was released.

Everyone of the 800 balloons bore a printed label addressed to Mr. Henry Brooke at the Ministry of Housing.

LAST WORD from bearded art student Mr. Ken Baynes, 25: "The St. Martin's building is just dull—intolerably dull."

SISTER ROWE HAS FLU

Evening Standard Reporter

Sister Helen Rowe, who has just left Buckingham Palace after attending the

On the march today . . . top-hatted Mr. Ken Baynes, 25, and Angela Heskett, 21. Both are art students.

UGLY

and oh! so out of date

PEMBRIDGE VOTER

BOROUGH COUNCIL ELECTIONS

THURSDAY, MAY 7, 1959

WHAT a hullabaloo in the High Street! The architects of tomorrow turned out in force to laugh at what the Kensington Council is doing today. They came to mock and protest at the design for a new Central Library. Ugly, they cried, and 300 years behind the times.

A century ago

UGLY? Maybe they were right. But the demonstrators should not have stayed in the High Street. There's plenty more that's ugly and out of date (and old and dirty, too) in Kensington, especially North Kensington. Labour protests but the Tories do not seem to care overmuch. The public baths date from 1888. The public library went up in Ladbroke Grove in 1891. And since then? Nothing. Not one public building has been constructed by the Borough Council this century.

All missing

OUT OF DATE? The Tories have been in power at the Town Hall since it was built — in 1880. And they are still stuck in the nineteenth century. That's why local young people have to go outside North Kensington for cricket, football, cycle racing, athletics or open air swimming. That's why 50,000 North Kensington residents have no public hall bigger than a schoolroom for meetings or dances, concerts or exhibitions—except in the months when off-the-bus-route Lancaster Road baths become the makeshift Argyll Halls. The Labour boroughs are not like this.

Unhealthy

UGLY? There's nothing uglier or unhealthier than an overflowing, smelly dustbin. But Kensington empties dustbins only once a week. Other boroughs clear theirs twice a week —and have been doing so for years.

MAY 7th - lovely day for a change!

67

was set up not by architects. Architects tend to come from the middle class. The question of being "a member of the professions" is important to them. Whereas art students are free spirits.'

According to Baynes, 'This all grew out of the idea, which happened in discussions in the bar, and in the library and so on. That, really, if you looked at the architecture in London, you could hardly find a building that one would call "modern".' '[Architecture] fell into two categories,' William Wilkins recalls. 'There was the very poor overblown revival of classicism of some kind or another. And there was some really terrible modernism.'

'What the Anti-Uglies wanted was more good modern architecture, the kind of work stemming from the Bauhaus,' Baynes relates. 'It's not a question of being "in keeping" with London. Great cities grow, change, challenge the people who live in them. We felt, just as in painting and so on, that London was beginning to be important, and so there should be an appropriate architecture. So we cooked up the crazy idea of having demonstrations about this.'

A core group coalesced around the founders, headquartered at 23 Cromwell Road. 'When I arrived, there were William Wilkins and Ken Baynes,' Newman says. 'They really were the start of Anti-Ugly.' Along with Newman, Wilkins remembers 'a chap in Graphics called Barry Kirk. A chap called Ron Fuller, and he had a friend called Nigel Adams. A girl called Angela Heskett. And Brian Newman's girlfriend Janet Allen.' 'Gerald Nason,' Baynes adds. 'Roddy Maude-Roxby was soon involved. And Pauline very shortly after it started.' 'I joined largely because it meant going around with Pauline,' Maude-Roxby says.

As for the name, 'There was a young lecturer called Michael Kullman, who was a left-wing radical,' Wilkins recalls. 'He'd been taken as an assistant in General Studies. As the thing developed a head of steam, it was he who said, "Well, what about it simply being Anti-Ugly?" And somebody else tagged on "Action".'

By March 1959, some seven months after it was formed, the group had produced a one-page manifesto (on crisply designed letterhead), the points of which bore the influence of architecture writer and AUA patron saint Ian Nairn, who in 1955 had already declared Britain's emerging postwar 'subtopia' to be an 'outrage'. Though the manifesto lists Baynes as chairman, Newman as secretary and Wilkins as treasurer, none of the three recall anything so formal. 'People swapped duties every day,' Newman explains. 'I don't know how it worked, quite honestly.' 'I don't remember any fallings-out at all,' Wilkins adds. 'It was a band of brothers and sisters. My subsequent career has suddenly reminded me of how unusual it was.'

If a desire for change and the art school as subversive incubator were two of the strands in the Anti-Ugly plait, the third was at once unlikely and definitive. 'The theatrical aspect of the Royal College was very vibrant at the time,' Baynes remembers. 'You can see a bit of influence on some of our methods. After the Second World War, there emerged a streak of completely off-the-wall humour, exemplified by *The Goon Show*. There was the same sort of feeling about Anti-Ugly. Whether anyone understood what it was that we were saying, I'm not entirely sure. But not only did we really believe it, it was also tremendous fun. I think Pauline got involved, really, because it looked fun.'

'The first Anti-Ugly event was planned for 10 December 1958,' Stamp reports. 'The targets were, first, Caltex House in the Brompton Road, an ungainly semi-modern development of 1955–57 by Stone Toms & Partners, dubiously enhanced by Franta Belsky's sculptures of horses, and the monumental neo-Georgian Agriculture House in Knightsbridge [headquarters of the Farmers' Union] of 1956 by Ronald Ward & Partners.'

Fifty Royal College of Art students paraded outside two new buildings in Knightsbridge yesterday crying: 'Pull them down'. The buildings are Caltex House, costing just under £1m and not yet completed, and Agriculture House, which cost over £500,000 and was opened two years ago.

The students, who have formed an Anti-Ugly Action Society, marched through Knightsbridge carrying banners and placards. It was the first of several planned operations. Their aim is better building.

The banners proclaimed: 'Ugly buildings are a sin', 'Must bad buildings speak for Britain' and 'Look around you'. The students marched from Hyde Park Corner to Knightsbridge accompanied by a drummer and a bugler.

– The Daily Telegraph

'For perhaps the first time in English history,' Robin Darwin declared, 'buildings were catcalled, booed and applauded as though they were a first night.'

The 50 paraders were ... clad, as the Times disdainfully noted, 'in lumpy coats, blue jeans, hats like tufts of gorse and, in one case, green boots'.

– The Royal Gazette

'We were marching through Knightsbridge,' Natalie Gibson remembers. 'And this incredibly tall, elegant woman came out of a shop, it was Bazaar, Mary Quant's shop, to look at this motley crew going past. And she said, "Oh, but you're all so ugly yourselves!"'

Operation Two, against a new Bank of England structure and Bracken House, both in the City, unfolded less than a week later, on 16 December. 'More Architecture – Less STODGE' read one of the banners, but the affair ended prematurely when the police declared the solemn beating of a drum a violation of a by-law within the district banning music without a permit. The next operation, however, on 15 January 1959 and also in the City, represented a step forward in AUA's sense of occasion. 'We learned that you needed not simply to get on the street, but to be able to create a story and an event,' says Baynes. 'Something that would attract press photographers and so on.'

HOME FOR BARCLAY SQUARES

The Anti-Uglies – that team of Counter-Attacking Royal College of Art students – have been at it again. Their latest victim is the proposed head office for Barclays Bank, a building which makes nonsense of any talk of replanning the City ...

– The Architects' Journal

Miss Janet Allen ... led about 30 fellow men and women students from the college, all wearing mourning clothes.

At the site of the new bank, where the foundation stone was being laid by Mr Anthony Tuke (chairman), the students put down their 'coffin' – it bore an inscription reading: 'Here lyeth British architecture' – and lit a candle at each end.

– Esher News and Advertiser

'It was quite revolutionary as a form of protest,' says Newman. 'Mock funerals.' Wilkins remembers 'a carnival air, and a great deal of excitement about it. Nothing of the sort had been seen before.' According to Stamp, 'the deposition of the coffin on the pavement and the lighting of candles around it provided a photo opportunity for the press as Allen and another glamorous RCA stained-glass student, the "Wimbledon Bardot" Pauline Boty, scattered rose petals over it.'

Though Pauline was a supporting player, her looks inevitably set her apart. In the 29 January edition of *The Architects' Journal,* beneath a photo of a bundled-up Pauline scattering rose petals, appears a curious bit of doggerel.

Sir –
The Pauline Gospel we acclaim –
But oh! The Pauline form:
Must thus be duffled honest frame
To keep La Boty warm?
– W.H.E., Coventry

The fourth action, against the Kensington Public Library on 4 February 1959, represented the high-water mark of everything AUA hoped to accomplish, and is remembered by one and all as the group's most effective.

STUDENTS PROTEST AGAINST LIBRARY PLAN
DEGENERATE, THEY CLAIM

Marching through Kensington the other day with a jovial rabble of about two hundred students, some in simulated seventeenth-century dress, many carrying angry banners, escorted by policemen treading solemnly in time with an ardently chaotic Dixieland band [The Temperance Seven]*, one began to feel like an extra in an Ealing comedy. But the joke was meant to be a serious one: it was operation four of the Anti-ugly Action, an unofficial Royal College of Art organisation that favours good contemporary architecture and demonstrates in protest against new buildings that it considers bad. The Anti-uglies target was the royal borough of Kensington's new central library, now under construction.*

    – Manchester Guardian Weekly

At the head of the procession came, wheeled in a bath chair, a figure representing an architect of the seventeenth century [Ken Baynes]*, labelled 'Three hundred years and still going strong'.*

The students had marched from the Royal College of Art in Cromwell Road, and arrived outside the present Public Library in Kensington High Street ...

    – Kensington News

Outside the reigning public library ... the town crier read extracts from the recent apologia by Mr Vincent Harris, the architect.

    – The Daily Telegraph

'Oyez, oyez, oyez!' balled the Crier [Barry Kirk]*. (Cheers, hoots, catcalls and blasts on a trumpet from the mob.) 'The new Kensington Public Library shall be a building of good manners' (Cries of 'It's horrible. Pull it down!') ... 'in modern English Renaissance style, in keeping with the Royal Borough.' (Yells of derision.)*

Raising his voice above the din, the Crier went on: 'It will be a manly type of building, and an example of dignified architecture.' (Cries of terrific protest.)

    – Kensington News

'An item on the television news caught my eye,' records Christopher Logue in *Prince Charming*, his 1999 memoir. 'The Anti-Uglies had demonstrated outside the new Kensington Central Library, with Pauline Boty, dressed as an eighteenth-century shepherdess, pushing a blindfolded, silvery-wigged man labelled "*ARCHITECT*" ... Miss Boty was questioned. She dismissed "What's a pretty girl like you doing at this sort of an event?" with a friendly grin, and went on to say that the building was an expensive disgrace. When the interviewer reported that many people thought it was "very efficient inside", Boty replied:

"We are outside."'

'Here's a disappointment for you: she was a somewhat peripheral figure,' Wilkins says. 'She came and went as the mood took her. I would say Pauline was brought forward by the media, rather than us.' Baynes is more sympathetic: 'She was a very, very busy girl, and she probably didn't give as much time to Anti-Ugly as we would have liked. The time she did give was tremendously useful. Because she was such a beautiful girl, she was apt to get the attention of reporters and people rather well. She fully recognized her worth to Anti-Ugly, and she was very good at playing that role.'

Though one is loath to dispute the founders, Pauline's participation was not, in fact, entirely casual. 'Anti-Uglies Probe Art Training', an April 1959 article in the *Kensington Post*, reports that AUA members 'are now forming a study group to make enquiries into the training of all artists. Particularly it will enquire into the training of architects and the kind of jobs open to them after studying.' Pauline is quoted: 'No-one seems to know what the standards of good architecture are. As far as we can see, people ask "people in the know" to suggest a good architect. What we want to find out is where the advice comes from, and why open competitions are not held more often.' Whether or not Pauline got involved in this forward-thinking exploration of competition-based commissions, what is certain is that a month earlier, on 2 March, she led AUA Operation Six, a second assault on Bracken House, which had opened the week before.

Yet an article published two weeks later in the *Daily Express*, featuring a photo of Pauline beside the headline 'Of all things she [pointing-finger icon] is secretary of the ANTI-UGLIES!' suggests a problem endemic to participation in public life: the difference between what one intends, and what the culture chooses to make of it. The article's tone suggests that, at least in this, one of her first forays into popular culture, Pauline was overmatched. In a way the story, and an earlier television appearance, established the character of the adversary she would confront for all her life.

MISS PAULINE BOTY assured me that it has nothing to do with policy, which is far above these things. But the fact remains that the 20-year-old Miss Boty, who is secretary of that very indignant organization the Anti-Ugly Action Society, is, well, very pretty indeed ...

But yesterday, the girl from the Royal College of Art, who might be seen any afternoon toting a protest banner through the streets, told me she had problems all her own.

'First, we've had some really worrying complaints about the way our members dress,' she told me. 'Their old cords and duffel [sic] coats are a disgrace to the organization, some are saying.

'I have to keep pointing out that they are, after all, only students in their working garb.'

The talk turned to buildings, which is the moment for every good Anti-Ugly to slip into crusading mode.

'I think the Air Ministry building is a real stinker, with the Farmers' Union H.Q., the Bank of England, and the Financial Times as runners-up,' Pauline announced.

Her own home? 'A 1930 "semi" in Carshalton, normally termed "desirable",' sighed Pauline. 'I don't approve, of course, but I daren't say anything or daddy would be upset.'

– The Daily Express, 16 March 1959

'Certainly newspapers were keen to pander to the prejudices of readers,' writes Gavin Stamp. 'The Daily Telegraph noted "duffle coats and ponytails, the twin badges of Anti-Ugly Action" ... ' Yet 'the prejudices of readers' also included the trivialization of women acid-etched by Sally Alexander and Nell Dunn. Thus, the miniature portrait of MISS PAULINE BOTY presents us with a bubble-headed blonde 'secretary' (what else could a girl be?) whose heart – ironically, given what we know – belongs to daddy. It suggests Pauline's challenge as she sought to subvert the way she was seen: to use her appeal to advance new agendas without being subsumed by the culture she proposed to change.

The challenge, in fact, had presented itself almost immediately, several months previous: on 11 December 1958, one day after AUA's first demonstration, Pauline appeared with Baynes, Wilkins and Maude-Roxby on the BBC's televised chat show *Tonight*. As co-founders, Baynes and Wilkins were obvious choices; Maude-Roxby, an undeniably theatrical presence, also made sense. But it was Pauline who elicited the most interest and, perhaps not surprisingly, the malice. 'They recruited Pauline because she was very glamorous, and it could not be said that the other of us were very glamorous,' Wilkins explains. 'So she became very much more associated with the movement than she might have.'

Tonight was hosted by Alan Whicker, described by Maude-Roxby as 'a smooth operator'. 'The interview had been rehearsed, there'd been preliminary discussions with researchers,' says Wilkins. 'And Whicker was to go down the line of us asking different questions of each one.' 'At first he seemed quite sympathetic,' Maude-Roxby remembers. 'But actually he was put off by the idea that people would complain about new buildings and so on. And put it to us that we were art students, we didn't necessarily know how to evaluate architecture.'

'He was due to end with Ken Baynes,' Wilkins says. 'And then, at the last minute, he put an unrehearsed question to Pauline.' It was, Maude-Roxby realized, a set-up. 'We had said, "Shall we dress?"' he explains. '"No, no, no, the whole point is, you're art students." We were asked to come wearing our "colorful clothes", as they put it. And then, at the end of the interview, he said to Pauline, "You speak of yourself as being anti-ugly. But if you don't mind my saying so, I think your own clothes are a mess." Something like that – something quite offensive.' 'And she stammered,' Wilkins recalls, 'and frankly, it made us look foolish.'

'And we rebelled!' Maude-Roxby declares. 'We said, "Mr. Whicker! In our opinion, that suit that you're wearing is incredibly tedious, and the choice of tie is quite unpleasant!" They were trying to get us out of the studio, and we just ignored that and went on shouting out at him. It was going out live, you couldn't stop it. People said it was extraordinary, that they'd had this spontaneous outburst, it made television more lively.'

'It's a good thing he never interviewed the sculptors,' says Gerald Nason. 'They would have dealt with him.'

So, one presumes, would have any of the three men on the panel (who in any case struck back immediately). Yet if Whicker felt that embarrassing a pretty blonde would be perceived as acceptable, even welcome, to the BBC audience, he proved to be culturally tone-deaf. 'In his sympathetic review of AUA's achievements published in April 1959,' notes Stamp, 'John Smith [founder in 1965, of the Landmark Trust] dealt with these "sartorial problems" and observed that "an elegantly suited TV interviewer may ask the Anti-Uglies why, if they are so concerned with lack of beauty in building, do they themselves wear such (pause, for a nervous laugh) ugly clothes. This old chestnut can be ignored, but when it does appear it is a certain sign that a movement is getting somewhere, and is worthy of closer examination."'

Anti-Ugly Action had its last demonstration, against a commercial block on St Martin's Place, in March 1960, winding down as its charter members left the College. Yet for a movement begun by a handful of duffle-coated students committed to effecting urbanistic change using cardboard coffins, tricorn hats and other weapons of serious fun, the group's mission was prescient and its impact significant. For Pauline, too, the benefits of Anti-Ugly involvement were multiple. It introduced a woman with an interest in social change to the mechanisms and experience of activism. AUA demonstrated to an artist who would eventually place issues of many sorts at the centre of her work the power of subversive wit when it came to changing minds. Pauline's engagements with print and visual media revealed the faces of friend and enemy, and enabled her to consider strategies for self-advertisement that might set her at the centre of her times as both participant and observer. Not least, Anti-Ugly showed a consumer of pop culture who was not yet a Pop artist an example of what might be described as Pop in action.

'He was splendidly mad in those days,' Ken Baynes recalls. 'Very, very "up for it". If you wanted somebody to take part in some completely madcap scheme,

Roddy was your man.'

Roddy Maude-Roxby's fine madness came to the fore when, following his ascension to the leadership of the RCA's theatre company, he took charge of the College revues. 'There was a small group, about four or five of us, who wanted to do these shows at the end of the terms,' he relates. 'Derek Boshier was one. So was Pauline. And it would be sort of ad lib, but we'd have ideas, and we'd run through them, so we'd know what we were on about.

'Once we got the thing rolling, we put up posters saying, "Anybody who wants to be in on it, bring us your ideas." And *masses* would come and say they wanted to be in it. David Hockney had a piece, which he wanted me to do. And I can't remember if I did do it or not, but I so much begged him to do it. Which was facial and bodily expressions of different types of cars that had been in minor accidents. A Rolls-Royce that's got a scratch.'

'There was a guy called Mark Berger, who was a great friend of David,' remembers Boshier. 'And it was he who got David to go on stage in one of these revues. David was dressed up in a frock, a dress. And wearing clogs, you know, like the Dutch wooden clogs. And David came on singing a song from the then-current musical *Oklahoma!* He was singing *I'm Just a Girl Who Can't Say No*, and changed the title to *I'm Just a Boy Who Can't Say No'*.

The revues unfolded on the junior common room stage and, as ever, the best adjective remains 'anarchic'. 'There was a running order, and sketch titles [for example, *Your Monet or Your Wife*], and it just went through the evening,' Maude-Roxby remembers. 'They were ragged as anything. And they were interminable, they went on miles too long. People went to the bar and came back, and the same thing was going on. The audience was usually quite drunk as well. They yelled back at you and stuff.'

'There were a couple of sketches which I messed up, because I couldn't remember the words,' says Geoffrey Reeve, though 'they were very tolerant of me. I got the laughs. "The stupid guy." There was one sketch with Tony Manzaroli when he comes on and turns on a light bulb. And then I come on and sniff around the whole stage, until eventually I'd come up to his armpit, and just engulf him with an embrace. And then the lights went out. That's the only one that I figured was any good.' 'There was always a spiff on ads,' Boshier says. 'The graphic designers did a whole series of advertisements. Which they acted on stage – "make your armpits charmpits".'

'Darwin would come and bring his friends,' Maude-Roxby recalls. 'And after each show, he'd say, "You really should do Shakespeare, you know. It'd be *so* impressive."'

Puerile though the descriptions might sound, Boshier believes the revues were an early manifestation of performance art, and Maude-Roxby heard from

College alumni who, after participating in America's first Happenings, recognized an affinity with the doings intoxicating the common room's intoxicated audience. (The 'legitimate' theatre also took notice: William Gaskill, Ann Jellicoe and Keith Johnstone of the Royal Court Theatre were regular attendees.) The experimental context, of course, spoke powerfully to Pauline. If, as Gwyneth Berman opines, her face-painting at Wimbledon with Jennifer Carey provoked an interest in the 'masks' of public image and alternative identity, and a fascination with role-playing, then participation in the revues offered Pauline a stage – quite literally – to try them out.

'Pauline was extremely beautiful and attractive, and that quality she just easily brought on stage,' Maude-Roxby says. 'She was flirtatious. She would be received that way, and she'd come towards the audience. Pauline sang the line, "Daddy wouldn't buy me a Bauhaus." The idea was given to her by [artist] Dick Smith. I can remember her singing, "I've got a little cat/And I'm very fond of that/ But I'd rather have a Bau-hau-haus!" When she was doing it about the second time, she said, "I've got a little cat – my pussy," and everyone went crazy.'

Nicholas Garland perceived her intentions. 'She was being a sort of dumb blonde while she sang it, and I thought, "There's something interesting about this,"' he remembers. 'People think she's that, and she's acting a parody of that, and somehow she's demonstrating that she's *not* that.

'Some people that Roddy talked to about Pauline made a point of the fact that she was not taken as seriously as her talents and gifts and intelligence warranted.

Left
A 'quasi revue'
set, 1962.

Right
Derek Williams
and Roddy Maude-
Roxby, onstage in
a revue sketch.

In a funny way there's always a problem when someone is as beautiful as that. But what I remember about Pauline is her mocking that "male gaze" look at her beauty. She knew how people thought she was. She defended against it by producing a sort of parody of that sort of behaviour. I admired it. I thought, "You're better than the people who are just saying you're a dumb blonde – you're *demonstrating* that you're not."'

'I remember one of the songs that she sang,' says Gerald Nason. 'It was very short: "Everybody loves my body/But my body/Is just a body to me." She wasn't a very good singer, but she could sing it in a very sexy sort of way. She wasn't laughing, she wasn't smiling. She just did it. It was funny as well as being beautiful. You're going to have me crying soon.'

'Granddad didn't like what she was doing,' Bridget Boty says. 'He'd see photos of her, which he didn't really approve of. Didn't like her lifestyle one little bit, he hated every part of it. I think one of the reasons why she probably came to the front of all the publicity was, she kind of wanted to show she was doing something, show him she was doing what she was saying she was doing. Not that it made him feel any better. They didn't really want something to stick out, did they?'

77

6

AT THE
ROYAL COLLEGE

OF ART

1958–1961
Part 4: 'Capital-P Pop'

But Pauline's main mission at College was neither to march nor perform – to 'stick out', as Bridget puts it. She had come to South Kensington to make art and, more particularly, to find her voice as an art-maker. As Pauline's métier proved to be Pop, let us take a moment to consider the movement's trajectory in Britain, prior to her arrival at the RCA and during her years there, when the style – the 'Royal College Style' of Pop in particular – came into its own.

'I don't know whether you know my story about the name Pop Art,' says Peter Blake. 'There was an English critic called Lawrence Alloway – he was a great mentor and a terrific champion of British Pop. He gave a dinner party, and I was explaining that what I was trying to do was to make a picture that was parallel to pop music. If you bought an Elvis record and played it, I wanted to make a visual comment on that, that you would read in exactly the same way. And he said, "What, a kind of pop art?" That's my version of the origination of the phrase. Add it to the others.'

As Blake's anecdote suggests, British Pop has more than one origin story. Yet, while different individuals and factions have claimed parentage, it is more accurate to say that the style – defined by Alloway, in a 1962 essay, as 'the use of popular art sources by fine artists' – alchemized out of something in the air at a particular moment in time: circumstances to which different people were drawn, in different ways, for different reasons. It was their contributions, taken together, that produced Pop. And perhaps no part of the story matters less than who coined the term.

The Independent Group (IG), a collective of artists, critics, architects and designers that met between 1952 and 1955, is typically credited with being the nest in which British Pop was hatched. The Group, which included the artists Richard Hamilton, Eduardo Paolozzi, Nigel Henderson, and William Turnbull, critics Alloway, Peter Reyner Banham, Toni del Renzio, and scholar-artist John McHale, and the architects Alison and Peter Smithson, coalesced out of their involvement with London's Institute of Contemporary Arts, which launched in 1947. The ICA supported the Group's formation, gave it meeting space, offered exposure to a wealth of artworks, ideas, and critical opinions – and, no less usefully, presented an ideological parent against which the IG could react and rebel.

The ICA's founders, notably Roland Penrose and Herbert Read, championed

Opposite
Peter Blake,
On the Balcony,
1955–57,
oil on canvas,
121.3 x 90.8 cm

'classical' modern art, exemplified by the prewar Continental avant-garde. Yet for Independent Group members – who were younger than the ICA leadership, had practical (rather than exclusively academic) training in areas like commercial design and aeronautical engineering, and were witnessing the shift of the art world's centre from Picasso's Paris to Pollock's New York – old-school modernism was not an end but a jumping-off point for an analysis of culture, with an emphasis on what they saw as a false choice between High and Low.

The IG's thinking evolved in two waves, with the first, undertaken in a series of meetings from September 1952 to June 1953, focused on, of all things, science. 'If there was one binding spirit among the people of the Independent Group,' Richard Hamilton observed, 'it was a distaste for Herbert Read's attitudes.' By this, Hamilton meant Read's – and by extension the Establishment's – belief in timeless aesthetic absolutes, which established a hierarchy that set the practitioners of fine art above the rackety quotidian swirl. The Group rejected this Platonic perspective, and the ruling taste that came with it, in favour of an 'empirical' modernism that acknowledged the impact of science, technology and mechanization on visual culture, in a time Banham described as 'The Jet Age, the Detergent Decade, the Second Industrial Revolution.'

Having posited an equivalency between the timeless and the transitory, the Group took the next logical step. 'To Alloway a serious analysis of American mass culture was a continuation of the concerns of the first session, where American mass-produced objects and images were at the cutting edge of technological progress,' notes IG historian Anne Massey. 'It was during the second phase of the IG, from '54 to '55, that earlier preoccupations with overturning the assumptions of modernism were incorporated with a serious analysis of American mass culture using largely American sources.'

This was a big deal in mid-1950s Britain, when the vulgar issue of the American comic book industry was considered so corrupting that many were legally prohibited. Yet the impact of the US mass culture machine on Group members recalls the enthusiasm shared by Gerald Laing and Nicholas Garland over the first bright spots to appear on Britain's postwar landscape. 'One of the great trainings for the public's eye was reading American magazines,' recalled Reyner Banham. 'We goggled at the graphics and the colour-work in adverts for appliances that were almost inconceivable in power-short Britain, and food ads so luscious you wanted to eat them.' To Banham, casting all this aside in favour of a Platonic ideal amounted to hypocrisy. 'We eagerly consume noisy ephemeridae, here with a bang today, gone without a whimper tomorrow – movies, beach-wear, pulp magazines, this morning's headlines and tomorrow's T.V. programmes – yet we insist on aesthetic and moral standards hitched to permanency, durability and perennity.'

In place of the timeless and universal, the Group proposed an ever-changing, populist visual culture that arose from the ongoing back-and-forth between savvy marketers and sophisticated consumers. Yet in a particular respect IG members proved not unsimilar to the likes of Read and Penrose: they made judgments and drew distinctions. 'The Group distinguished between traditional, craft-based popular culture and the new, mass culture by the use of the term "pop art",' Massey relates.

By the time the Independent Group had its final get-together in July 1955, it had launched ideas that would resonate throughout the 1950s and 1960s, and certain of its members remained influential. Undoubtedly, the second-wave Pop artists, many of whom emerged from the RCA's Painting school in the early 1960s, would have been aware of the Group's work. But its retrospective claim that the IG participants had been the 'Fathers of Pop' – the title of a 1979 documentary about them – isn't entirely accurate. For one, most of the 'Hockney Generation' regarded their forebears, notes Massey, 'as a rather insular clique, whose work was little known'. And the younger artists who put British Pop Art on the map – and certainly Pauline – hardly needed the Independent Group to hip them to the visual potential of popular culture.

More to the point, what Massey calls 'the strenuous attempts on behalf of subsequent historians to establish a respectable heritage for 1960s Pop Art'– a narrative to which Alloway and Banham contributed, with essays that, she writes, 'attempted to carve out a niche for the IG in the Pop Art lineage' – sowed confusion. The Independent Group concerned itself with 'pop art' – that is, mass-produced visual media – as a means of analysing popular culture. 'Pop Art', conversely, was a *style,* one that incorporated mass-produced visual media into paintings, sculptures and other fine-art genres. It is Pop with a capital P that Pauline and her comrades practised – however much, or little, it may have reflected the ideas put forth by the Group.

So what *were* the origins of capital-P Pop?

In his 1962 essay *Pop Since 1949,* Alloway named Francis Bacon as Britain's first Pop artist, citing paintings that drew on Eadweard Muybridge's motion-study photos, and imagery from Sergei Eisenstein's 1925 film *Battleship Potemkin.* The Bacon connection, however, is more tenuous than the work of two IG members: Eduardo Paolozzi and Richard Hamilton.

A tirelessly creative multidisciplinary artist, Paolozzi remains principally known as a sculptor of often monumental works (some influenced by that IG fan favourite, science fiction). But he maintained an interest in visual material of every sort, which he collected voluminously. While living and working in Paris, from 1947 until 1949, Paolozzi amassed a trove of mainstream American magazines and pulp

Right

Richard Hamilton,

Just what is it that makes today's homes so different, so appealing?,

1956, collage,

26 × 24.8 cm

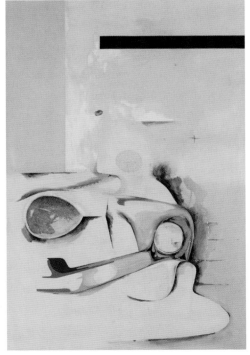

fiction paperbacks, which he procured from former servicemen studying abroad on the GI Bill. These became the raw material for a series of small-scale collages that, in 1952, the artist used to illustrate a lecture – entitled 'Bunk' – which he presented at the Independent Group's inaugural meeting. Some were no more than pages torn from magazines, but others – notably *I Was a Rich Man's Plaything*, which incorporates the word 'Pop' (beside the muzzle of a gun) – are layered constructions that make unexpected connections between quotidian images, and produce wit, perplexity, provocation and pizzazz. Though they have, as Massey notes, 'acquired a mythical aura, often cited as the first examples of British Pop Art or even Pop Art', the collages were meant as research material, and did not become 'art' until 1972, when Paolozzi made screen-printed versions for exhibition.

Like the 'Bunk' series, Richard Hamilton's 1956 collage *Just what is it that makes today's homes so different, so appealing?* is frequently cited as the foundational work of British Pop. Also like 'Bunk', Hamilton's effort was otherwise motivated: it was created as a catalogue illustration, and a poster, for *This Is Tomorrow*, a landmark exhibition at London's Whitechapel Gallery. And again as with 'Bunk', Hamilton's collage, measuring roughly ten-by-ten inches, wasn't seen as a stand-alone artwork until years later. Yet, as the Pop Art historian Marco Livingstone observes, 'the collage remains an extraordinary prophecy of the iconography of Pop': the references Livingstone lists include '20th-century technology, popular entertainments and systems of modern mass communication ... convenience foods, domestic appliances and advertising imagery ... the eroticism of pin-ups and muscle-man magazines', and 'even an early use of the word Pop in the larger-than-life piece of American candy held up by the body-builder'.

Interestingly, Hamilton's paintings from the same period lack the collage's density, specificity, obviousness, and decibel level – they are, in fact, quite the opposite. While such works as *Hommage à Chrysler Corp.*, *Hers is a Lush Situation*, *She*, and *Pin-up*, all from the late 1950s and early 1960s, deal with the American interdependence of marketing, sex and money, Hamilton's paintings are elegant, restrained, and spare, sensual in form and soft of colour, surreal in their mechanical /human conflations and Cubist in spirit, and most of all allusive rather than explicit. Though clearly at home in Pop, the presence of the modernist fine-art tradition – indeed, the pictures' sheer beauty – invites the viewer, not to see the obvious, but to consider the imagery's ambiguity, and ponder alternate interpretations. 'If you ask who I think is the best Pop artist in the world, without a doubt, for me, it's Richard Hamilton,' says Derek Boshier.

But for Pauline – and perhaps, Boshier's comment notwithstanding, for her Painting school contemporaries – the most influential first-generation Pop artist was Peter Blake. Unlike Hamilton's cool classicism and ambiguous subtext, Blake's early paintings are autobiographical and emotional; they show a clear connection

Opposite left
Eduardo Paolozzi,
I Was a Rich Man's Plaything,
1947, collage,
35.9 × 23.8 cm

Opposite right
Richard Hamilton,
Hommage à Chrysler Corp., 1957,
oil, metal foil,
and digital print
on wood,
122 × 81 cm

Peter Blake (left) and Richard Smith at the Royal College of Art, circa 1956.

to folk art and what Massey calls 'traditional British rural crafts and ways of life ... barge painting, tattooing, circuses, gypsies, fairground decoration and patchwork quilts.' Blake, moreover, was an RCA painting student from 1953 to 1956, and remained involved with the life of the College, befriending and encouraging new arrivals. Thus he served as artistic example, comrade-in-arms and, not least, generous mentor.

Regarding the work, Blake's own origin story is instructive. 'When the Second World War started, I was seven, and I was evacuated twice during that period of time,' he remembers. 'So I wasn't with my parents, and I missed my childhood. A lot of what I'm about psychologically links to that. I wanted to be a painter, and at Gravesend School of Art, they said, "You'll never make a living as a painter, do graphic design" – "Commercial Art", as it was called then. I did a year of a two-year commercial art course, tried for the Royal College – I sent one painting – and was accepted into the Painting school.'

The work Blake began to produce reflected his life as a teenager in Dartford, southeast of London, whose graphic sensibility – he began at Gravesend at 14 – interacted naturally with the folk and naïve art he discovered around him. 'My contribution to Pop Art at that point was autobiographical,' he says. 'I was a working-class little kid. So the phenomena of childhood, of professional wrestling, football and boxing – that's what I was painting about.'

Blake's 'circus' paintings, made during and just after College, reflect this precisely. Created on boards and panels, each features a fictional fairground or sideshow attraction, rendered with an almost cartoon garishness, and scratched and battered so as to suggest a piece of authentic memorabilia. The works express Blake's delight in the world of his subject matter and, in the almost obsessive level

Left
Peter Blake,
**Siriol, She-Devil
of Naked Madness**,
1957, oil and
collage on panel,
76.2 × 21.6 cm

Right
Peter Blake,
Girlie Door,
1959, collage
and objects on
hardboard,
121.9 × 60.3 cm

of detail, a surprising strain of emotion. Most evident is the bravura character of Blake's accomplishment: the erasure of his abundant artistic talent, in the creation of a perfectly rendered 'found' piece of Pop.

Though not as autobiographical as *Boy with Paintings, Self-Portrait with Badges* or *Children Reading Comics,* in which he 'appears' with his sister, Blake's Pop works from the late 1950s and early 1960s are also personal. They dovetail with another of the painter's great obsessions: fandom, particular as regards the music of his day, artists such as Chubby Checker, Brian Wilson and Chuck Berry. Engaging more fully with pop music, foregrounding an iconography of pin-ups, Hollywood stars and rock'n'roll idols, Blake shifted his approach: switching to actual found objects and, rather than detailed renderings of things like badges and comic books, collage. This may have further subsumed his painting chops, but it replaced them with an iconic style that helped to define British Pop (though Blake's technique of running a selection of images or designs along the top of a canvas – a motif Pauline 'sampled' frequently – was, the artist acknowledges, taken from the American Pop maestro Jasper Johns). These works also capture the appeal of Pop Art at its most celebratory, a condition Pauline was to indelibly describe as 'a nostalgia for NOW': the idea that the pop cultural life of the moment derived an extra frisson from the awareness – even as you were living it – that life's best moments are legendary.

The painters who were contemporaneous with Pauline at the RCA – and comprised, along with individuals attending London's other postgraduate schools, the core of second-wave British Pop – were Derek Boshier, David Hockney, Allen Jones, R B Kitaj, and Peter Phillips, who began in 1959, and Patrick Caulfield, a 1960 arrival. This group did indeed share certain preoccupations with its predecessors, but the generations were more different than alike; moreover, given that Kitaj was an American almost exactly Peter Blake's age, and Jones got kicked out of College after a year, they themselves were not so comfortably categorized. Nonetheless, the inventors of what became known as the 'Royal College Style' helped birth an art historical movement, one as distinct and influential as Impressionism or Surrealism.

'The student of 1959 is less easy to teach because the chips on his shoulder, which in some instances are virtually professional epaulets, make him less ready to learn,' observed Darwin of this cohort, 'yet this refusal to take ideas on trust, though it may not be congenial to the tutor, may in the long run prove to be a valuable characteristic.' Among the traits the late 1950s students shared, their youth proved especially meaningful. Not only did this encourage the scepticism that both annoyed and attracted Darwin, it also made the artists natural recipients of the mass culture machine that supplied the raw material – the visuals *and* the sensibility – of Pop.

This was a point of departure from American Pop, whose practitioners were by and large older and more detached from the imagery upon which they drew. Yet for Allen Jones, and for many of his contemporaries, the art across the Atlantic offered inspiration. 'I understood that one should be bold and not have any qualms about what one should or shouldn't do in paint,' Jones recalls. 'That was the exhilarating lesson of American art.'

In fact, the lesson took. 'One of the great pleasures of British Pop lies in its very openness, in the sense that anything is possible, that any found or invented image or any subject can be the occasion for a work of art,' notes Marco Livingstone. 'A personal commitment to subject matter is a distinguishing feature of the art produced in the early 1960s by the RCA painters.' Despite drawing, to a degree, on American mass culture, the Pop percolating at the Royal College remained grounded in European fine-art traditions. A painterly quality – evidence of the hand – was abundant, as was a celebration of colour. To Jones, moreover, who believes that, despite British claims to the contrary, 'Pop Art was an American thing,' the principal difference between the two was that 'European artists never abandoned illusionistic depth', whereas 'it was a tenet of American painting that the fact of the surface was a part of the subject of the picture'.

Also unlike American Pop, which tended to focus on single iconic images (for example flags and targets) or, as with Andy Warhol, the repetition of an image, 'the artists working in Britain,' Livingstone observes, 'continued to work more within the European traditions of relational composition,' by which he means a 'preference for taking the eye on a visual journey ... to create narrative.' This characteristic, to which British Pop lent itself naturally, the historian cites as a defining trait of the 'Royal College Style'.

However much was shared, their independence of spirit, emphasis on self-expression and openness to subject matter made the work of the Royal College painters notably diverse. 'I think it's quite interesting how all the British Pop artists had different agendas and came from different places,' says Boshier – indeed, a look at what he and David Hockney chose to do with toothpaste, in the former's culturally critical *The Identi-Kit Man* and the latter's sexually explicit *Cleaning Teeth, Early Evening (10pm) W11,* makes the point unforgettably.

Boshier was the most socially engaged painter of his cohort, and the most sceptical of America: rather than painting pop stars or pin-ups, he drew on his reading of books like Vance Packard's *The Hidden Persuaders* to create canvases that addressed the malign effects of American mass marketing on the consumer, and the encroachment of American capitalist values on other nations and political systems. Patrick Caulfield's work could not have been more opposite: using hardboard and house paint to replicate the flat affect of signage, mixing this with a kitschy, paint-by-numbers approach to landscape, objects and figures, he rendered both high-art quotations and the components of everyday life in a deadpan style at once amusing, emotional and, at times, tinged with menace.

'It's astonishingly assured and ahead of its time, I think by far the best work he ever produced,' says Nicholas Garland of David Hockney's RCA output. His assessment is, to be sure, debatable, yet Hockney's student paintings – which drew on the 'untutored' language of child and outsider art, cartoons and graffiti to obliquely expose the artist's most urgent interests, yearnings and desires – still deliver the shock of the new. Hockney also experimented, in *Tea Painting in an Illusionistic Style,* with a canvas in the shape of the box of Typhoo tea it depicts, but it was Allen Jones who maximized this gambit. Though he remains best known for his notorious 1969 *Hatstand, Table* and *Chair* – furnishings made from lifelike mannequins of submissively positioned, semi-naked women – at the decade's start he created colourful 'bus' paintings that engaged, Livingstone notes, 'a specifically Pop notion of relating the object quality of the painting to a particular subject' – an epiphany Jones arrived at while teaching art to pre-teens. 'If you see a child's drawing of a vehicle, they'll draw the box with the wheels underneath, and tilt the box forward, put some lines behind it, so it looks as though it's going fast,' the artist explains. 'And I thought, "That's a bloody good idea for a painting!"' Jones built rhomboid-shaped canvases that, via their tilt, conveyed the sense of a bus's forward motion, to which he added anecdotal vignettes – 'using the language of gestural abstraction but to a figurative end' – capturing the everydayness of urban existence.

David Hockney (left)
and Derek Boshier at
the Royal College of
Art in 1962, before
Hockney's painting
**We Two Boys Together
Clinging**.

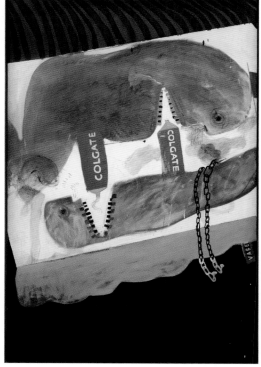

R B Kitaj – older, American, intellectual and strongly attached to the European tradition – resisted the Pop label (as did Hockney) and was only two years at the RCA; his references were largely literary/historical rather than pop cultural. But he impressed his fellow students as an example – 'We were all influenced by Kitaj in terms of his professionalism, and his work ethic,' Boshier recalls – and via his 'use of found imagery and quotations of style and technique', notes Livingstone, which gave his Pop-inclined friends a template for the free organization of canvases using their own iconography. More importantly, Kitaj believed in art as a personal journey, which affected everyone, Hockney especially. 'He told me that I should look upon painting as a means of exploring all the things that most interested me, and that I should paint pictures that reflected this,' said the artist, who foregrounded his homosexuality when it was, in England, still illegal.

Peter Phillips was, in a sense, the outlier: the youngest of the group, attracted to the rough energy of engines, pinball games and shooting galleries, trained from the age of 13 in such craft skills as technical draughtsmanship, silversmithing and heraldry. Yet at the College, Phillips produced fully realized works of lapidary Pop: inspired to a degree by board-game formats, his paintings were organized compositions that integrated abstraction and figuration, and with their cool glamour – and great size – resembled their American cousins.

Phillips's preference for big pictures, however, spelled trouble. Much has been made of the encouraging, laissez-faire attitude of the Royal College tutor-practitioners. But towards the Pop painters who arrived in 1959, they behaved just like teachers everywhere. According to Livingstone, 'Phillips painted his Pop pictures at home rather than in the studio provided for him in the College, since he had been berated by staff and threatened with expulsion during his first year for painting huge abstractions.'

In fact, Jones believes, 'The staff were very reactionary, stuck in the Euston Road and Pissarro and Post-Impressionist thing. The faculty thought that the year was somehow getting away from their ethos and a couple of times they called everybody together and said, "Listen, your first year here, you should study from the Life room and from nature, and you can be creative in your final year." We were all in the Life room at least three days a week, and all working hard, but they decided that they would make an example of somebody. And they put a pin in the list, and it happened to be me! On the last day of the summer term, when most people are going off on holiday, they just gave me the push.'

Jones ended up at Hornsey College of Art – from which he had graduated the year before – doing a two-year teacher training course.

In 1963, Carel Weight, then the RCA's Professor of Painting, observed that '[w]hen Mark Rothko recently visited the College, he seemed astonished that students painting in such contrasting styles could work together in such complete harmony, often stimulated and inspired by one another'. Though Rothko's surprise says as much about him as the Painting school's comity, it reinforces how essential was that camaraderie to the cohering of these independent voices – still developing, still students – into a distinct and genuine movement. This was borne out by the 1961 Young Contemporaries exhibition, held at London's Royal Society of British Artists (RBA) galleries. The show, an important showcase for new artists, was overseen by a committee of students, and in 1961 Phillips was the committee president, Jones the secretary; according to Livingstone, Lawrence Alloway, an exhibition juror, suggested that the Royal College painters present a 'united front' by rehanging the show so that their work could be seen together.

Jones remembers it differently. 'As everyone was going home, Peter and I looked at the hang, and we said, "This just looks like an ordinary Sketch Club, rather like the summer show at the Academy,"' he relates. 'By that time, it was clear that the group of artists at the Royal College' – of which, despite his expulsion, he considered himself one – 'were onto something different. So Peter and I rehung the whole show, and basically faced off the Royal College students with the Slade, which was very much what I called "struggle" painting. I remember we gave Kitaj one wall.' The home team was generally well represented: like Kitaj, Hockney, Jones and Phillips each got four, Boshier showed three pictures, and Caulfield had two – 21 in total.

Jones's dismissal of the Slade work indicates the rivalry between the two, which Nicholas Garland, a student there prior to his Royal Court gig, felt acutely. 'I was taught that the god was Cézanne, and that the people who came after – who were our tutors – were descended from Cézanne,' he explains. 'I don't think the Royal College people took any notice of the Slade people at all. But we at the Slade looked at the Royal College people. I thought they'd taken a bum steer – that Pop Art stuff, it's a dead end. When Pauline talked about nostalgia for the present, I thought that was just silly, though I wouldn't probably have said so. And it was typical of the Royal College people that they would formulate an idea like that.'

Whether or not the difference between the two would have been so stark had Phillips and Jones not re-jigged the presentation is hard to say. But when the Now of Royal College Pop faced off against the Then of the Slade's dark, impastoed landscapes, still lifes and portraits, a charge was ignited. According to Livingstone, 'This exhibition was considered the breakthrough for British Pop Art.'

Today, Pop's enduring appeal is evident, as is its influence – what are the RCA-era David Hockney and Jean-Michel Basquiat, if not kindred spirits? What is less well known is how much of an impact British Pop's second generation had on their predecessors: in the early 1960s the work of Blake, Joe Tilson and Richard Smith drew inspiration from the younger artists, and the goodwill flowed in both directions. 'We were influenced, after we'd started to do Pop Art, by the encouragement we got from Joe Tilson,' Boshier remembers. 'Joe owned a house, off of Kensington High Street. It was a meeting place, a salon, where everyone hung out. It's not mentioned enough, and I always mention it now. It's a very important part of Pop Art.'

What Livingstone describes as Tilson's 'central role in bringing together the disparate intentions of his colleagues into something resembling a unified moment' was literalized in a singular collaboration: Tilson's 1963 *A-Z Box of Friends and Family* – quite literally a box, which incorporates specially commissioned small contributions from many of British Pop's major figures. Included in the alphabetized cavalcade are Blake (B), Hockney (D), Jones (J), Kitaj (K), Phillips (P), Hamilton (R) and Smith (S), as well as a piece by Tilson himself, listed under Z. The effort, at once a work of fine art, a celebration of talent and friendship, and a time capsule, seems to capture everything that was best about British Pop in its breakout moment – a genuine example of Pauline's 'nostalgia for NOW'.

Joe Tilson,
A-Z Box of Friends and Family, 1963,
mixed media,
233 × 153 cm

7

AT THE ROYAL COLLEGE OF ART

1958–1961

Part 5: 'To think I've got someone like that for a daughter!'

From 30 November until 29 December 1961, twenty of Pauline's artworks, primarily collages but at least one painting (*Gershwin*), were featured in *Blake Boty Porter Reeve*, a four-artist exhibition at the AIA Gallery, off Leicester Square in Soho. The show was organized by none other than Charles Carey, who was on the Artists International Association committee, in response to a suggestion by its chairman, the painter Adrian Heath, that the gallery present something to do with the 'new' movement called Pop. 'I got four people who were doing work roughly in the same area,' Carey recalls – in addition to Pauline and Peter Blake, there were Christine Porter and Geoffrey Reeve – and the outcome, he believes, was 'the first exhibition of Pop Art in England'.

According to Carey, the work Pauline showed had been completed within the previous year; as she graduated from the Royal College at the start of July 1961, it may be assumed that much of what was on display represented Pauline's mature student work. The precise contents of the show remain beyond verification, as some of Pauline's collages no longer exist, and so cannot be matched exactly to the titles listed in the AIA programme. But in January 1962, Pauline appeared in *Pop Goes the Easel,* a BBC documentary about a day in the life of four Pop artists – the others were Blake, Boshier and Phillips – and in the sequence showcasing her work can be seen a number of the works Carey exhibited, including some of those presumed lost. Moreover, prior to shooting, Pauline did a preparatory interview with the film's director, Ken Russell, in which she described her intentions regarding specific pictures, and also talked about her interests and enthusiasms, and the motivations underlying her creative impulses. Thus we have a record – incomplete, yet illuminating – of what Pauline had been doing as an ostensible stained-glass student, and where she was upon embarking on her professional life.

This is useful, for the obvious reason that Pauline was *not* a member of the gang of RCA painters who developed second-wave British Pop. It is true, moreover, that Pauline's claim on Pop at this particular moment has been questioned by Marco Livingstone, who wrote that she 'can be said to have become a Pop painter only in 1963, when she painted a series of pictures based on photographic images of public figures', and, as will be seen, by Derek Boshier. But given that her time at College was increasingly consumed by a medium better suited than stained glass to what she wished to express – collage – and her initial forays into painting, it is more accurate to say that in 1961 Pauline was finding her way to a personal interpretation of Pop. After all: if Pauline *wasn't* a Pop artist, why did Carey

Opposite Pauline in December 1961, during the run of **Blake Boty Porter Reeve** at the AIA Gallery in Soho.

feature her in England's first Pop exhibition, and Russell solicit her to co-star in *Pop Goes the Easel*?

There is, of course, an obvious answer to that question. A less apparent, more interesting one can be found in the work on view in the film, and the years of effort that led up to it.

'She would have been doing stained glass and the early collages by the time we met,' Blake remembers. 'I recall that there was quite a lot of black in the stained glass – they were dark. Technically, it would have been quite heavy leading.' Pauline's classmate Gerald Nason saw the same. 'The lead uses up quite a lot of the picture,' he explains. 'So they were very dark by the time she'd finished with them, because she never did anything huge. Very sort of thick, very dense, lots of bits put together.'

Pauline's dilemma was evident: her stained-glass panels, based on image-saturated collages, were disadvantaged by the physical constraints of the medium. She could turn its limitations to her benefit: a circa 1958 self-portrait on display in

Above
Pauline's sometime boyfriend David Cripps designed the cover of the AIA programme.

London's National Portrait Gallery suggests a lively spirit muzzled by an enveloping lead vine. But increasingly, Pauline's collage production became an end in itself.

'We all did collages then, even for people's birthday cards and things,' Natalie Gibson recalls. 'But Pauline's were quite Surrealist.' 'They were very Surrealist, weren't they?' Blake affirms. 'We both used the same kind of iconography. I imagine by then I was interested in Hannah Höch, Schwitters. You couldn't make a collage and not be influenced by Schwitters and Max Ernst. It's like, if you're cutting something out, it's instantly a Schwitters. There's no point in hiding it.'

In Pauline's collages can be seen borrowings from all three artists: Ernst's interest in Victoriana; the graphic abstractions and pop cultural samplings of Schwitters; and, in Höch's photomontages, juxtapositions of scale, an interest in politics (including sexual politics), a dry humour and a touch of the macabre. But a no less important influence, according to Boshier, was the now-forgotten 'collage novel' series by the American artist Norman Rubington, which he published under the extravagantly phoney pseudonym Akbar del Piombo in the late 1950s and early 1960s. Inspired by Ernst's foundational 1929 collage book *La Femme 100 Têtes*, Rubington used 19th- and early 20th-century steel engravings as his source material to create fantastical and spooky, highly satirical genre tales, primarily pictorial but with bits of text that helped hold the stories together even as they exacerbated their absurdity. To contemporary eyes, the six Akbar del Piombo books are recognizable as graphic novel precursors, and remain every bit as addictive.

'I have four of them: *The Boiler Maker, The Hero Maker, Fuzz Against Junk,* and *Is That You Simon?*' Boshier reports. '"A Far-Out Book" series, from the Olympia Press in Paris and, in New York, the Citadel Press. I bought them because Pauline got them, and we thought, "Wow, they're great."' Nonetheless, the books reinforce Boshier's belief that Pauline's collages were not Pop. Rather, 'They were nostalgic, Victorian things, like what Max Ernst did if you went back half a generation.'

Boshier's recognition of Ernst's influence – on Pauline and Rubington alike – is accurate. But what she responded to in the Far-Out Books, one suspects, was not so much their Victorian quality as the singularity of Rubington's Pop sensibility – its cinematic character, deadpan tone, unflagging outrageousness and wit, and especially his assaults on every sort of hypocrisy. And there was something else: the books' dreamlike atmosphere, the kind of 'logical illogic' authored nightly, in the mind, by Morpheus.

Pauline had a fascination with what might be described as the reality of dreams, and made it the subject of her (now lost) thesis, in which she paired passages from Poe, Rimbaud, Baudelaire, Apollinaire and others, as well as her own writings, with collages that were, as she put it to Ken Russell, 'sort of expressly dreamlike'. In her preliminary interview with the director, Pauline explained the aspects of her 'quite vivid dreams' that influenced her work.

Above
**Untitled (with
Lace and Hair
Colour Advert)**,
circa 1960–61,
collage and
paint on paper,
39.7 × 37.2 cm

Opposite
Siren, 1960,
stained glass,
42.5 × 55 cm

Often dreams seem more real than life, because as you're actually dreaming, you focus on each thing – you know, if you're talking to somebody in a dream, you aren't aware of the room around you and what's going on or a bird singing outside or anything like that. You're just aware that you're speaking to somebody and you just see them, and there's nothing else really to interrupt that, and so you get this kind of strange kind of intensity about it. And in these, I was trying to do that – you know, cut out all the other things that were to do with it and just get the straight thing of that odd feeling.

Speaking of her collages, Pauline noted another dream phenomenon:

I just liked the idea of something happening without other people sort of taking any notice at all – something terrible and ridiculous at the same time ... If you accept extraordinary things as everyday things, then they become all the more extraordinary.

Pauline's fascination with dream logic also dovetailed with one of her pop cultural obsessions.

Science fiction films are all – I like the way they start off. Everything's very normal and everyone's behaving quite normally. And it would be a dead boring film at the beginning unless you knew some monster was going to appear at the end. And then slowly halfway through, people begin to get puzzled ... [Y]ou don't know what's happening and that builds up a certain kind of fear. And again, it can be ridiculous, you know, it can get to the point of ridiculousness where it just becomes funny. And there're these two different things all the time.

By the time of the AIA show, Pauline's interests, influences and working methods had coalesced into something resembling a style, one that is displayed – alas, in black-and-white – in *Pop Goes the Easel*. Of the 15 collages shown in the film, 11 can be reasonably identified as having come from Carey's exhibition. Only five are known to still exist, and just two of those – *A Big Hand* and *Picture Show* – are among the ones that Pauline spoke about with Russell.

Even so, *Easel* offers up some revelations. *Siren,* a collage that Pauline did use as a stained-glass template, confirms that her intentions got diluted in translation. And the film shows an intriguing edit: *Untitled (with Lace and Hair Colour Advert),* a still-extant collage that derives its impact from an arrangement of pink lace, a magazine cutting featuring rows of kiss curls and lips, and a bathing-suited pin-up girl – all encircling a man's hirsute hand, holding that of a baby – originally featured a photo of a woman resembling Elizabeth Taylor along its left-hand edge.

Pauline's comments to Russell on her collages are also revealing: exposing the sometimes provocative, sometimes comic thinking behind the images, and welcoming us into the artist's particular sensibility.

The Wreck of the Hesperus involves a simple juxtaposition: in the foreground, in the lower half of the picture, three people herd sheep in a bucolic forest clearing, while behind them, beyond the tree line and set against an expanse of sky, an ocean liner goes down, nose first.

I saw this photograph of the Titanic going down, which I thought was tremendously dramatic, you know, and very odd ... And then there was this, just this print I had lying around, and which I liked very much and which was a kind of Victorian painting. And I just put the two together because I thought they looked extraordinary, you know, sort of like a horror dream. Only some people find it terribly funny and some people hate it, you know ... When I did some at home and my mother saw them, she said, 'To think I've got someone like that for a daughter!'

Resembling a tableau by the silent film fantasist Georges Méliès, *Siren* is divided into quadrants: a fountain featuring a column surrounded by jets and flumes of water; a face, seemingly carved from a cliffside, with a huge, obscenely gaping mouth ('a 16th-century Mannerist cave doorway from the garden of the Duke of Bomarzo,' Sue Tate reports); an ornate hand gripping a smouldering object; and a bunch of bananas. At the centre of this phantasmagoria stands a plump 19th-century hoochie-coochie dancer.

One of my favourites ... It took ages and ages. I took lots of what I thought would be sort of Freudian symbols and what have you. And it's all really based on sex the whole time, you know. Like bananas and fountains and that huge mouth.

And the lady is obviously a sort of – well, she was a Victorian pin-up from the Gold Rush.

In *Here They Come Again,* a gigantic American football player leaps over the top of Blenheim Palace, while behind the fortress-like 18th-century structure, three equally outsized, unlikely figures stand beneath a sky filled with orbs.

Clockwise from top left
The Wreck of the Hesperus, Here They Come Again and **Darn That Dream**, all circa 1960–61, as they appear in **Pop Goes the Easel**.

The things up in the air are planets or where they come from or they're spaceships – whatever you want them to be. And that's an American footballer, because I think they look a bit how like I imagine a spaceman would look stepping out of Blenheim Palace. And behind him actually is a monkey. Then there's Fidel Castro, and then there's a woman on the telephone in her corset – she's communicating with them and explaining what's going on. And that also has that thing of, you know, people so big that they make everything else look either ridiculous, or frightening, or amusing.

One of the most layered of the lost collages, *Darn That Dream* takes its title from the American Songbook standard about someone who possesses his (or her) loved one only while asleep. On the left, the head of a desiccated-looking Somerset Maugham – at the end of a thick branch and with a grinning woman's face in place of an eyeball – regards a topless woman (on the right) wearing a pillbox hat made of meat and holding an upside-down bottle as though it were a tennis racket, with Brendan Behan's head floating at the bottom. The woman's torso grows out of a corseted figure with two heads – male and female, the latter seeming to whisper into the man's ear. Two more faces appear at the figure's shoulders: Jerry Lewis, and an announcer proclaiming Castro's victory. (In the film, as Pauline and Blake study the picture, she describes it as a 'rude-y', and in fact *Darn That Dream* was the one that upset Pauline's mother.)

I set out for it to be an erotic one – erotic and macabre at the same time. There are all sorts of sort of phallic symbols – that sort of bottle she's holding, having meat on her head, and the fruit being where it is [at the corseted figure's posterior]. *And I had Somerset Maugham's face in this. I thought it would look a bit like soil erosion ... It's a head at the same time as being sort of a landscape.*

One of Pauline's most attractive qualities was the genuineness of her enthusiasms, a quality evident in *Picture Show*. Loosely zoned as a triptych, with a gold background, the collage features some of Pauline's fan favourites: political (Franklin Roosevelt, the Greek Cypriot anti-colonialist freedom fighter Georgios Grivas), literary (Proust, Rimbaud, Colette), and others celebrated for their beauty, style and capacities (Mesdames Pompadour and Récamier, Doña Isabel de Porcel, Marilyn Monroe). The selection reveals the catholic breadth of Pauline's interests; her sexuality turns up, metaphorically, in Beethoven's quill pen, a cherub holding up Big Ben and a man's finger pressing a doorbell as a woman pensively listens.

For that I selected lots and lots of things I liked. I had the idea of a gallery and people looking at pictures and some of the pictures might be alive, you know ... It's just a picture show. But there are things in it that just sort of happen.

Though she doesn't speak about them, two of Pauline's most effective collages also appear in the film. In *I Surrender Dear*, a woman allows herself to be kissed by her formally dressed suitor (who holds a giant egg, a droll expression of what he expects from her), while behind them a regiment of soldiers stands with upthrust bayonetted rifles – offering, to him, erotic encouragement and, to her, coercion. *Untitled (Hand, Secateurs and Children)*, a nightmare fairy tale set in a botanical garden, features two ladies in bonnets and a top-hatted gent, chatting in an *allée*

Left
Gershwin, 1961,
oil on board,
97 × 127 cm

Right
**Untitled (Red, Yellow,
Blue Abstract)**,
circa 1961,
oil on board,
97 × 126 cm

bordered by banks of towering succulents – oblivious to the two young girls above, being lifted away by a giant female hand gripping a pair of pruning clippers, the blades holding one of the children by the neck.

Much happens in the picture show of Pauline's collage work. One is drawn into a world of narrative alternately obvious and oblique; sexuality at once light-hearted and disturbing; revolutionary politics; hero worship; surreal alterations of scale, often with 'a big hand' (the title of a particularly dramatic collage) as the focal point; above all, a mix of dream logic and pulp sci-fi, stirred into juxtapositions of the mundane and the menacing. In these student works, Pauline seems most comfortable in a state of hypervigilance, one reflective of her life experience: a sensibility alert to the fact that everyday life teeters at every moment on a precipice – a stumble away from comedy, absurdity or catastrophe.

'I remember her showing me her paintings,' Nicholas Garland relates. 'Within them, there might be strong drawing and painting of a head or something like that, but it was in amongst lots of other funny things. Even the paintings were like collage, made up of fragments. And I thought, you know, nice, decorative. If I sound like a sort of pompous asshole, I was. Art students are very good at encouraging each other, and we learned to look at work we didn't like very much but found something to admire. I would have been skilled at finding something nice to say.'

Given that some of the paintings Pauline would produce in the five years between graduation and her death did indeed employ collage – actually or in representation, as a sort of *trompe l'oeil* – Garland's memories of combinations of fragments make sense. Yet despite his admitted snarkiness, Garland's judgment suggests that, in her student years – and however confident she was as a collagist – Pauline's mature painting style remained elusive. This was borne out by the paintings she did, in fact, choose to show: colourful geometric abstractions in the manner of Sonia Delaunay, an influence she did nothing to hide – a circa 1960 gouache on paper was called *Untitled (After Delaunay).*

But there was another inspiration, one that gave Pauline's abstractions a more individual character. This was evident at the AIA in *Gershwin* and perhaps – given its title – *Ziegfeld Line*: the visual culture of the 1930s, Hollywood musicals in particular.

I think they're super. The kind of shapes they used, and just the songs and dances and everything, it sort of – you can't explain it – it's just an atmosphere really. I think I partly try and do this with some of my paintings, but some of them I sort of combined a bit the dream thing in with a much more abstract thing.

To a notable degree, Pauline succeeded in translating the vividness she found in prewar film production design, choreography and music into paint. Though they could not be more different in style, *Gershwin* and other of Pauline's abstractions offer the same unambiguous joy found in Mondrian's late-career paean to Jazz Age Manhattan, *Broadway Boogie Woogie.* But it did not come easy and, at least with Russell, Pauline was candid about that.

It's very hard for me to do at the moment. I just think that it might not come out more and more. And at the moment they're much more inclined to be kind of flat patterns. And I'm trying to – I don't know what I'm trying to do. I'm just doing it, I think.

I'll know it when I've done it. You see, I did some more collages and for me, you know, I can now look back on them – they're over a series of years – and I can see more or less what I was doing. With the paintings, I'm so sort of involved with them at the moment that perhaps I – I can't even say what I'm trying to do. To be vital I suppose, but that's it.

Pauline's work was not included in the Young Contemporaries exhibition that featured her fellow students' work and solidified the significance of Pop.

Instead, at the age of 23, she received her Stained Glass diploma and graduated. Yet the record shows her three years at the Royal College of Art to have been fruitful ones. She had partaken of everything the College, at that shining hour, had to offer. She had herself contributed to its vitality, as an activist, entertainer and personality. Certainly, Pauline had, to borrow a phrase, burst joy's grape against her palate fine. Most remarkably, while executing a degree in a subject in which she entertained only moderate interest and was not entirely suited to her talents, Pauline worked consistently, and on her own, in other media, producing work that – if not as recognizably Pop as that of the RCA's painters – drew on the qualities of the 'Royal College Style'. In particular, her collages possessed in abundance that most central characteristic of British Pop: Livingstone's 'personal commitment to subject matter' – enthusiasms that Pauline, at last beginning adult life in earnest, was excited to share.

'It's a horrible thing when people just look at things and walk away, and that's it, you know?' she told Ken Russell. 'Because after all, you do things for people, I think, really, and even if you might say, "Oh I only work for myself," you can't really work for yourself ... I'd like my things to relate to everybody in the end. Always.'

8

HELLO,
CRUEL WORLD

1961–1962

'When Pauline left the Royal College, she really didn't have a clue what to do,' Ray Bradley says. 'She was definitely an active painter. But how do you paint if you haven't got any money, and you can't buy paints, and you can't buy canvases, and you can't pay your rent?'

Bradley might have added that, prior to graduation, Pauline's intentions were very much in play. In her student file, there is a handwritten note requesting that the registrar, John Moon, contribute a letter of recommendation to accompany her application for a 'graduate assistantship' at Mills College, a women's arts institution in Oakland, California; her note indicates that she'd also solicited testimonials from Lawrence Lee and Michael Kullman, 'as I need three separate references'. (Moon's letter of support, dated 3 March, mentions her Anti-Ugly and theatrical activities, affirms that she is 'well qualified', and concludes that 'she is a young woman of intelligence and character, and I feel sure would make an important contribution to the staff of any college'.)

Pauline also applied to the Arts Council of Great Britain, asking to be considered for their New Designers Scheme, which would have enabled her to work as an assistant set designer. For this, she received a letter from the principal. 'I think in fact you can be assured that Miss Boty is rather an exceptional student who has certainly made her mark here during the last three years,' Darwin wrote. 'She is, I know, very interested in working for the theatre, and I think her general intelligence and her all-round talents would make her very successful in such work if she could have the opportunity of learning more about it. She is an exceptionally nice and attractive girl who, I am sure, would get on with the staff of any theatre who took her in charge.'

Neither panned out, though both reflect Pauline's multiplicity of abilities and interests, and her uncertainty, observed by Nicholas Garland, about which to prioritize. In fact, Pauline did better than might have been expected of a 23-year-old art school graduate: by the end of 1961, she'd had a stained-glass work, *Sheba Before Solomon,* included in a touring Arts Council exhibition, finished her AIA show and begun modelling for print ads, two of which appeared in the RCA magazine *ARK*. But prior to *Blake Boty Porter Reeve,* in the timeworn tradition of creatives everywhere, the first thing Pauline did was get a waitressing job, at Terence Conran's debut restaurant, the Soup Kitchen – London's first French bistro, featuring the city's second Gaggia espresso machine – which had moved from its original location to Wilton Place in Knightsbridge. As Charles Carey

Opposite Pauline and her boa, in the penultimate scene in Ken Russell's **Pop Goes the Easel,** filmed at Richard Smith's studio.

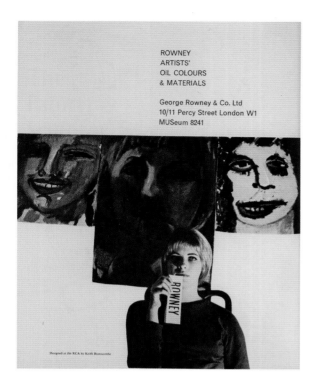

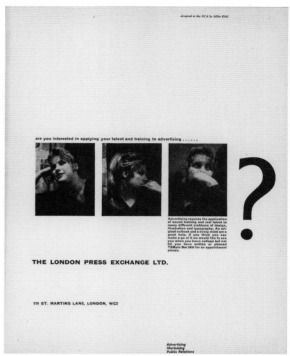

helped at school, so too did Jennifer Carey in life: a Soup Kitchen employee (one of her murals adorned a wall), she got Pauline the gig. Celia Birtwell worked there simultaneously. 'There was a till that we would re-jig up, because Pauline wanted some money to buy stretchers for her canvases,' Birtwell recalls. 'And then I was made the manager, and all my friends would come and get the key off me and then go and raid the fridge to get some steaks for their boyfriends. I lost my job letting all the bloody pals borrow the key, I tell you. Never mind.'

Pauline also moved, to a bedsit at 80 Addison Road near Holland Park, a 19th-century house featuring a central stair and an expansive garden. The upper floors had been subdivided into single rooms, and Birtwell had the space beside Pauline's. 'My room was at the front, and didn't get the sun,' she says. 'But I was able to borrow a French daybed, and I had a screen that kind of hid my little kitchen. Pauline had the big beautiful room that overlooked the garden.' Like Pauline, who was determined to be self-supporting, 'I can remember being *so poor*,' Birtwell says. 'We had those stoves, where you had paraffin in them. There was a shop in Shepherd's Bush and it was really cheap, and you'd go buy these tins of beans and sardines, and warm them on this paraffin stove.

'Everybody went to Henekey's, the pub, which was on the corner of Westbourne Grove and Portobello Road. Anybody you ask of my generation,

Left
ARK number 28,
1961, designed by
Keith Branscombe.

Right
ARK number 24,
1959, designed by
Mike Kidd.

that's where everybody hung out. Everybody would go on a Saturday afternoon, and there was always a party to follow. It had bentwood furniture in the garden, a big garden that we'd always sit out in in the summer.'

80 Addison Road belonged to Jon Manasseh, an antique dealer whose gallery, Façade, was in Westbourne Grove, and whose singularity, variously recollected, captures the savour of the times. 'He was quite extraordinary, this bearded sort of rather marvellous-looking guy,' says Birtwell. 'He came from a rather rich Jewish family, I think they came over here in the twenties, and he was the black sheep.' 'Quite exotic,' affirms Natalie Gibson. 'Lived with his parents in Camden Hill when I first met him. His parents were very peculiar. They didn't talk to each other, they communicated by notes, and he was the go-between.' 'He had Cointreau at the side of his bed, and a great big bowl of Quality Street chocolate,' Birtwell recalls. 'I met him in Henekey's. He was always in the pub sort of looking around with these dark, brown-velvet eyes. Quite a shy man in a way, but very eccentric. He used to wear moleskin trousers with braces, and they were always a bit high over his tummy.' As for the house, 'Jon had bought it from this extraordinary woman called Mrs. Van der Elst,' says Birtwell. 'In the basement there were her husband's ashes. It was all very sort of spooky and rather fabulous.'

Also on the premises, off and on, were two of Pauline's College cronies. 'I had a very small studio, which I shared with Peter Blake,' says Derek Boshier. 'And every day when I was in, I'd walk the five steps and knock on Pauline's door and we'd have instant coffee. We were big instant-coffee people. We'd hang out. Whatever the local gossip was. Who was going out with who, what was happening, films, everything.'

Immersed in this *rêve de la bohème*, Pauline may have been as cash-strapped as Birtwell. But one person, apparently, thought otherwise: Bridget Boty believed 80 Addison Road to be just off Grosvenor Square, in the posh heart of Mayfair. 'Somewhere along the line, some money went down,' she says. 'Because presumably she rented the house, near the American embassy. But it might have been one of her boyfriends who owned it.'

Bridget's recollection – so startling, given Pauline's actual circumstances – is provocative. It may have simply been a misunderstanding on her sister-in-law's part. Or, if this is indeed a story Pauline floated, it might have expressed a seemingly out-of-character impulse to put forth a firmer financial, even 'respectable' front for her family. Perhaps Bridget is misremembering. Yet on just such powerful undercurrents can a house sail from Kensington to Mayfair.

That struggle – between embracing the hipster's absence of guilt and vulnerability, and claiming recognition in a determinedly bourgeois clan – was evident to Bridget that spring, at her wedding to Arthur, where she and her same-age sister-in-law first met. 'She was in Mary Quant-type stuff – she came in one of her posh hats [designed by her friend James Wedge],' Bridget recalls. 'And she knocked me out, 'cause I was very country. People were all amazed at her, they all remembered her afterwards. But she was in the back. Very, very quiet. Terribly quiet. And none of her family kind of told her to join in. I expect Nana probably did more at the wedding with her than I did. It was rushed, terribly rushed, because we had to do it in a week, and had the farm to run. And Arthur forgot the licence, didn't he?'

It was, for Pauline, a season of transition. But if she needed reassurance, it was presently to come her way. On Sunday 25 March 1962, Pauline became a culture figure – at least to the audience of three and a half million that watched *Pop Goes the Easel.*

From the BBC publicity department:

MONITOR cameras spent a day – from dawn until midnight – with four young artists who between them have won critical acclaim, exhibition prizes and Arts Council awards. Each of them has sought inspiration in the world of pop singers, pin-ups, spacemen, wrestling and the Twist.
'We're battered and bombarded day in and day out with images of horror and bug-eyed monsters' says Peter Phillips. 'The imagery is fictitious but nevertheless it's there – we're sort of knocked for six by this mass-media stuff'. Derek Boshier uses American images 'not because I'm in love with them but because of their symbolic meaning – the way Americanism has crept into the social life of the country'. Pauline shares their preoccupation with symbols which despite their ironic or fantastic juxtaposition are clearly recognizable ... 'Things like beer cans may become a new kind of folk art; they're like paintings on pin tables: something else that people haven't really looked at before.' Peter Blake, the eldest of the four, summarises: 'I wouldn't paint a bowl of fruit or a still life with a wine bottle or a petal falling off a flower with a piece of dew on it; I'm not interested. I paint what I like.'

Monitor debuted in February 1958 as television's first regularly scheduled arts programme. Among the original directors was John Schlesinger; when he moved on, to pursue a feature film career that peaked, in 1969, with *Midnight Cowboy,* the show's sharp-eyed producer, Huw Wheldon, engaged Ken Russell – who made his own mark in features, also in '69, with *Women in Love* – to take Schlesinger's place. *Easel,* Russell's 19th outing for *Monitor,* was the first to fill its full 45-minute length.

'I remember we met in the Downbeat Club in Soho, on a hot summer afternoon,' says Peter Blake. 'And he proposed the idea to me. He already wanted

Pauline in it. I don't know how he met her. But he probably thought that she was filmic, and visually wonderful.' A July 1962 article in the *Leicester Evening Mail* reports that Pauline was 'spotted' by Russell at the *Blake Boty Porter Reeve* exhibition, though Geoffrey Reeve remembers suggesting Pauline to the director, along with Boshier and Phillips. 'He started to tell me about this film, and I got really enthusiastic,' Reeve relates. 'And he said, "Do you know anyone else who'd take part, I need some other people to make a group." We chatted, and said goodbye, and I never heard any more until they'd announced who was going to be in it. You get used to things like that.'

Pop Goes the Easel was the name of a 1935 Three Stooges comedy short, and *Monitor* borrowed it for what proved to be nearly as antic an affair. 'It was a good film – the actual texture of the film is brilliant,' Blake believes. 'Though in the introduction, Huw Wheldon was incredibly patronizing about it, wasn't he? It's the most negative introduction I've ever heard, I think.'

In fact, the effect is comic. Following the *Monitor* main-title animation, underscored by the show's serious-but-bracing theme music (from Dag Wirén's *Serenade for Strings*), the camera pans across a reproduction of Pauline's collage wall, with its many film and rock'n'roll stars … and arrives at the notably un-Pop mad-eagle visage of Wheldon, who appears amidst the others as a kind of party-crasher. He addresses the audience and, mindful of its expectations, cushions the upcoming blow, though peculiarly:

Above left

'She came in one of her posh hats,' Bridget remembers of Pauline's appearance at her 1961 wedding to Arthur (**above right**).

Good evening. Our programme tonight consists of one single film that we have made about four young artists. They're four painters who turn for their subject matter to the world of Pop Art. The world of the popular imagination. The world of film stars. The Twist. Science fiction. Pop singers. A world that you can dismiss if you feel so inclined, of course, as being tawdry and second-rate. But a world all the same. In which everybody, to some degree anyway, lives, whether we like it or not. Film stars aren't film stars for nothing, nor are they received as film stars for no reason at all.

Having pre-emptively scolded three and a half million people for their narrow-mindedness, Wheldon introduces the quartet, whom we observe at work: Blake, 29 at the time, cutting a door in two with a handsaw; Phillips, 22, polishing the frame of a painting; Pauline – 'she's 24 – 24 yesterday, in fact', so 23 during the shoot – applying glue to a collage cutout; and finally Boshier, also 24, tapping a nail into the side of *First Air-Mail Painting* (we see the back of it, with the title scrawled under 'Boshier R.C.A.' and, beneath that, the price: £100).

The film then begins with a prologue: an outing at Bertram Mills Circus, inside the Grand Hall at London's Olympia, the four riding bumper cars, at a shooting gallery, and generally larking about, underscored by James Darren's *Goodbye Cruel World (I'm Off to Join the Circus)*. Next, Russell launches his 'day in the life' motif, showing us the artists following their rituals; each receives roughly eight minutes of screen time, in which artworks are shown and thoughts heard in voice-over. This is followed by three set-pieces: a wander through Portobello Market, to the tune of Gene Chandler's *Duke of Earl*; the four enjoying a wrestling match; and finally the most famous sequence, a raucous Twist party in which can be glimpsed Hockney, Maude-Roxby and other scene-makers. Then a coda, set to Bach's *Concerto for Four Harpsichords*: the artists back at their solitary work – concluding with Pauline in close-up, brushing at one of her canvases.

'Some of it was contrived,' Blake recalls. 'It wasn't convenient to find an actual wrestling match at that point in the filming. So what Ken did was, he got a film of an existing wrestling match, and sat us in a row, as though we were in a crowd. I think we may have watched the film and reacted to it in some way. Whereas other sequences, like the circus, were relatively uncontrived. Some of it was nerve-wracking. Just to walk down Portobello Road with a film crew was relatively alarming.'

The penultimate scene was filmed at Richard Smith's studio on 3 February, a house with plain brick walls that answered Smith's desire for a New York-style artist's loft. 'The party was there,' Blake says, 'and that was mad.' According to Adam Smith, 'The BBC laid on a dozen bottles of Beaujolais and a dozen of beer to get the party rolling, and roll it did.' 'Everybody got very drunk,' Blake affirms. 'The cameraman climbed up onto the beams, and he got drunk. Ken got drunk. It was a good party.'

As is often the case with the art of cinema, many of the BBC notes documenting the shoot, which consumed 17 days between 20 January and 8 March, deal with money. A *Monitor* staff member asks the network's lawyer to handle a complaint from Peter Phillips's landlady at 58 Holland Road, regarding filming without her permission. Jon Manasseh appears, hustling the BBC for a ten-guineas-a-day 'facilities fee' by claiming that Russell stored equipment in an empty room. And there is an invoice authorizing payment of 25 guineas per artist for the first four days of filming, with a note appended regarding Blake: 'He is an artist of some repute compared to the others who are only youngsters and just starting. There is a possibility that in addition to this four days filming he <u>may</u> be asked to the dubbing session for commentary or something. If he is then we'd have to add to this fee.'

Other notes relate to the initial set-piece in Pauline's segment: the nightmare from which she awakens in the morning. It was filmed in a curving third-floor corridor of the BBC's then-new Television Centre in White City, an unpromising environment (staff referred to it as 'the Doughnut') that Russell put to good use. The sequence is arresting, its characters effectively sketched on a BBC info sheet:

Miss D R Gribble. Someone representing 'authority' ... Woman in wheelchair ... Very austere uniform-type dress. Very formal, with high collar in dark material and long. Black stockings, black lace-up shoes and black kid gloves. Could help be given to 'scrape' hair back for the sake of severity. Will be wearing dark glasses ...
Miss Henny Schudde ... Miss Hanne Schmidt ... Miss Anne[gret] Loose ... These three girls need to look as though they represent an 'Institution', i.e. live or

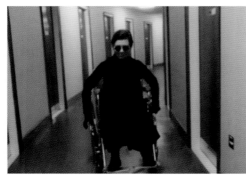

work in one ... [Their dress is] very stiff and 'uniform'.
    Miss Pauline Boty. An art student resenting 'authority' ... Own clothes.

The obvious Teutonic character of Pauline's adversaries was made explicit by the casting of the young women: 'These three German girls ... may be required to say just a phrase in German to establish that they are German ... Suggest as they are students we give them two guineas each for half a day's work.'

In the sequence, which follows an early-morning establishing shot of 80 Addison Road's façade, we find Pauline kneeling in the corridor, with its institutional lighting and loud HVAC system, studying an array of drawings laid out on the floor. Abruptly, one of the *Mädchens in uniform* advances on her, the others arranged at intervals behind to amplify the threat. Walking across the drawings, the girl hurls scolding German until Pauline leaps up and slaps her. At that, the 'authority' in the wheelchair appears, expressionless, eyes hidden, rolling over the drawings like a one-woman tank korps. The soundtrack explodes into a stew of electronic music, a ringing alarm and a pounding heart as Pauline takes off down the corridor, staccato editing heightening her terror, the wheelchair in close pursuit. Reaching an elevator, Pauline bangs on the call button, leaping in just as the door closes on her nemesis. Within, she sighs with relief ... turns ... and spies

Above Pauline's nightmare, filmed in a corridor of the BBC's Television Centre in White City.

the woman in the chair! Pauline frantically grabs the elevator's emergency phone – and abruptly sits up in bed at 80 Addison Road, the nightmare banished.

Russell was 35 when he made this, his first full-length *Monitor,* and understandably anxious to extract the maximum from the chance. Jane Percival claimed that the sequence was based on an actual nightmare Pauline related to the director, but given the BBC production notes – and the clichéd character of the scene's content, a farrago of shopworn tropes – this seems questionable. More likely, Russell saw an opportunity to unleash his penchant for provocative flamboyance, and took off from the interest in dreams Pauline related in the show's preparatory interview.

In this, the sequence is not unique: *Easel* reveals a director (fairly, like most directors) most inspired by that of which he could take creative ownership. We see it, not only in Pauline's scenes, but those featuring Peter Phillips. Blake and Boshier are handled fairly straightforwardly: there are clever editing interpolations and inspired flourishes of sound and image, but mostly we see and hear artists at work. The hipster-handsome Phillips, however, Russell presents as a kind of international man of mystery: he makes his entry, in black turtleneck and smart sport coat, in the back seat of a tailfinned Ford Galaxy, its top down (it is the cusp of February), being chauffeur-driven by an ultra-hip Black man (the actor Danny Daniels) as Cannonball Adderley's *This Here* floods the soundtrack. However Phillips actually began his days, surely this wasn't a part of it; presumably the painter told Russell that he drew inspiration from board games and pin-ups, and the director, inflamed by Phillips' glam look, spun this into the swinging tale of an artful Harry Palmer, complete with a sexy blonde bird playing pinball in his room as he paints. (In her book *London's New Scene,* the art historian Lisa Tickner reports that Phillips actually 'shared rooms with three other men, the pintable was rented, the blonde lived upstairs and the film suggests much more space than he enjoyed'.)

Russell's creative fevers were in fact a departure from the usual parade of art-film talking heads, and arose from more than careerism. 'I found working on a film with these amazing pop artists to be a very liberating experience,' he recalled in 1991. 'I sort of got infected with this new spirit, this new revolution and I got rid of this old documentary heritage.' The result, as Tickner observes, is less a film about Pop Art than Russell's attempt at a Pop Art film. Yet if this is admirable, it also had the effect of substituting the director's reality for that of his subjects (the articulate Boshier excepted). Consequently, Pauline emerges less as an artist than a peculiarly ambiguous figure.

This becomes evident once our heroine, awakened, realizes that the boys are out in the garden, waiting to be let in. We see her famous room as they arrive; as Blake asks about a face in the wall collage ('That's Natalie Wood, in *Splendor in the Grahss,*' she lilts musically), Boshier picks up an LP, and Phillips

flops on the bed, Pauline makes coffee on a hot plate (one of several prominent fire hazards). This tableau of a contemporary artist's life is underscored, oddly, with Fred Astaire's 1937 version of *A Foggy Day in London Town*, which rises as the camera zooms into a close-up of Pauline, reflected in a mirror as she backcombs her haystack-in-a-hurricane hair. The shot lasts just over a minute – an eternity in screen time – and though a voice-overed Pauline begins, at about the three-quarter mark, to describe the influence of dreams on her collages, the visual point is in fact a celebration – a *deification* – of youth, style and glamour at the dawn of a golden age. As the image lasts and lasts, as we contemplate her fierce combat with that impertinent hair, Pauline achieves, before our eyes, a kind of apotheosis: she transforms into a figure as stunning, as unforgettable, as Marilyn or Bardot. Whether or not this was Russell's intent – the take was made on the shoot's last day and may have answered a need for filler – it is one of the film's most indelible moments. In 60 seconds, a legend is born.

Yet as the shot dissolves into a review of Pauline's collages, the soundtrack offers up spooky, harp-infested 'dream' music, then a sappy waltz played by an old-fashioned dance orchestra, and the star's anointment curdles: Russell has seized on the Victorian aspect of Pauline's work and is making camp of it. Her commentary is a scripted encapsulation of what she related in the preliminary interview.

I've always had very vivid dreams and I can remember them very very easily and I've used the kind of atmosphere of the dreams in my collages.
I think there are two things about this, and one is that I often take the moment before something has actually happened and don't know if it's going to be terrible, or it might be very funny. The other thing is that if something very extraordinary is actually happening and yet everyone around isn't taking any notice of it at all.

Above Ken Russell transformed Peter Phillips into an ultra-cool, international-man-of-mystery-style hipster (complete with chauffeur-driven Ford Galaxy).

However enlightening this might be, the music undermines the content, producing an experience best described as twee. The narrative regains its footing in the next beat, in which Blake and Pauline review her collages; the exchange is notable, for what we learn about the work, the affection between the two and Pauline's engaged, undeniably sweet persona. Then it is nostalgia time again, a string of Hollywood musical excerpts: a production number from *Top Hat* (1935); Fred Astaire, fleet-footed; four-year-old Shirley Temple dancing frantically, set to Astaire's up-tempo version of *They All Laughed*. Again we are treated to a scripted reduction of Pauline's pre-shoot musings.

I've always enjoyed the Thirties and musicals, and I've seen all the Fred Astaire and Ginger Rogers films, and some Shirley Temple as well, and I suppose I've just absorbed all the shapes they use and the atmosphere, and it's just come out in my paintings.

There follows a cut-to-the-music montage of details from the paintings, focusing on their 'Deco' aspects, subtracting meaning and context. Coming off this peregrination, a campy finish: a close-up of Pauline, in top hat and white tie, doing a cutesy-poo lip-synch to Shirley Temple's 1934 rendition of *On the Good Ship Lollipop* (according to Gwyneth Berman, this was taken from an RCA revue sketch).

Above A legend is born: Pauline's back-combing close-up, a single shot lasting just over a minute.

From a cinema-history standpoint Pauline's segment intrigues, as Russell went on to make over-the-top music-themed features, including *The Boy Friend*, *Lisztomania* and *Tommy*, the origins of which can be seen in Pauline's Temple turn. Yet, as was the case with her Anti-Ugly press experiences, the director was trading on Pauline's persona for his own purposes, at the expense of her reality. Of course, as the saying goes, nobody put a gun to her head; millions of people

saw her work, she was in first-class artistic company and it was in Pauline's character to try new things, to say *why not?* Moreover, 'Boty apparently had the greatest control over her section' of the film, Berman records in a thesis footnote, in part because she shared with Russell an admiration for contemporary French cinema. Unlike the RCA revues, however, where Nicholas Garland watched Pauline subvert the perception of her as a gorgeous bubblehead – to enjoy herself, entertain others and make a point – she is precisely *not* in control in *Easel*, and consequently portrayed untruly, as a kind of cliché.

And yet. In the movie's *vérité* moments *la vraie* Pauline shines, and this is almost poignantly the case in the party scene, with its revels set to *Twist Around the Clock*. The sequence has turned up in multiple productions about the period, and even amusingly misidentified: in a documentary about the landmark British rock'n'roll TV show *Ready Steady Go!* Dick Smith's loft is passed off as the *RSG!* green room. But one wonders if it would be so regularly sampled absent Pauline.

To be sure, everyone is having a well-lubricated blast – Blake's opaque eyes suggest he's barely staying upright – but taking their Twist rather seriously. Not Pauline. She disports with the reckless freedom she so admired in her heroes, commanding the revels with a raucous effervescence that is, truly, show-stopping. We see her twisting solo with a feathered boa, showy and provocative, and shaking boobs and booty at top speed before a severely overmatched Boshier. But it is the first sighting that stands out: dancing with Boshier, sensing the camera's presence, she turns to it and winks – three times – signalling innocent anything-goes fun, the purple promise of sin and a slight, surprising dash of detachment – a mix that seems to capture Pauline, the participant and the observer, *in toto*. Watching the moment today, some six decades after it first beamed out across Britain, one feels Pauline's true singularity – that, and the tragedy of her loss.

Left Pauline lip-synching to Shirley Temple's rendition of **On the Good Ship Lollipop.**

Right Peter Blake asks questions about **Picture Show** as Pauline looks on.

'The whole thing nailed me,' remembers David Alan Mellor, the art historian and curator who, in 1993, launched Pauline's rediscovery. 'I was 13, growing up in the English Midlands. English working-class life, it wasn't poverty, but it was meagre. The wonderful treat would be to have an instant curry. And by chance I saw this *Monitor* documentary. And here was this vision of something wonderful, of freedom and gaiety. It does sound like a roll call of clichés, but remember those clichés about the sixties weren't in place at that time. This is why that film is so foundational – *so* foundational. This really was a revelation, and Pauline was part of that revelation. She is like the golden goddess figure, who brings that forward. I'd not started going out with girls, but I didn't know any of my female peers who looked remotely like this, she just looked so extraordinary. And that wonderful voice. Very *posh* voice. I mean, you heard a voice like that, you realized it belonged to a student who probably owned a suede coat.

'She is far more than the paintings,' Mellor adds. 'She's like the harbinger of something, a cultural revolution and a great liberation. Pauline will always be associated with this. She is the shape of Englishwomen to come.'

'I've got a funny feeling that Nana wouldn't have liked Granddad to see it, so probably kept it quiet,' Bridget Boty says. 'He'd probably have grumbled, and she'd rather him not grumble. What the eye doesn't see, the heart doesn't grieve over, does it?'

The BBC 'Reaction Index' gave the show a score of 47: 'the lowest figure given to any programme in the *Monitor* series since its inception in 1958', according to a 24 April 'Audience Research Report', which also detailed the reasons.

Because they felt that such 'torments of the imagination' were beyond their ken, and also anything but pleasing for consideration on TV, a large proportion of the sample audience deplored this investigation into what they supposed is the beatnik level of the world of art. Certainly many viewers thought it unworthy as a subject for a Monitor *'probe', and were obviously sorry that the promoters of the programme thought fit to pay attention to such 'over-played sensationalism' ...*

Other viewers, indeed about a quarter of the sample, were interested, even if, mainly, in a wry sort of way, in the purpose of the programme as certainly affording 'a remarkable insight into the disturbed and frightening world' inhabited by some young people today. From this point of view, several said, the whole background (including the Twist session) of this recorded day in the company of four young artists ... and their pictures seemed 'a better criticism of the disintegrating civilization we live in' than the work it set out to introduce ...

Another but much smaller group who found the programme really stimulating and worth-while would have liked to have seen more of the finished work of these artists (particularly that of Pauline Boty – 'a girl who shows considerable talent') rather than seeing and hearing so much of how they evolve their ideas. As an Electrician put it, 'one did not get enough time to know whether one was looking at a painting by the artist, or montage or what have you'.

Punch's critic, Bernard Hollowood, called it 'a long film riddled with cinematographic clichés, and a rigamarole of pretentious eavesdropping'. Arthur Calder-Marshall, reviewing *Easel* in *The Listener*, enjoyed Pauline's nightmare, 'a pastiche of the sort of Ufa production that was had in the nineteen-thirties', but felt that 'if it was intended to show us the work of these artists, explain what they were trying to do and evaluate their achievement, the programme was a failure ... the director was far too concerned with his own art effects to allow me to consider theirs.'

Peter Phillips was with the naysayers. Interviewed in 1964, he indicated that *Easel* presented Pop as 'a bit of a giggle' rather than a serious art movement (one to which he'd dedicated his life). What did Pauline think? Fortune was often her ally, and being chosen to co-star in a high-visibility production was fortune at its most fecund. Perhaps it also revealed how double-edged luck can be. After 'beautiful', the adjective most often appended to Pauline is 'confident': Richard Hollis felt it in her paintings, and Nicola Wood speaks for the multitudes when she says, 'I never saw an unconfident Pauline.' Surely this was the woman who arrived at the RCA in 1958 – but was she the same one who emerged, from that 'ridiculous little screwed-up world', as she called the College in a letter to Jane Percival, in '61? Watching *Easel* – seeing herself, as Mellor describes her, as a 'fantastic, mythical flora reborn from one of Leonore Fini's paintings from the'30s into the epoch of Pop', but also (to paraphrase André Gide) understood too quickly – was Pauline's confidence shaken? If we choose to see her application to Mills College and pursuit of an Arts Council grant as a tincture of uncertainty – if giving a Grosvenor Square address expressed a small wish for respectability, Carshalton-style – did the 'Pauline Boty' that Russell reflected back to her enlarge that tincture and cause her to wonder: am I the real deal? Phillips may have bristled at what Tickner calls the 'obliquely sinister aura of bohemian cool' Russell laid upon him, but he remained a committed painter. So did Pauline – but she also began to act. Was this the inquisitive magpie instinct that charmed Nicholas Garland, or an oblique expression of self-doubt?

Impossible to say. But it remains one of life's few unassailable verities that one never knows where a thing will lead. Pauline may have started acting to pay the bills, to explore another aspect of her talent, to hide from doubts about the seriousness of her artistic commitment. Whatever the motivation, acting, it would seem, produced an unexpected outcome: it unlocked her potential as a painter.

Opposite Pauline makes a friend of the camera, and the audience, in the often-sampled (and, upon occasion, incorrectly ascribed) party sequence.

9

THE ART
OF ACTING

1962–1963

'She looks good, doesn't she?' says Peter Blake of Pauline in *Easel*. 'I wonder if that set off a want to be an actress that wasn't there before.' In fact, Pauline had revealed a passion for performing as far back as *The School for Scandal*, at Wallington, and drawn considerable joy from her meta-glam turns in the College revues. But if *Easel* inflamed her interest, what actually launched Pauline as a professional actress was her affair with the director Philip Saville, whom she met on New Year's Eve 1962 at the Chelsea Arts Club, three weeks before Ken Russell began shooting. Saville's interest was instant. 'I saw this startlingly beautiful woman and powered my way through about fifteen blokes to talk to her,' he told Sabine Durrant.

> **Nell:** *Have you chosen your men in the past?*
>
> **Pauline:** *I've mainly chosen them. But the married man I got involved with literally chose me. It was the first time in my life someone had pursued me so violently. He did it from a terribly romantic point of view and he had an extraordinary sort of chemical effect on me, a feeling – he always gave me a sort of fantastic feeling of 'ahuhah', sort of escape, somehow, complete sort of escape and nothing to do with the kind of ordinary things you know. And also he talked in such a romantic language all the time. 'This is fantastic and I've never felt like this' and most people don't – I mean most Englishmen find it very difficult to express themselves in ways like that and to actually hear it spoken is an extraordinary thing. It's slightly frightening as well, you know. You think 'Oh my God, what are you talking about? This is ridiculous.'*

One of the busiest and most highly regarded practitioners in British television, Saville had begun as an actor in 1948, at 18, and directed his first TV film, *Curtains for Harry* (co-written by his first wife, Jane Arden, and Richard Lester, the future director of *A Hard Day's Night*), in 1955; when he met Pauline, he was well into a long run on the dramatic anthology series *Armchair Theatre*, for which he directed 45 instalments between 1956 and 1972 (along with a good deal else). An innovator on the order of his American contemporaries John Frankenheimer and Sidney Lumet, Saville specialized in live, multi-camera productions in which carefully blocked actors and camera moves, and well-timed edits, braided the director's visual acuity with the high-wire immediacy of theatre. 'I never worked with him, we weren't each other's cup of tea,' Tony Garnett says. 'But I thought he was brilliant. Very sharp stuff.'

Opposite An actress prepares: Pauline backstage at the Royal Court Theatre, in which she appeared in **Day of the Prince**, 13 May 1963.

To Michael Lindsay-Hogg, the wunderkind director of *Ready Steady Go!*, Saville 'was a very sort of debonair guy. Nicely dressed. Lean, tall, handsome. Sort of mischievous. Always seeing the joke, not taking himself too seriously. Had a lot of relationships with women.' The description suggests a rather conventional figure. Thus it is surprising that Jane Arden, to whom Saville was married from 1947 until her suicide in 1982 (though the couple separated in the 1960s) – and with whom he occasionally collaborated – was his utter opposite: an actress, dramatist, filmmaker and radical feminist whose own work was challenging and not infrequently confrontational, even brutally so.

'My mother was way ahead of her time,' says Sebastian Saville. 'She was a uniquely brilliant, incredibly talented, totally compassionate person. My mom's friends came from every spectrum – psychoanalysts, artists, who'd come round for these dinner parties that would go on for days. She had this women's theatre group – it was more like intensive group therapy with about ten or fifteen 20- to 25-year-old women. And of course everyone taking LSD and smoking pot.' Amidst it all, 'My dad would go off to work. They were living parallel lives.'

Sebastian does not dispute the idea that, in response to the director's perception of his wife's creative and intellectual superiority, Saville *père* became an epic womanizer, leading to epic rows. 'He had this voracious appetite for young actresses – he had affairs with hundreds,' Sebastian says. 'I think me not remembering my young childhood was a desire to block out the constant fighting that was going on. It was like watching a caveman with a club fighting a samurai warrior with a very sharp sword.'

Given the circumstances, one can understand Saville's attraction to a talented, independent woman with a strong personality, yet who offered a less challenging alternative to his domestic circumstances. That – along with her other attributes – was Pauline. 'I fell very heavily under her spell, like so many young men did at the time,' the director acknowledges. 'She naturally captured so much of me. And what we had, it was just a tremendous relationship.'

'Philip Saville usually turned *Armchair Theatre* actresses into girlfriends, but with Pauline it was the other way round,' notes Adam Smith. The director cast her in her first dramatic TV role – as the 'Irish tart' Anna – in the *Armchair Theatre* production *North City Traffic Straight Ahead,* which aired on 22 July 1962.

'I encouraged her to be an actress,' Saville affirms. 'I thought she'd be good. I thought she'd be good in anything that she attempted to do.' 'Because he wanted to control her, I'm sure,' believes Tracy Tynan. 'Jane Arden he couldn't control, and was totally competition to him.' If this component existed, Saville's main motivation seems more elemental. 'She looked great, and she had an aura,' he says. 'At that time, I thought all the great people, the best people, you know, gave off an aura. But then again, of course, when a man falls for somebody, the aura

Above One of the speculative set designs, for Jean Genet's **The Balcony**, that accompanied Pauline's 1961 Arts Council application for an opportunity to work in theatre.

appears. She was always very surprised that I had such a high appreciation of what she was doing, because she never valued her acting.'

If indeed she held a low opinion of her abilities, the question of what, to Pauline, acting was meant to mean (to borrow a phrase from Samuel Beckett) – consciously or otherwise – is difficult to ascertain. Given that waitressing was unremunerative, and that Pauline would begin teaching stained glass and mosaics in the Murals department of Hammersmith School of Art in September – a job she held for more than a year – her sister-in-law's assessment seems plausible. 'I'm sure she did acting *and* modelling for money,' Bridget believes, affirming Pauline's determination to be self-supporting. 'She didn't ever say she enjoyed it. It just happened that somebody had asked her to do this, and it was money at the end.'

Acting also raised Pauline's profile, offering opportunities to promote her work and, indeed, her philosophy. 'Painter Pauline Turns Actress', a *Leicester Evening Mail* article occasioned by *North City Traffic*, reports that 'now she's "officially" an actress, she won't give up painting ... "I think one should paint so much a day even if one feels terrible. It's like exercising, for a ballet dancer." She doesn't want to choose and disapproves of people who tell her she should ... "I am serious about acting but I don't see why everybody should specialize so much. I shall go on painting, too."'

As had been the case at the RCA, Pauline's attempts to craft a public persona on her own terms were often kneecapped by the culture. 'A saucy-looking blonde with a high-jumper's legs' is the description in a *Sunday Mirror* article on the day of the broadcast. 'A Star May Be Born', published in the *Mirror* six days earlier, features a photo of Pauline in her white fedora, winking at the camera. 'Stop winking at me, luv,' begins the piece – 'I know your secret,' which proves to be 'she does not care about stardom – well, not all that much ... She would be equally happy to be a painter and is currently working on a painting of Marilyn Monroe.' The ending reduces Pauline's art to that commonest of denominators: 'Her pay for her first TV role will earn her far more cash than she charges for a painting.'

Given her prior dealings with Fleet Street, this sort of treatment could hardly have been a surprise, nor did it prevent Pauline from having headshots taken and inserting one in *Spotlight,* a casting directory. Conceivably, acting for the camera might have constituted research: the last time Pauline saw Charles Carey – by chance on a London street, in 1966 – she told him that she wanted to become a filmmaker. But Pauline might have had an entirely different motivation, one expressed to Nell Dunn.

Pauline: *Painting you do alone, you know, you sit there and it's your own terrible fight or your own lovely bit, whichever sort of phase it's in but it's really terribly alone and you make the whole thing yourself the whole construction is, you know – but acting you're a part of a team, a lot of people are dependent upon you, you are very dependent on other people and the conception is the writer's and director's. The part is something to do with your own idea obviously you know, the way you are and everything, but it's a part of the something instead of being a thing alone in itself.*

Whether or not being 'a part of the something' represented a wish to shift the exclusive burden of a project's success off her shoulders – whether or not painting was truly a calling, as it was for her *Easel* co-stars – Pauline's attraction to group endeavour fits with her social, performative nature, her involvement with Anti-Ugly and the revues. It may well have influenced her end-of-college interest in a theatre internship. According to Sue Tate, a pair of speculative set designs for Jean Genet's *The Balcony* were created to accompany her Arts Council application; one hard-edged, featuring flats with images evoking left-wing agitprop, the other layered with floral wallpaper and lace – both presided over by a horizontal band of collage featuring female lips and faces – the designs represent an imaginative, layered use of the proscenium space, a clear vision of what a production might look like, and an enthusiasm for the work.

And work was gotten. In October, between graduation and the AIA show, Pauline scored a prime commission: she created the poster for the first production

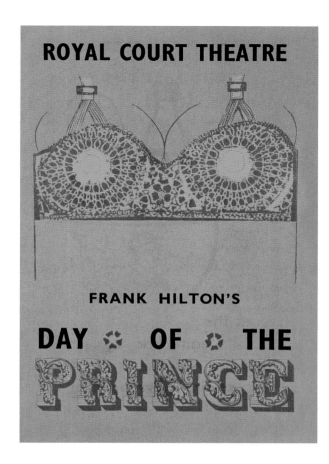

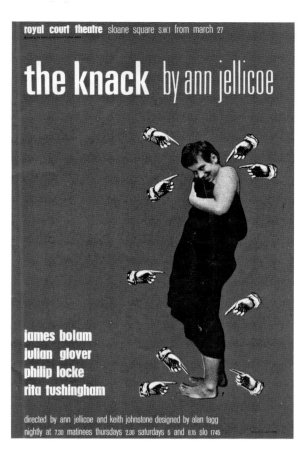

of Ann Jellicoe's comedy *The Knack*, at the Cambridge Arts Theatre; when the play moved to London's Royal Court Theatre in March 1962, her witty design – featuring a coy, naked Rita Tushingham wrapped in a towel, with nine 'finger-pointing' icons (similar to the one in the *Daily Express* article about Pauline's AUA participation) aimed at different parts of her body – served as the programme cover.

In May of the following year, with several TV roles to her credit, Pauline made her stage debut – as the golden bra-wearing virgin bombshell Virginia – at the Royal Court, in Frank Hilton's *Day of the Prince*, directed by Keith Johnstone. Pauline also designed the cover of the programme, featuring an extravagantly garish bra reminiscent of those in Blake's faux folk-art fairground paintings, and an S-shaped board game for the centrefold, a droll take on the play's bizarre doings. For someone seeking to be part of an artistic collective, wearing two creative hats at a place as central to London's cultural life as the Royal Court was a coup, a challenge she largely met. Her graphic design work conveyed a crisp, hip élan, and Johnstone appreciated her: 'She was so full of life that her skin seemed hardly able to contain her.'

THE ART OF ACTING

'There's a whole lot of things that you want to do, and somewhere in amongst them, there's you,' observes Roddy Maude-Roxby, wisely. So it might have been, in theatre, for Pauline. She perhaps felt that the solitary existence of a fine artist ill-suited her, or even that – for the moment, at any rate – she didn't have something to say. That road, however, went untravelled. Pauline's last known completed painting, *Bum* (1966), was meant as a set design for *Oh! Calcutta!*, Kenneth Tynan's risqué stage revue. But it wasn't used, and other than her Royal Court efforts, she did no theatrical graphic design work.

This is unfortunate, as design represented a more sustainable path to collaborative creativity than acting. Pauline appeared in one more play, 1963's *Afternoon Men* at the Arts Theatre Club, and her turns before the camera, beginning with *North City Traffic* for Saville and concluding with an amusing silent bit opposite Michael Caine in *Alfie* (released the month following her death), numbered in the middle teens; these included another film for Ken Russell, a TV show directed by the legendary Michael Powell and a mini-series. But the nearly unanimous view of those in her circle is that, however much they wished her well, Pauline lacked the craft, talent and, perhaps ultimately, the commitment to replicate on stage or screen that which made her so naturally sensational. 'I thought it was a waste of time,' says Geoffrey Reeve. 'When it was good fun' – by which he means the College revues – 'that's probably how it should have been. When it started to get serious, then it didn't work.'

Reeve's judgment appears to have been ratified by *Day of the Prince*, a one-joke affair about a wholesome white virgin waiting for her 'prince' to come; when a Black man named Prince turns up, her family of oddballs decides there's something off about him but can't quite put their finger on it. Race is never mentioned – ultimately, Prince is rejected because he bites his nails.

Pauline received her usual press attention – 'Pauline Boty will be marked "absent" when her class reassembles at ... Hammersmith today,' the *Daily Express* announced, '[f]or 24-year-old art mistress Pauline has landed her first part on the London stage.' And she scored a rave from what might be characterized as the hometown paper, *Hammersmith & Shepherd's Bush Gazette*: 'a few weeks ago she was a teacher at Hammersmith Art College, unknown. Now she's the brightest comedy prospect in the whole of London, star material ... Pauline, the Shepherd's Bush girl from Addison Road. As a comedienne, she's top of the class.'

Others, however, were less kind. According to the *Birmingham Daily Post*, '[I]f Pauline Boty the blonde is inclined to skid off into shrill squeaking, she is decorative enough for her purpose.' As for *The Times*: 'The only glaring flaw is the shrill posturing Virginia of Pauline Boty, an actress who seems noticeably underequipped for the professional stage.' Her director did not entirely disagree.

'She read well at the audition but it emerged later on that she was not gifted in movement, not good at the dance that was required by the play,' Keith Johnstone recalled. 'Hard work would have improved this, but it was probably a brain thing. And anyway she had other fish to fry.'

'I felt that she tore herself in two,' says Peter Blake. 'She shouldn't have gone towards the theatre. She should have stayed as a painter. She had to split her life pretty much down the middle between being a painter and being an aspiring actress. It was too much to ask.' Blake's assessment of her talent aligns with other of her friends: 'She never could quite hide herself. I can understand why Julie Christie got the parts and she didn't.'

His comment refers to the central disappointment of Pauline's avocation: she screen-tested opposite Tom Courtenay for the part of Liz, the free-spirited young woman in John Schlesinger's 1963 film *Billy Liar*, one of the roles that made a star of Julie Christie. 'Tom Courtenay came to the house when they were talking about making the film,' Celia Birtwell remembers. 'He was rather handsome. Rather attractive. He was quite nice to all of us, actually. I think we'll leave it like that. And of course Julie Christie got the part, but it was very, very close, whether she got it or Pauline would have got it.' 'They kept on calling her back, and we all thought, "She'll get the part,"' Maude-Roxby says. 'And then when we saw the film, we reckoned that they'd dressed Julie Christie very much as Pauline. That they were quite taken with her looks and choice of clothing, her personal style.'

These recollections bring to mind the famous line from John Ford's 1962 Western, *The Man Who Shot Liberty Valance* – which Pauline, a great fan of the genre, might well have seen, in between auditions, in the year of its release: 'When the legend becomes fact, print the legend.' Whether or not Schlesinger drew on Pauline's style or personality for Christie's performance (in which Liz's nature is telegraphed via the nonstop swinging of her handbag) is a matter of speculation. What is not is how close Pauline actually came to getting the part.

'She was a good type for the part is all I know,' offers Tom Courtenay via e-mail. 'What I do know is that I tested with 3 girls: Pauline, Topsy Jane who played my girlfriend in *The [Loneliness of the Long-Distance] Runner* and Julie C. Topsy got the part and we started filming with her. After a couple of weeks she was replaced by Julie. I know I was more convinced by Topsy in the tests. She was more believable. Please don't ask me about Pauline as an actress. I couldn't comment constructively.'

In fact, the film's most unhappy event had to do not with Pauline, but the talented and singular Topsy Jane, who was married to Tony Garnett. 'Topsy had a choice of either going to Stratford, to work for Tony Richardson, or to work with John Schlesinger on *Billy Liar*,' Garnett says. 'In the end, she decided to do *Billy Liar*. She was under enormous pressure from John. And Tom Courtenay was

calling every day. So she went off, and no mobile phones then or Internet. So we just said, "See you in a few weeks. Hope it goes well." And two or three weeks later, she appeared back in London. She'd been sacked. John said her eyes were giving nothing to the camera at all. She was overweight. Dank, lazy, chain-smoking. The psychiatrists diagnosed her as schizophrenic. And she was more or less like that for the rest of her life.'

Perhaps because of their resemblance to one another, and that both were icons of their place and time, there is another Julie-related legend: that Schlesinger's 1965 film *Darling* – which won Oscars for both Christie and screenwriter Frederic Raphael – was based in part on Pauline's affair with Saville. 'I must confess that I had never heard of Miss Boty,' Raphael explains via e-mail. 'The only "researched" element of [*Darling* protagonist] Diana Scott derived from the life and loves [of] the late Beth Rogan, whom I met a couple of times before writing the script. Most of what is in the character came out of my imagination, supplemented by whatever gossipy things emerged from long sessions with John Schlesinger and [producer] Jo Janni.'

(Speaking of legends: surely the most astonishing one is that Pauline brought Bob Dylan to London in 1962, his first trip outside the US. In fact, Saville related in a 2016 conversation, Dylan owed his luck to Jane Arden, who'd seen him performing in Greenwich Village, found him extraordinary and recommended him to her husband, who cast him in *Madhouse on Castle Street*, a television play which the BBC broadcast on 13 January 1963. Though Pauline and Saville did

Above
Pauline commissioned a portfolio of head shots from John Timbers, who'd taken the **North City Traffic Straight Ahead** production stills.

collect Dylan from the airport upon his arrival, they had other plans for the evening, and so parked him at a very surprised Jane Percival's flat at 34 Blenheim Crescent, where he joined an in-progress dinner party – attendees included the painter Anne Martin and the dramatists John Arden and Michael Hastings – and, singing for his pheasant, performed extempore the songs that, presently, would make of him a *true* legend.)

As Ken Baynes and William Wilkins observed of Pauline, in connection with the notice she received as the Marianne of Anti-Ugly, she enjoyed the attention but kept it in perspective. So it was with acting.

> **Nell:** *And is the admiration nice?*
> **Pauline:** *Well I don't think you really get admiration. I think that you might get people who think it's marvellous to be an actress because they think of it as being glamourous but that's really got nothing to do with anything. I mean that's a completely false thing. I think one of the terrible things about people setting out to be actresses – I think this is mainly to do with girls more than men – is that they are kind of taken up with the glamour idea or 'I'm on the stage' you know, all this kind of thing which I think I – I would like admiration. But I would hate to become terribly aware of it. If someone is being terribly effusive about me or something I've done then I shut off because you mustn't let yourself be affected by this.*
> **Nell:** *Why, do you think you'd get conceited or what?*
> **Pauline:** *Because it's very easy to get things out of proportion and really and truly if you think about it there are millions of other people who are much better than you anyway. And – well I think it can be very destructive.*

It was. In the last years of her life – in Pauline's own estimation, as shall be seen – the drug of regular television gigs, by distracting her from her true work, became a contributing factor in her depressions. And yet, paradoxically, Pauline grasped something essential about the effects of acting on the personality, which was of benefit to her development as a painter.

> **Pauline:** *I think it's nice seeing yourself being somebody else which isn't quite you but is all based on you, because it's always based on you, in acting I think. But you've assumed another identity in a way so that you can show yourself much more because you're not being yourself, you're saying, well really I'm supposed to be Anne Smith or something, and so you can really be much more yourself.*
> **Nell:** *You mean that it isn't really an escape from yourself, it's giving yourself another dimension?*
> **Pauline:** *Well I think it can be a release.*

Beginning at Wimbledon, continuing more decisively at the RCA, Pauline developed an ability to stand at a distance from herself, to both enjoy and exploit the one-two punch of her looks and persona. If she was understandably more cautious at secondary school, recognizing (as a smart, sensitive teenage girl is wont to do) that making light of one's sexual allure is more effective *and* more prudent, at College Pauline was mature and secure enough to deploy her powers more impactfully. As an Anti-Ugly, Pauline used the press she received to bring attention to the architectural blight encroaching on postwar England; vamping it up in the revues, she employed the spell she cast as a bombshell to convey the fact that there was more to her – to any woman – than met (or perhaps didn't meet) the eye. But though her stained glass, collages and paintings were 'personal', at the start of 1962, she had yet to use the figure of 'Pauline Boty', so effectively deployed in life, to achieve an artistic transformation.

Acting, we may plausibly posit, changed that. As she explained to Nell Dunn, the assumption of a fictional identity enabled Pauline to release aspects of her true self that might otherwise have lain dormant, or even unrecognized. This was a revelation, and from there it was a short leap to an understanding more transformative, more profound: that playing the character of *yourself* can deliver no less of a release. For Pauline, it opened the way to a more comprehensive, fully actualized self-ownership, to putting responsibility to herself ahead of what others might want or think.

As Pauline had learned time and again – from Wallington to *Pop Goes the Easel* – getting the world to see you the way that you see yourself is an iffy proposition. But the cultivation of her double vision, the apprehension of herself as a fully engaged participant and a detached observer of that participation and what it might mean, could be especially useful in the one arena that Pauline could indeed control: painting.

'She was a bit lazy as a painter,' Saville says. 'She wasn't one of those people who had to get on with it. She had a laissez-faire attitude. That's what I meant by lazy. She didn't work very hard. She would do it, and she would say, "Come round and see this painting, this new one. I hope you like it." It was more of a joke to her really.'

To be charitable: it is likely that Saville couldn't comprehend someone whose approach to work wasn't the same as his. Because, certainly, he was wrong. At Wimbledon, Charles Carey observed, Pauline was more interested in making ideas than making art. As 1962 progressed, as she increasingly set the character of herself at the centre of her pictures, Pauline began to make both. In so doing, she found her style.

10

BREAKTHROUGH

1962

When Clive talked about her, he said, "I know I can't explain it, but there was always something of herself in her paintings,"' remembers Tariq Ali. 'He said, "Tariq, I really wish you'd met her." I said, "Seeing her paintings, so do I."'

In the breakthrough year of 1962, Pauline painted in her room on Addison Road, beside her brass bed, her overbrimming tables and mismatched chairs, her wall collage beneath a shelf of books, her record player and space heater, mantelpiece and gas cooker, all of it crowded and carpeted with artefacts and curiosities, the bright autumn leaves of everyday life. It was, for Pauline and her peers, a commonplace condition, one that, according to Caroline Coon, affected the character of their work. 'We didn't have the money for massive studios,' Coon explains. 'We were painting in space that was more domestic. It was why all the English Pop artists' works are small of scale, in contrast to the Pop American artists, who were able to do these massive canvases. In lofts.'

Pauline's circumstances, in which she remained intimate with the physical aspects of her existence and the ideas and emotions they provoked, may also have amplified her presence in her pictures, their increasingly personal character. Looking at those canvases from the perspective of the present, it is surprising to learn that some in her circle, in effect, disapproved of them. 'I think her stained glass is actually better than her pictures,' admits Geoffrey Reeve. 'She had a long way to go in using the qualities of paint.' Gerald Nason's verdict? 'A bit slapdash, I thought then. I don't think she was careful enough.' Most curious is the view of Pauline's boon companion Derek Boshier. 'At that time, I liked her collages,' he says. 'And I think often, funnily enough, if I'm really, really honest, I think sometimes, and I emphasize sometimes, some of Pauline's paintings looked better in reproduction than when you see the actual surface. There's something – sometimes – unskilful. But,' Boshier adds, 'I changed my mind. I learned to like her work from an exhibition I saw called *Bad Painting*, but respected as bad painting, so it was almost anti-painting. So it was okay to be not totally neat.' (The critic Thomas Crow, by contrast, refers approvingly to Pauline's 'rough-and-ready manner of handling oil paint'.)

It is perhaps unfair and too easy, especially given Reeve's and Nason's admiration and affection, and Boshier's gallant, tortured effort to qualify his ambivalence, to say that their critical perspective is particularly male. But it does miss the point in a way that Celia Birtwell's view, which ignores technical considerations and aims for the heart, does not. 'I went to see a show of her work

133

in Wolverhampton, and I just thought, "God, she was bloody good,"' she says. 'It was so alive. I think it's very much of its time, very much to do with the Pop Art movement, but then she had her own personality as well. I think they're very joyous, sort of luscious. It brought it all back to me, that period of our lives.'

Birtwell's effusiveness, her recognition, in the work, of Pauline's personality – 'joyous', 'luscious' – and the evocation of a moment in time, provoke a question: *what is skill?* Is it technical proficiency? If so, then Pauline was indeed not among the most able painters of her generation. But if skill is defined as the ability to convey a highly personal point of view, in a distinctive, singular and uncompromisingly direct creative voice – to make the viewer feel, understand, *connect* – then Pauline's skilfulness was rivalled, in her day, only by that of David Hockney. In every artistic movement, we encounter artists whose proficiency can astonish, and those who can make a visceral connection with an audience. There are of course individuals who can do both, and others whose proficiency is so astonishing that it becomes a kind of connection. Had she lived beyond 28, Pauline's craft would surely have improved; the two *It's a Man's World* pictures and *Bum* reveal the benefits of experience. But her skill at connection, connection through self-revelation, became evident the moment she got onto her style. 'There was always something of herself in her paintings,' Pauline's husband told Tariq Ali. That was fully on display in 1962.

Pauline was not the only woman in London at the start of the 1960s to enjoy an apology-free sex life. But as Boshier, Natalie Gibson, Roger Smith and others observe, she was unusually frank about her objects of desire (and her feelings about them) and is nearly unique among female artists of the day to make that frankness, and those feelings, the subject of her work. The Belgian Pop painter Evelyne Axell, about whom more presently, mined similar terrain. But Pauline's approach was distinctly her own.

'I joked with Clive once, I said, "What do you recognize about her in the Belmondo painting?"' Ali relates. 'He laughed and said, "She wanted to fuck him!"' *With Love to Jean-Paul Belmondo* can fairly be described as the first fully realized 'Pauline Boty' painting. It features one of her Pop heroes. It celebrates Belmondo in two ways, at a remove as an iconic component of popular culture, and up close as someone she would like to bed. The picture is infused with Pauline's personality – not only her sexuality but more particularly her wit, expressed in the rude enormity of the rose, which seems to spew out of Belmondo's hat like a crimson mushroom cloud. ('The flower symbolizes the female vagina,' Coon observes. 'And it sits on his head.') It is, by virtue of its sexual forthrightness, feminist in character. Most distinctively, with its row of five hearts across the top of the canvas,

its warm red-orange colour palette and the depiction of the star, in black-and-white, as human – with an elongated chin, a bit of flyaway hair – *With Love to Jean-Paul Belmondo* conveys delicacy of feeling as well as passion, an understanding of and solidarity with its protagonist, that elevates what might have been a ribald joke into an affecting work of art. 'In the image of the latest French star,' writes the art historian Kalliopi Minioudaki, 'Boty's passion for New Wave cinema, her quest for "present-day" idols and her sexual desire came inextricably together.' Minioudaki also observes in *Belmondo* Pauline's undoctrinaire, instinctive sexual politics: 'By identifying handsome men with the objects of her Pop fandom, she recast the female Pop artist as desiring young woman, while further redeeming the erotic pleasures of pop culture's consumption by women.'

Though dated '62' on the edge of the verso, Pauline either reworked the canvas or took her time: Michael Ward's 1963 photo of the artist posing in front of it reveals an unfinished bit beneath the chin. Whatever the case, the effort proved worthwhile. Many of those interviewed for this book cited it as their favourite among the artist's paintings (indeed, when *Belmondo* sold at auction in June 2022, the hammer price – £1,159,500 – set a Boty record) and when, in the 1980s, a teenage Boty Goodwin got her own first flat, on Chalcot Road in London's Primrose Hill, it hung at the top of the second-floor stairs – its four-by-five-foot expanse, recalls Boty's friend Stephanie Duncan, consuming much of the landing wall. One imagines that so unambiguously joyful an expression would have offered reassurance, from the mother about whom Boty fantasized but never knew.

Belmondo, of course, was a distant figure, a hero. In *Portrait of Derek Marlowe with Unknown Ladies*, Pauline moved things closer to home. She met Marlowe, most famous today for his 1966 novel *A Dandy in Aspic*, in 1962, when he profiled her for *Scene*, an arts-and-pop-culture-themed weekly; the story made the cover of the 8 November issue, along with a nearly full-page photo, by Michael Seymour, of Pauline curled on her Addison Road bed.

The piece is thin in all respects, memorable mostly for its opening sentences – 'Actresses often have tiny brains. Painters often have large beards. Imagine a brainy actress who is also a painter and also a blonde and you have PAULINE BOTY' – and, too, for Pauline's oft-quoted observation regarding nostalgia: 'Mainly we have a kind of nostalgia for the present, for NOW. People have this kind of nostalgia for Victoriana and we have nostalgia for things that are now ... It's almost like painting mythology, only present-day mythology – film stars etc.'

Surely the article's most fertile by-product was Pauline's affair with the writer, or rather the artwork that arose from it. How quickly the first led to the second is not clear – the Tate Britain, which acquired the painting in 2018, gives the date as 1962–63 – but if *Belmondo* is the earliest recognizable 'Boty', then *Marlowe* is the first painting to offer us Pauline's simultaneous expression of enthusiastic engagement and cold-eyed critique.

The portrait of Marlowe, which consumes most of the canvas, presents him in black (his hair and sweater) and pale blue (his skin) against a medium cobalt background. The pose is teasing, seductive: chin on hand obscuring half his mouth and left cheek, cigarette between fingers cocked beside his left eye, and meeting our own eyes directly with a gaze both dreamy and bemused. The Marlowe we see is as his one-time flatmate, the playwright Tom Stoppard, described him: 'laconic, smiley, quiet, and darkly good looking'.

Along the left side of the portrait there is a vertical strip of darker blue, with five grey-black shapes that resemble sideways chess pawns, but that the Tate Britain's description identifies as film sprocket holes (albeit abstract): thus what we are seeing is a photograph or, more likely, a frame from a motion picture – if Belmondo, rendered in black-and-white, is an icon of world cinema, then Marlowe, brushed in sexy, nightclub shades of black and blue, features in a production of Pauline's own making, he is her personal, blue-movie dreamboat.

And then there are the 'unknown ladies', confined to a narrow horizontal band along the picture's top (the Tate describes it as a frieze). In contrast to the portrait, they are distorted, smeary and clown-garish, the quartet of faces cut off at the forehead and chin, brightly lit against a red background, their impact frightful and crude.

Yet they are not entirely unknown – we have seen them before. Their look and arrangement approximate the horizontal bands of collage Pauline created for the stage designs that accompanied her 1961 Arts Council application: the collage appears in her renderings of Scenes I and V of Genet's *The Balcony*, which takes place in a brothel. And one of the ladies in particular – the second from right – seems inspired by a photo, created by Geoffrey Reeve, for the autumn 1962 issue of the RCA's magazine *ARK*, in which Pauline appears – smiling, slightly out of focus, eyes closed – beneath three men peeking through a transom.

The painting is not hard to parse. Pauline's depiction of Marlowe is savoury: it reveals affection, intimacy, a touch of hero worship, a bit of rue. But as the frieze indicates, Pauline is all too aware that, to her matinee idol, she is just another of the conquests drifting above his life, useful but a blur, no more memorable than a prostitute and perhaps less. 'For the men of that generation, women, even women from the past, were sexual objects,' says Caroline Coon. 'Not really wholly human. It wasn't Pauline's fierce, profound intellectual ability that impressed those men. It was all about how beautiful she was. Very annoying for her. Well, yes.'

This objectification was personal to Pauline but also cultural. Her painting is a comment upon a time in which men were stars, lovingly sighed over, and women were relegated to the margins (in the case of *Marlowe*, literally). Pauline offered her own experience in the talk with Nell Dunn:

Above
**Portrait of Derek
Marlowe with Unknown
Ladies**, 1962–63,
oil on canvas,
148 × 142 cm

Pauline's affair with Derek Marlowe followed his article about her in **Scene**. The frieze at the painting's top drew on Pauline's set design for **The Balcony**, as well as Geoffrey Reeve's comic photograph.

Nell: *Men think of you just as a pretty girl you mean?*

Pauline: *No, they just find it embarrassing when you start talking about – I've met so many men who get slightly embarrassed – they're a bit square probably. If you – well for instance you know there are lots of women who are intellectually cleverer than lots of men but it's difficult for lots of men to ever accept this idea, and they often feel 'Well anyway I'm a man and being a man is lots better than being a woman.'*

Nell: *If you start talking about ideas and things they just think you're putting it on?*

Pauline: *Well not that you're putting it on, they just find it slightly embarrassing, and you aren't doing the right thing you know.*

Marlowe also returns us to critiques of Pauline's abilities. These were voiced, not only with diplomatic discretion by friends, but harshly and in public: following her inclusion in the 1993 Barbican Centre exhibition *The Sixties Art Scene in London* – a resurrection of sorts, the first high-profile display of her work in decades – the art critic Waldemar Januszczak, appearing on the BBC2 programme *The Tonight Show*, called Pauline a 'bad' and 'derivative' artist whose reputation rested on being a 'dolly bird'. Unfortunately for the critic, he shared the stage with Caroline Coon. 'Boy, did she lay into him,' remembers David Alan Mellor, the exhibition's curator. 'Caroline, God bless her, took him to bits for it.'

The inaccuracy of Januszczak's judgment is demonstrated by the portrait's elegance: not only the nuanced capturing of Marlowe's character, but the very slight softening that suggests movement, a cinematic coming to life. If the unknown ladies are by contrast unsubtle in their ghoulishness, it is not a failure of skill – but rather because Pauline had a point to make.

Pauline also painted female stars – individuals for whom she felt not an attraction but an affinity – most memorably Marilyn Monroe. To illuminate her complex sense of kinship, let us first consider the woman Pauline chose *not* to paint, despite the multitude of comparisons made between the two: Brigitte Bardot.

Whether or not B.B. interested Pauline as a subject, in a sense, it wasn't necessary: if creating a work of art can be an act of self-exploration, then there would have been few revelations to be gained from delving into the French star. In her 1959 essay *Brigitte Bardot and the Lolita Syndrome,* Simone de Beauvoir offered a sketch of her protagonist that almost perfectly captures Pauline. 'People who know B.B. speak of her amiable disposition, her kindness and her youthful freshness,' Beauvoir writes. 'She is neither silly nor scatterbrained, and her naturalness is not an act ... She is blooming and healthy, quietly sensual. It is impossible to see in her the touch of Satan, and for that reason she seems all the more diabolical to women who feel humiliated and threatened by her beauty ...

```
              I
The tree outside is faint
falling away in the blue light
of the rain.
Look
Their hats crammed onto
tight lowered heads
scurry, scurry in the rain
Rain - so gentle - so soft
like the kiss of a cloud,
They run from it
It pours- abandoned
Throwing itself onto the hard
                    unfeeling
pavement
Shut your eyes to it
run away from it
No escape no
it falls - falls
- everywhere
slowly pouring out
its melancholy yearnings
its forgotten memories
in palpitating sadness
- weeping forever
The gulls scream
over desolate wastes of cities
beating their wings in the rain.
                    P.V.B.
```

```
              II
On a morning, pale
From a dewless night
Three, in a car, knowing
A brown thought less day
Was theirs
Lifted the veil.
Though they had vowed
Never, never.
Never look up,
Keep your eyes down and
Smell the right smells.
    So.
    They jumped.
    They shrieked.
    They yelled.
    They trumped.
Leaving their grey, grim right
                    behind them.
    Into the sun
    Into the sea.
Make love in the woods
Roll in the grass
Chew the rich, sticky blades
Blow silver in the wind
    Free as air
Laughing, naked in the sun
                    P.V.B.
```

Left
Two of Pauline's poems, published in **Newsheet** – one despairing, the other ecstatic.

Right
The artist posing with **Celia Birtwell and Some of Her Heroes**, 29 October 1963.

But the male feels uncomfortable if, instead of a doll of flesh-and-blood, he holds in his arms a conscious being who is sizing him up. A free woman is the very contrary of a light woman ... Children are forever asking why, why not. They are told to be silent. Brigitte's eyes, her smile, her presence, impel one to ask oneself why, why not.'

As someone who had long been asking *why, why not*, Pauline didn't need to explore Bardot. The issues confronting Marilyn Monroe, however – the challenges she faced and her mixed success (to say the least) in overcoming them – were not unsimilar to those which harried Pauline. If Bardot might be said to be the unconflicted version of the artist, Marilyn represented the flip side, and it was perhaps for this reason that Pauline made her the subject of four paintings – before and after the star's death by suicide, on 4 August 1962, at the age of 36.

To Roddy Maude-Roxby, the connection was clear. 'I think Marilyn Monroe would have fascinated her because of the impossible life she was leading,' he says. 'That she's, like Pauline, someone who's seen by the world as very beautiful, and then exploited. The films are made, and quite often have missed the value of Marilyn Monroe, of allowing her to just be there rather than involving her in

Lewis Morley
remembered his
September 1963 photo
session with Pauline
as being relaxed and
unforced, perhaps
a consequence of
their personal
relationship.

a ludicrous story. If you don't watch out, the world commercializes you, and in a sense, Pauline could have ended up like Marilyn Monroe. And when she paints Marilyn, she's saying in some way, "I feel for that woman, who needn't have died the way she died, and needn't have been in a whole lot of films that were quite often cruel with her."'

Pauline did indeed watch out – but the world commercialized her in any case. Like Marilyn, she discovered the exceptional difficulty of being oneself, without losing that self to a culture too quick to make assumptions and judgments.

Following her emergence as an Anti-Ugly, Pauline became one of the most photographed women of her time, captured by, among others, John Aston, David Bailey, Roger Mayne, Lewis Morley, Geoffrey Reeve, Michael Seymour and Michael Ward. Frequently she is depicted at, or with, her work; beginning in 1963, Pauline began to appear nude or semi-nude before her paintings, sometimes mimicking the poses of the figures in the compositions. Most indelible is Morley's September 1963 image of Pauline beneath *Belmondo*, sprawled prone on a ratty divan, wearing nothing but a look of lurid promise and the dirt on an upraised foot, in imitation of Marie-Louise O'Murphy's pose in Boucher's famous portrait. That O'Murphy was a mistress of Louis XV makes plain Pauline's view of *le roi* of 1960s French cinema and her desired relationship with him.

Who suggested what is unknowable, but Pauline surely responded to the personality of the photographer, the dynamic of the moment, the waxing and waning of imagination and nerve. The 29 October 1963 shoot with Ward was notably fruitful. Pauline posed with *Celia Birtwell and Some of Her Heroes*, a nearly full-length portrait of her flatmate, holding a rose and standing before a white wall, to which are pinned images of, among others, Brando, Elvis, the Everly Brothers and David Hockney. In the painting, Birtwell's blouse is unbuttoned, exposing her bra, and she wears jeans; Pauline mimics her sitter's pose in Ward's photo, and her shirt is open (revealing an identical bra), but the jeans are missing: instead, she wears a horizontally-striped Mary Quant bikini bottom and low-heeled boots. (Thomas Crow's description of Birtwell's pose – 'insouciant provocation unconcerned with conventional propriety' – more accurately describes the painter.) In another photo, Pauline stands before *Tom's Dream*, a canvas centred on a woman in flower-covered panties, her face obscured by the gauzy, purple-pink top she's pulling over her head with crossed arms; in the picture, Pauline again copies the action in the painting, although we see her grinning hugely at the camera, and she wears thigh-highs and a garter belt under translucent knickers.

In the 1960s and 1970s, a number of artists, including Yayoi Kusama, Yoko Ono and Carolee Schneemann, created photographs and performance pieces in which the exposed female body was a central thematic component. Pauline's sessions with Morley and Ward were more light-hearted and improvisational, a far cry from

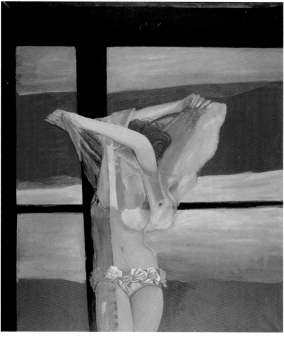

Ono's 1964 *Cut Piece*, in which she sat sphinx-like as audience members snipped off her clothes, or Schneemann, in 1975, reading from a scroll of paper as she extracted it from her vagina. Indeed, to her friends, Pauline's 'cheesecake' shoots (to borrow Adam Smith's word) were cheeky, nervy, but at root a lark. 'I can see her thinking that it'd be fun to pose nude with her paintings,' says Tracy Tynan. 'Why the fuck not, you know?'

That is one way to look at it. Another is through the lens of Nicola Wood's aforementioned observation regarding a difference between the sexes: that while women suffered from a 'dual personality thing', wanting to be dolly birds *and* taken seriously, 'men never had to dally with those two opposites – they were just men, and they did whatever they wanted and it was right'. Accordingly, as Pauline – as other female artists – sought to claim male prerogatives, they found that what might be a bit of fun for a man could become, for a woman, perilous. Writing about Pauline and her contemporaries, the curator Sid Sachs described a 'beauty trap': 'The attractiveness of these artists created a dilemma. On the one hand, it provided mechanisms of acceptance in the social arena. Being unafraid of public nudity enhanced social access for bold women of this generation ... Recognition as a model/performer ... was not the same thing as validation as an artist, a double standard that haunted these women. Attractive artists who also modeled and/or acted ... were trapped by the superficial gaze of capitalist glamour.'

Surely – yet Pauline sought to live beyond the snap of the trap's teeth. This was true as well of her contemporary and acquaintance Evelyne Axell, and a consideration of the two together is instructive. Like her English counterpart an alluring, attractive sometime actress with a sportive attitude towards sex and self-exposure and a penchant for provocative insouciance, Axell's paintings, notes Kalliopi Minioudaki, 'radicalized Pop's fetishistic fascination with consumer objects by channeling their eroticization into the service of female desire through female fantasies of erotic consumption'. What she calls 'Axell's dirty jokes' include canvases in which female tongues apply themselves to ice cream cones with salacious relish, and the artist's *Erotomobiles*, featuring cars – driven by women – that serve as veritable arsenals of pleasure, with switches, shifts, pedals, etc., braiding polymorphous ecstasies with the boundless freedom of the road. (In a tragic irony, Axell's early death, at 37, came in a car wreck.)

Where Pauline and Axell cross paths in particular is in the inclusion of their own naked bodies in self-created versions of that touchstone of Pop art, the pin-up. They did it differently – Axell obliquely, by serving as her own model for erotically charged artworks (some painted on Plexiglas, and with fake-fur pubic hair, giving them heightened tactile allure); Pauline explicitly, by posing with her paintings – but, Minioudaki asserts, the intention, the impact, were the same. '[A]xell and Boty embraced the feminist potential of the pin-up as pop culture's

Opposite above
Evelyne Axell, photographed by her husband, Jean Antoine, and **Le Petit Espace Vert**, 1970, her resulting artwork.

Opposite below
Pauline having a good time with her painting **Tom's Dream**.

genre of the sexually aware and in-control woman to flesh out their shared sexual politics through a thoroughly Pop vocabulary, in effect aligning themselves with a series of artists before and after them that range from early twentieth-century burlesque performers to fin-de-siècle "bad girls" ... an ultimate revision of the sexual object into sexual subject. Axell's Amazons of desire and Boty's pin-ups solicit [the male gaze] to sabotage its phallocentric logic through their makers' own radical narcissism.'

Depending upon one's tolerance for art criticism, one can give this credence or, as regards Pauline, credit Tynan's belief that it was all in good fun. Likely it was both. If we assume even moderate intentionality on Pauline's part – and why should we not? – then Minioudaki has a point. Indeed, her thinking about the artist adds a useful layer to our understanding of Pauline's work and life both: '[Boty] repeated the pin-up from a "mobile" point of view that allowed her to either look at pop culture's sexualized image of women as ... celebrating its empowering propagation of female sexuality, or to expose the pin-up as a site of patriarchal oppression by ventriloquizing men's view of it.' Noting 'the centrality of photojournalism in making London the epitome of the Swinging Sixties', describing the model as the 'new elite' of the decade, Minioudaki observes that Pauline was able to leverage her position within the moment to defy 'the passivity of the photographer's model' by engaging in a 'strategic uncovering'. '[B]y inserting her work, along with her body, in a photo shoot ... she made a statement as an embodied female painter, and by excessively mimicking the sexualized poses of the feminine in popular culture, she both parodically exposed them as sexist topoi [i.e. stock formulas] and affectively embraced them as empowering vehicles of female sexuality.'

Pauline and her Belgian sister, Minioudaki points out, occupied a two-woman niche among female Pop artists: as actresses and public figures, they 'directly experienced Pop culture's objectification of women'. Yet 'incarnating Pop's "bad girls"', they engaged in a 'subversion of women's object position in both high and pop culture': '[Pauline and Axell] discovered strategies that allowed them to tackle the problem of "woman-as-image" without relinquishing the pleasures either of their body or of their consumption of popular culture, but in fact pronouncing them from the heart of Pop.'

If it is fair to assign lucid artistic and political motives to Pauline's pin-ups, we must also – especially in light of her Marilyn obsession – consider who had, as it were, the last laugh. Perhaps because Axell was mentored by Magritte, her *oeuvre* was more substantive and stylistically consistent – because her self-representation was more consciously 'artistic' and her nudity (mostly) contained within her paintings – the Belgian received a response more closely aligned with her intentions. The ways in which Pauline's cheesecake was sliced, on the other hand, could not have been more different from what she desired. 'For a three-page spread in *Men Only*, headed "Pauline Goes Pop", Boty initially posed with her work and a poster for the AIA show,' Sue Tate reports. 'However, on returning to the office John Aston, the photographer, was reprimanded and sent back by his editor "to get something more racy" for the *Men Only* audience. Four of the seven images used are seductive poses without work. The text, while it does discuss her thoughts on Pop, also describes her as "blonde, long, with grey blue eyes". It reduces her to "a pet, darling and symbol" of the Pop artists and ends on her acting career ... [W]hen Ward's image of her with Belmondo was used on the cover of *Men Only* in 1964, it was cropped so she appeared naked and there was no contextualizing text, not even a caption, to anchor her identity *as the artist*.'

In a 1965 issue of the soft-core magazine *Tit Bits* – headlined 'Pauline has a contract to thrill' – the editors cropped out the artworks from Ward's photo session almost entirely, and used an alternate take of the *Tom's Dream* photo, in which she wears different knickers and has more of her shirt off. Recalls Natalie Gibson, 'She wanted to draw attention to the paintings, but quite often the painting got left out. She was cross about that. She felt she'd been double-crossed.'

The 1962 Marilyns predate the cheesecake. But Pauline had, via her Anti-Ugly activities, already been objectified by the press and made sport of on television, already seen the 'Pauline Boty' she sent out into the world subverted, turned into a sexist joke. Not by inclination given to woe-is-me-ism, Pauline seems to have largely laughed off the public traduction of her intentions. But as Maude-Roxby observes, she recognized this aspect of her experience in Marilyn's, and the four paintings she produced before and after the star's suicide effuse the emotion Derek Boshier observed at the start of August 1962: he never saw Pauline cry so hard as when Marilyn died.

One of the paintings is difficult to judge: now lost, it exists only in a John Aston photograph from the first *Men Only* session. Based on a publicity still, by Richard Avedon, for *Some Like It Hot*, it depicts Marilyn with a lock of hair falling across her forehead, with one of the beads of her extra-long necklace between her teeth; Pauline, standing before the painting, replicates the pose. (*The Only Blonde in the World* – Pauline's best-known work – will be discussed in the next chapter.)

Regarding the other two: their difference reflects what we may presume to be their chronology. *Epitaph to Something's Gotta Give* references Marilyn's last, unfinished film, which shut down production on 12 June owing to its troublesome star. Though the footage remained unseen for decades, *Life* magazine published production stills, featuring Marilyn taking a topless night-time dip in a pool, in its 22 June issue, and Pauline replicated one of the swimming photos as her painting's centrepiece. An epitaph typically commemorates, in written language, someone who has died; in this case the language is visual, the deceased is a film and the

message is the opposite of mournful. Effectively a collage rendered in oils, four red-orange circles hover around Marilyn as she enjoys the water – the picture's background is rendered in the same intense hue – and these, according to Sue Tate, had a special significance for Pauline. 'While at the RCA, [Pauline] had discussed with her boyfriend, Jim Donovan, the fact that no one had tried to picture the female orgasm, describing hers as "lovely, lovely" orange circular shapes, streaming outward with an audible "pop, pop, pop" and she painted him a sketch.'

The painting's celebration of sexual empowerment is reinforced by the encore appearance of the Victorian pin-up from Pauline's *Siren* collage, set against an orange circle surrounded by a ring of green – an inclusion that places Marilyn in the great continuum of iconic erotica. Bold blue streaks, extending from the right-hand side of Marilyn's image, give balance to the composition, and suggest that, though *Something's Gotta Give* may be dead, the star's story retains a road

Epitaph to Something's Gotta Give, 1962, oil on hardboard, 127 × 106.5 cm

on which to go forth. Pauline has thus subverted the idea of an epitaph: making it not an end, but a foreshadowing of better times to come.

That was not to be, and *Colour Her Gone* – the title borrows the last line of Kander and Ebb's exquisite 1962 song of lost love, *My Coloring Book*, changing the pronoun's gender – reflects Pauline's mood. The four-by-four-foot oil on board is a triptych of sorts, with two abstract panels, featuring ribbons of pink and green on a grey background, flanking a portrait of Marilyn – taken from the cover of the November 1962 issue of *Town* magazine, but also closely resembling Geoffrey Reeve's photo of Pauline in *ARK* (and perhaps chosen for that reason). It is not a complex painting. The portrait features Marilyn at her most iconic and alluring – her most 'legendary' – with a grit-teeth smile that hints at both boundless erotic promise and a certain desperation; there are roses in front of and behind her – not in this case sexual stand-ins, but a gift from the artist, lovingly bestowed (in Ali Smith's novel *Autumn*, a character notes that 'the roses have curled up round her collarbone, like they're embracing her'). The flanking grey panels are painted over the rose-covered backdrop: they are encroaching over Marilyn's image and will soon obscure her.

As both *Belmondo* and *Marlowe* make clear, Pauline was more than capable of making a statement when she so chose. But with *Colour Her Gone*, Pauline preferred to express only emotion: depicting a 'hero' in whom she saw aspects of herself, festooned with flowers, as the grey waters closed over her. (Intriguingly, the painting appears in Ken Russell's 1963 television film *Bartok*, in which, in a highly stylized sequence, Pauline plays a prostitute who entices a client into her room, where he's robbed by two thugs as he's about to have sex with this seductive honey-trap. *Colour Her Gone* hangs on the wall. Perhaps Russell was doing a favour for a friend in need of exposure.)

Pauline's work appeared in two exhibitions in 1962. The first, in June, was called *New Art* and was up for two weeks as part of the Festival of Labour at London's Congress House. A brief newspaper notice, featuring a photo of Pauline hanging her contribution (an abstract canvas) above the infantilizing headline 'All my own work!', suggests one reason why the artist identified with Marilyn. The second, *New Approaches to the Figure*, at the Arthur Jeffress Gallery, ran from 28 August through 28 September, and featured three works by Pauline. Two – *Red Manoeuvre* and *Epitaph* – were paintings. The third, called *Doll in a Painted Box*, was as the title suggests: a doll with lush black hair, dressed in a peasant blouse and skirt and sporting knee-high boots, in an orange-coloured wood box. Judging from Pauline's picture, leaning on the piece and regarding the camera with a world-weary air, in the January 1963 issue of *Vogue*, it is about three feet high

Colour Her Gone,
1962, oil on
hardboard,
121.9 × 121.9 cm

and physically substantial.

Though not as well known (or highly regarded) as her paintings and collages, Pauline created a number of dolls, which Celia Birtwell observed in her room on Addison Road. 'They were made of white fabric, they had white faces, she put beauty spots on them, and they'd have black curly hair,' Birtwell remembers. 'They looked quite Spanish, they were very Goya-esque.'

Pauline's doll-making seems to have been a manifestation of her restless creativity – she was not, like the innovative Jann Haworth, an originator of Pop soft sculpture – but *Painted Box* was an exception. Its genesis can be found in her conversation with Nell Dunn:

> **Pauline:** *One of the awful things about being in a situation going out with a married man is that you're kind of sitting in your little box of a room waiting for a phone call, you know, and for them every now and then they go up to this box and lift the lid and take you out and it's lovely, you know, and then they put you safely back in your box and they go home to children or something like that, you know ... and I hate that kind of inactive thing. I can't stand it, and it just got to a peak when I thought 'Well this is just incredibly boring' ...*

Pauline persisted with him for a year and a half, until she met Clive Goodwin and married him ten days later. But evidently, Philip Saville – or the unequal nature of their relationship – had exhausted Pauline's patience before 1962 was out. Adam Smith describes *Painted Box* as Pauline's 'first overtly feminist work' and whether or not that is strictly true, it was evidently motivated by her dislike of being a passive participant in a relationship, entirely at the mercy of a married man's availability and whims.

In a 2014 e-mail, Smith (who died in December 2019, at 58) noted that Pauline had described herself to an interviewer as a feminist 'in 1963 – Wednesday 31 July, to be precise ... but I resist the voguish impulse to overstate this'. Smith meant that the idea of Pauline as proto-feminist, in his view, had been applied retroactively, by those wishing to see the artist as being in the political vanguard. Yet Pauline's artworks, interviews and public statements – her *actions* – paint her as someone who struggled against the then-prevailing notions of what a woman could or should expect, what she could or should do, and, above all, how she could or should be. And in her breakthrough year as an artist, as Pauline made 'Pauline Boty' the protagonist of her work and thus came ever closer to finding her style, the feminist and the flibbertigibbet began, increasingly, to merge.

BRIDGET BOTY

I knew a different Pauline than comes out in all the papers.

It wasn't until about two years after coming down that we really sat down and talked troubles. And it was always where the next pay cheque was coming from. It was always to do with money, she was always terribly short of money, always short of money. A lot of the art she did, nobody paid for, I think. And she was always stressed, and she was modelling, she dieted down to a model size. And that didn't do her any good. Nana always thought that that's what caused the cancer. Smoking as well of course.

She'd've liked to have made a nice living painting. Her painting was what she'd left home to do. And I think perhaps some of the time she was thinking – don't we all – that what she set out to do isn't going to quite come out what she thought it might. I expect when you sit down to a painting, and it must go wrong occasionally, it must drive you crackers. Perhaps her paintings weren't quite so good as she thought.

She never lifted a paintbrush while she was down here. She'd come down here when she was worried. I felt she wanted to leave London behind when she came. I think she wanted to see that other people were living a life and also being worried about things as well, but coping. I think she got very close to the edge of pushing her life too far for a while, and probably was tipping over the edge occasionally. I mean, a good sleep does you a world of good, doesn't it? And I'm sure some of the life she led, you didn't get many good nights, because there was always somebody interfering somewhere along the line. Late nights, and you wanted to get to bed early. I don't think that happens in London, does it?

If it was fine, she'd go out in the wood for three or four hours, just walking. We've got some lovely woods out the back here. The more I think about it, we probably only saw each other two hours every weekend she was down here, because she'd be up in the wood, and say, 'Oh, that does me a world of good.' She didn't grate, she didn't get in the way, you know? She wanted a bit of peace and quiet. London can't give you what that wood does, so that was it.

She would have breakfast about ten o'clock, go out in the wood, and then about half past four or five, she'd come back and eat the remains of the dinner that we'd had at one o'clock. She used to diet the whole week, but when she came down here, she never once said, 'I can't eat that.' She used to have half an apple pie. She'd eat a big meal, and she'd go to bed early. Just restored.

She was just happy. She always used to say, 'Oh, I feel so much better going home. Now I've got to go on a diet from now until next weekend.'

And the boyfriends came and went. I'm sure I've met some very famous people, but I don't know. I used to leave them to their own devices. Bed was made. I was intrigued about the boyfriends. You know, 'How many have you got?' And she says, 'You know, they change.' But it was all in fun. I always felt she was being used a bit by the older men, I must admit. And then I thought, 'Well, she's old enough. She's been around enough to know what's going on.' I think that's why she had some of the boyfriends she had, you know. Older men – well, they were the ones that could afford to take you out to the right places, aren't they? There were one or two her age came down. I think they were students, they were all wearing funny clothes. Quiet. But I probably frightened them!

I have lived with the self-portrait – it was Pauline quite young, very, very young. I saw the look that's in the self-portrait's face when she used to come down here: *I don't know what I'm doing.* To me, I can see Pauline every time I look at it. It's got a kind of sadness about it.

I think the other lot have got it just a bit wrong about what Pauline was like. I think she was quite a frightened person. She had a lot to be lonely or sad about.

Untitled (Self-Portrait), circa 1955–56, oil on sketching paper, 56 × 38 cm

11

BREAKOUT

1963

'I like a woman who can do things. You know, a really swinging bird.
It's important she look sexy. But she must have that other thing as well. She must
look as if she could become Minister of Pensions.'

    – David Frost on why Pauline Boty is 'the perfect girl', 1963

'Radiant sunshine' though she seemed to most, the post-RCA Pauline may have been beset, as her sister-in-law believes, by fears both artistic and personal. Yet 1963 proved to be her year. Following a March magazine profile in *Men Only*, Pauline debuted in *Day of the Prince* (for which, as noted, she designed elements of the programme) at the Royal Court on 14 May – two days after being called, in the *Sunday Mirror*, 'Britain's top pop artist' – and had three paintings exhibited at the Midland Group Gallery in Nottingham, in a Pop Art show that opened eleven days later. A 2 August story in the *Evening Standard* and an appearance, the following week, as a featured dancer on the first instalment of the TV show *Ready Steady Go!* were prelude to her three-week run in *Afternoon Men* at the Arts Theatre Club, which began on the 22nd. *That* show overlapped with the opening, on 10 September, of her first solo exhibition, at the Grabowski Gallery, which itself ended a day before Pauline began as a regular contributor on BBC radio's *The Public Ear* in October (a month in which she also worked on Ken Russell's television biopic *Bartok*); Pauline closed out her annus mirabilis with a Marilyn-tinged turn on the television series *Maigret*, air date 17 December. Not least, on 24 June, Pauline celebrated 1963's halfway mark with her marriage to ex-actor/sometime TV producer-presenter/future literary agent Clive Goodwin, some 240 hours after being introduced to him by, of all people, Philip Saville. If she was, in Bridget's view, a person with much to be lonely or sad about, the year Pauline turned 25 was balm to her travails.

Perhaps influenced by the left-of-Labour activism of her new husband and his circle – or her own engagement, which included Bertrand Russell's anti-nuclear Aldermaston marches – several of Pauline's canvases that year were 'political', overtly or in effect. One was infused with the artist's acidic wit: *Big Jim Colosimo* features a flattering photo-realist rendering, based on a 1914 newspaper picture, of the Chicago racketeer, positioned against a rich blue background, and with BIG JIM (above) and COLOSIMO (below) integrated into multicoloured, chevron-patterned banners of the sort found in Peter Blake's pop star portraits.

Opposite
Pauline with her
lost painting
July 26th, October
1963.

155

Big Jim Colosimo,
1963, oil on canvas,
63 × 79 cm

156   **BREAKOUT**

As for why Pauline selected the obscure Colosimo rather than his better-known contemporary Al Capone: perhaps the string of brothels that made his fortune, Colosimo's alleged charm and expensively purchased political influence, and corporate-style organizational skills made him, in Pauline's eyes, an American archetype. Whatever the case, by borrowing the graphics Peter Blake used for Elvis and the Everly Brothers to present him, Pauline's point is unmistakable: in corrupt, capitalist America, it's the pimp who's Pop.

Pauline's ongoing interest in Cuba materialized in two works that combined collage (*trompe l'oeil* and actual) and painting: the now-lost *July 26th* (named for the date of the 1953 attack on the Moncada barracks, which launched the revolution) is centred around the figure of Fidel – it can be seen, with a laughing Pauline sprawled on the floor before it, in Michael Ward's October 1963 photo – and the heroic *Cuba Si,* described by Brooks Adams, in a 1993 *Art in America* review of Mellor's Barbican exhibition, as 'a painted response to the Cuban Missile Crisis ... which with its brightly colored composition of concentric circles bedecked with folkloric patterns and maps of Cuba, seems like a send-up of American imperialism on many levels'.

(The painting also had, for the artist, practical significance. 'She'd got a big commission for a Cuban, and she was in the middle of that, and she was worried that it wasn't going right, and she wanted the £1,000 it was going to bring in when she was finished,' Bridget remembers. 'In the beginning she was saying, "Oh, it would be lovely to get that money, I'll pay what I owe." And she was so happy when they were pleased with it. That was the only time I think I ever saw her excited.')

Arguably the most effective of Pauline's painted collages, also political in tone, is *Untitled (Sunflower Woman).* The central figure – her waist encircled by an enormous yellow sunflower – is a 'gesturing giantess' writes David Alan Mellor, 'a gyrating figure who might be dancing the Hitch Hike'. This joyful bombshell, however, Pauline used as a billboard to display what Mellor calls 'the composite melodramas of modernity': above the sunflower, consuming the woman's arms and chest, the grille of a Mercedes, a machine gun-firing gangster and a smokestacked factory; below the waist, the phallic Hindenburg explodes at her crotch (a darkly ribald joke) as a terrified blonde flees across one thigh and an owl glares balefully from the other. *Sunflower Woman* is frightening and exhilarating both: at once nightmarish – an icon of femininity, 'radiant sunshine' at her waist, besmirched by corporate/industrial capitalism – and, thanks to the force and felicity of its design, sublime.

To the anonymous collector who commissioned her lost painting about the Profumo affair, *Scandal '63,* Pauline wrote, '[L]ike a number of other English painters (egs. Blake and Hockney) I am interested in the technical difficulty of mixing styles in pictures like, for instance, the representational and the abstract,

in hopes of achieving some kind of synthesis.' Pauline managed such a mix adroitly in *Scandal*, and the means by which she achieved it speak to how she practised her craft, as well as her interests, in a picture that combines three of them: sex, politics and sexual politics.

The 'scandal' involved Secretary of State for War John Profumo's relationship with the teenage libertine Christine Keeler, which – thanks to Profumo's lies about it, and Keeler's simultaneous involvement with various high-society and demimonde figures (and a Soviet naval attaché) – brought down the Conservative government of Harold Macmillan. Pauline conveyed her interest in the affair to the French artist, anarchist and all-round provocateur Jean-Jacques Lebel, whom she met through her husband. 'I remember vividly Pauline, Clive and I saying, "Wow! Here we are, breaking our backs trying to bring down these imperialist governments and getting nowhere but getting our skulls beaten by the cops,"' Lebel says. 'And here's this charming, beautiful young lady, with her Swinging London sexuality, pot-smoking Mary Quant mini-skirted body, bringing down

Above
Cuba Si, 1963,
oil and collage
on canvas,
125 × 96 cm

Opposite
Untitled (Sunflower Woman), 1963,
oil on canvas,
78 × 95 cm

The first version of Pauline's lost painting **Scandal '63** (opposite), seen here in September 1963, features Christine Keeler as a somewhat conventional figure. That changed after the artist saw Lewis Morley's photograph (above left), which Pauline made the focus of the finished work (above right).

the whole British government! Sleeping with the right guys, this extraordinary woman did the job. It was a real Dadaist event, interpreted by us, of course.'

Visiting the couple at their London flat, Lebel was struck by Pauline's observation that 'Keeler was a radical by instinct rather than for intellectual reasons – that some people have this radical instinct that others don't,' he recalls. 'I remember Pauline saying – even though she herself was a very quiet person and not radical at all in the way she led her daily life – she still considered Keeler a sort of beacon of womanhood. She was very admiring of her freedom, her way of life.'

Pauline executed two takes on the same canvas. Both versions include, across the top, a frieze featuring four characters at the heart of the business: Aloysius 'Lucky' Gordon, a Jamaican-born jazz singer, whom Keeler accused of rape; Profumo himself; Stephen Ward, the fashionable osteopath that brought Profumo and Keeler together; and Johnny Edgecombe, a petty criminal and Keeler paramour, who slashed Gordon's face and fired gunshots through Ward's door, and whose arrest got the scandal rolling – 'the four men in Christine's life who suffered imprisonment, disgrace, and death', Pauline wrote.

The major difference lies in Pauline's portrayal of her protagonist. In a September 1963 photo, the artist posed with her in-progress first attempt, in which Keeler is depicted as a mod if proper young lady, handbag swinging à la

Julie Christie in *Billy Liar*, striding through an as-yet unresolved scramble of images, including a rosette, a woman's sexually ecstatic face, a man resembling the Notting Hill slumlord Peter Rachman – lover of both Keeler and her co-adventuress Mandy Rice-Davies – and a gun. But in a photo taken four months later, Pauline stands behind the finished painting, in which Keeler now appears as she does in Lewis Morley's world-famous black-and-white photo portrait, her nudity artfully concealed by the chair she's straddling. Below the frieze, the painting sets the monochrome Keeler against a hot red-orange background, across which flows a river of semi-abstract collage, characterized by the artist as having 'a kind of garish sensuality one might associate with Christine'; though hard to parse in photos, the ecstatic woman's face remains, as does the rosette, at the centre of which is the provocative number 69.

Pauline was forthright about the latter's significance. 'The figure 69 refers to the 69th sexual position,' she wrote (without, alas, naming the preceding 68). '[I]t seemed very important to contain in the picture a reminder that although all kinds of lessons can be shown from the case about political and moral corruption; for the people immediately concerned (and represented in the picture) the case was about sex.'

Pauline's reason for revising her original composition (the portrayal of

Keeler in particular) goes unrecorded – by September she would have been aware of Morley's photo, which had been published in the 9 June edition of the *Sunday Mirror* – but it might have been motivated by Macmillan's October resignation. If before, Keeler had seemed to Pauline like (in Kalliopi Minioudaki's formulation) 'a proper and fashionable new London girl' to whom things happened to happen, following the government's collapse she might plausibly have become, as Lebel suggests, an icon of sexual freedom and its obliterating power in the face of the patriarchy's conniving and hypocrisy. Thus Pauline's appropriation of Morley's artful pin-up: what was once an object of men's lewd fantasizing is now an emblem of women's self-empowerment.

Interestingly, *Scandal '63* occasioned what was likely Pauline's first Continental exposure as a painter. When in May 1964 Lebel mounted his *Festival of Free Expression* at the Centre Américain des Artistes and featured a selection of paintings, Clive prevailed upon him to include *Scandal*, which he brought to Paris himself. 'Clive thought, rightly so, that this would be good for her, to be invited to an exhibition where there were people like Warhol and Richard Hamilton,' Lebel says. 'He was pushing her to be more outspoken, more outward-looking, with her art.'

Given the autobiographical character of Pauline's maturing work, and her own posing, in which she remade the pin-up into an emblem of confident female sexuality, it is reasonable to see Christine Keeler, in *Scandal '63*, as the artist's surrogate. In two other of the year's creative issue can also be found Pauline substitutes, notable for being – like Keeler – avatars of the emerging 'new' woman.

The aforementioned *Celia Birtwell and Some of Her Heroes* features Pauline's flatmate – shortly to become one of London's hottest fashion-textile designers – her shirt unbuttoned, standing before a collage featuring Brando, Elvis, the Everly Brothers, David Hockney with his artwork *The Hypnotist* (from a photo by Snowden), a heart, a target and the number 6 (sampled from Peter Blake), and, for good measure, Haile Selassie and Archduke Franz Ferdinand. Birtwell did indeed pose, but in her own estimation the connection ends there. 'I don't think it looked like me at all,' she declares. 'And it was quite funny, because one of my "heroes" was David Hockney. And I hadn't really met him when she painted that picture. They were *her* heroes.'

The other work, *5-4-3-2-1*, remains one of Pauline's most famous, in large measure for its sexual exuberance. Between the numbers of the title, emblazoned across the top of the canvas on a fairground-style banner ('she often visited Battersea Funfair', Berman reports), and the picture's bottom, featuring the head of a dark-haired young woman, her wide, open mouth seeming to cry out in pleasure, there stretches a semi-abstract object: a rose – Pauline's preferred vaginal metaphor, here extended to include extra labial petals – surrounded by

thick black cross-hatching suggestive of pubic hair. To the right of this erotic storm-cloud, there is a yellow banner, on which is written 'OH, FOR A FU' (the remaining letters clipped off by the canvas edge). 'That was confrontational on her part for that time,' observes Marco Livingstone. 'For a woman to make openly sexual and erotic paintings raised eyebrows then – she wasn't making demure work as a young female artist.' To Pauline, this was second nature. According to Charles Carey, 'She felt that consciousness of her body was something she should celebrate. Pauline was interested in the erotic side of life, which she felt was neglected in the art world. Her work was quite sexy.'

The painting's inspiration has long been thought to be a television landmark, the rock'n'roll music and dance programme *Ready Steady Go!* – which, on its 9 August debut broadcast, featured an appearance by Pauline, demonstrating the Twist as part of a dance competition judged by the band leader Joe Loss. How Pauline secured her spot is unknown; the programme's historian, Andy Neill, suggests that 'Clive Goodwin had known *RSG!* creator Elkan Allan since the 'fifties, so she could have had an entrée there, seeing as she and Clive were married in June.' Whatever the case, both Pauline and Derek Boshier danced regularly during the show's first seasons.

Yet the link between painting and programme is inaccurate. Manfred

Left
**Celia Birtwell
and Some of Her
Heroes**, 1963,
oil on canvas,
122 × 152 cm

Right
5-4-3-2-1, 1963,
oil on canvas,
100 × 125 cm

Mann's song *5-4-3-2-1* eventually became the *RSG!* opening theme, and the ecstatic woman – Pauline's stand-in here, as was Birtwell elsewhere – bears a resemblance to the show's presenter, Cathy McGowan. But, in fact, the painting was finished by September 1963, McGowan began (in a subordinate capacity) in November, and *5-4-3-2-1* didn't start *RSG!* until January of the following year. Thus we have interesting coincidence, not creative inspiration. Most likely, Pauline took the numbers from the American space programme – as the countdown to that blast-off known as orgasm – and the picture's pleasure-loving brunette is, as *RSG!* director Michael Lindsay-Hogg puts it, 'a generic woman of the times'.

It is unsurprising that Pauline chose female culture figures, specific or otherwise, to represent her. Though she made a near-avocation of having her photo taken with her pictures, the artist only produced one conventional self-portrait, and that was in her teens: revealing the vulnerability and self-doubt her sister-in-law perceived during farm visits. *That* self, the private Pauline, is absent from 1963's pictorial cavalcade, replaced by the popular personality she cultivated – the observer/participant – to bring us sexual freedom, New Left politics, proto-feminism and other concerns.

Thus the pictures can be read as exercises in exposure and concealment, the work of someone who does and does not wish to be known – with one exception. In what might be described as her Pop self-portrait, *My Colouring Book*, Pauline offers a version of the self that Bridget saw, using the by-then well-established conventions of the style to reveal more intimate emotions and experiences.

My Coloring Book (in America the 'u' is omitted), with music and lyrics by John Kander and Fred Ebb, was introduced by Sandy Stewart on *Perry Como's Kraft Music Hall*, a television variety show, in October 1962, and recorded the following month by Barbra Streisand. By the end of 1963, it had been covered multiple times, by singers of both sexes – proving almost impossible to ruin – and established itself as a minor but distinct American classic. Although *Coloring Book* is not rock'n'roll but rather a work of standard popular music, it apparently made an impression on Pauline, who borrowed the last line for the title of her Marilyn portrait *Colour Her Gone*, then appropriated nearly the entirety of the lyrics, applied via Letraset directly onto the finished canvas, for her 1963 painting. The subject is lost love: the protagonist's paramour has abandoned her for 'another' and her grief is expressed in colours that shade into states of being – 'lonely', 'empty', 'gone'. Much has been made of Pauline's sexual swagger. But prior to meeting Clive, and despite many affairs, her major relationship had been with a married man who, as she put it to Nell Dunn, kept her in a box; it is not surprising that, however swashbuckling Pauline might have seemed, she'd have taken *My Coloring Book* so personally. And with her painting, the artist succeeded in doing what all those vocalists failed to manage: she took ownership of the song, and made it her story.

Pauline crafted various changes to the lyrics. One of them was substantive: she cut the prologue that sets up the song's premise.

For those who fancy coloring books
As certain people do
Here's a new one for you
A most unusual coloring book
The kind you never see
Crayons ready?
Very well
Begin to color me

This Pauline reduces to 'this is my book an unusual book this is my colouring book', in red-orange capital letters tucked into the painting's upper left corner. Pauline may have executed the edit for brevity's sake, but it makes a significant change in perspective. In the prologue, the song's protagonist casts herself in a passive role, asking her audience to take their crayons and colour her in. Pauline's perfunctory set-up extracts the passivity and, crucially, puts the 'crayons' back where they belong: in the hands of the creator.

Pauline's edit also jettisons the song's central conceit, which reminds us that colouring books are for children – those, moreover, content to stay between lines drawn by other hands. Instead, she presents six vignettes – three over three – each corresponding to a different verse, paired with the appropriate lyrics. Slightly overlapping one another, different in style, character and emotional texture, the images unfold cinematically: six 'scenes' chronicling aspects of a loss, each with its own subtitles eccentrically mixing upper- and lower-case lettering, as though hand-scrawled in a state of heartbreak.

these are the eyes that watched him
as he walked aWay
colour tHem grey

A ghostly face, barely visible, the eyes hidden behind dark grey-tinted granny glasses ...

this is tHe heart tHat Thought
he Would always BE TRUE
Colour IT BLUE

... a pair of blue valentines, one light, one dark, one atop the other, both layered over the top of a rainbow ...

THEsE are the arms that Held Him
and Touched Him
& lost hiM SomehoW
COLOUR Them empty noW

... a blonde, her features indistinct, her robust arms tightly hugging, from behind, a man-shaped void ...

My Colouring Book, 1963, oil and Letraset on canvas, 152.4 × 121.9 cm

These are the beads I wore
until she came BETWEEN
COLOUR THEM GREEN

... an arrangement of thick green circles, evocative of the red ones Pauline painted to signify orgasm, draped over a square orange background ...

this is the room I sleep in
and walk in and weep in and hide in
that nobody sees
colour it lonely please

    ... a surprisingly formal chamber, with a bed in an arched niche, floral print wallpaper and drapery, a rococo armchair, a doll's house set atop a tabouret table – a room that seems all the more abandoned for its stage-set elegance ...

THIS IS THE BOY
THE ONE I DEPENDED UPON
COLOUR HIM GONE

    The last image – of the lost love – is anti-romantic: a black-and-white photo-realist portrait of a leather-jacketed tough, eyes in semi-shadow, cigarette between tight lips. And Pauline has made a small, significant change to the lyric: Kander and Ebb's 'man' has been made a 'boy'.

    My Colouring Book remains unique in the artist's *oeuvre*: though words and phrases appear in other of her paintings, this is the only one that is, as it were, required reading. Like a chef who buys a can of soup, then doctors it into something original, Pauline empowered the song's protagonist, matured and personalized the imagery, transformed the fragile lyrics into graffiti – and by stripping away the song's plaintive delicacy, brought the anguish at its heart directly to the fore. As well, and in the best Pop spirit: by transforming a hit song into a projection of her own lived experience – her own heartbreak at the hands of a 'boy' – Pauline demonstrated precisely what it means to be a fan.

    1963 also continued Pauline's dialogue with the movies. If her choice of Belmondo as a subject was hormonal, the protagonist of *Monica Vitti with Heart*, which depicts director Michelangelo Antonioni's frequent siren of angst in full face, her black-and-white visage nestled in a red valentine, may have been an expression of Pauline's passion for avant-garde European film. One can also imagine her admiring – envying – the mix of enigmatic reserve, emotional and intellectual expressiveness, and Italian chic, lightly dashed with *il sale della terra*, that made Vitti the cinema's leading modern anti-heroine. Indeed, the title can be read two ways: as a description of the painting's content, or a green-eyed-monstered comment on what Pauline had in abundance and what some might

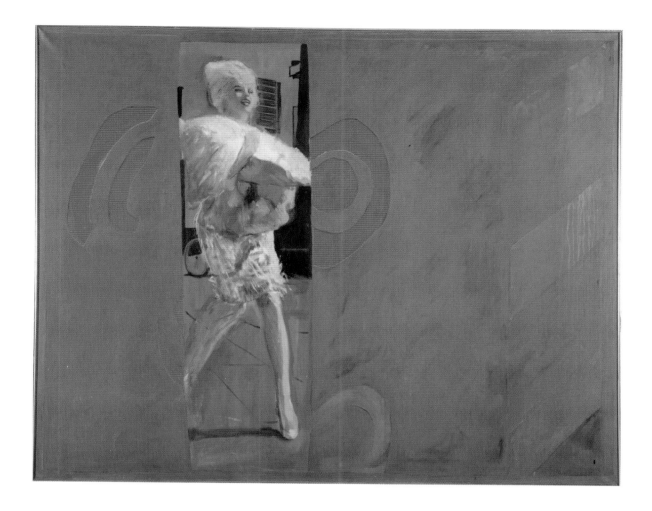

Opposite
**Monica Vitti with
Heart**, 1963,
oil on canvas,
65 × 80 cm

Above
**The Only Blonde in
the World**, 1962,
oil on canvas,
153 × 122.4 cm

have seen as the cool Vitti's sole deficiency.

Though the commonly accepted date for *The Only Blonde in the World* is 1963, this appears to be incorrect. In the delightful and fascinating 1964 documentary *Dieu est-il Pop???* (*Is God Pop???*), directed by Evelyne Axell's husband, Jean Antoine – the all-star cast of which includes Rauschenberg, Rosenquist, Tilson, Phillips, Jones, Donaldson and Magritte – Pauline, standing good-student-style before her painting, reveals that it was completed in 1962, prior to Monroe's death. Discovering that the artwork is a celebration, not a memorial, inevitably alters one's view of it; but either way, *The Only Blonde* pays tribute to Marilyn as unsinkable and eternal – in Minioudaki's description, 'a model of beauty, glamour and empowering sexual awareness, rather than a casualty of Hollywood's spectacle'. Pauline's rendering shows the star, her full-figure image taken from a publicity photo for Billy Wilder's 1959 classic *Some Like It Hot*, seeming to emerge from between two fields of brilliant green (decorated with abstractions reminiscent of the artist's Hollywood-musical paintings): breathlessly on the run, face ecstatic, shapely legs in racehorse motion, her vibrant body about to burst from a shimmering chrysalis of chiffon. ('Boty conveys her Monroe figure,' notes Thomas Crow, 'with confident imprecision.') If many of Pauline's pictures invite a feminist reading, *The Only Blonde in the World* – a title the artist might have conferred upon herself – weights towards the personal. Given her identification with Marilyn – her own 'betrayal' and trivialization by the media, and ambiguous engagement with the dramatic arts – Pauline may well have decided that, for both blondes, 'forever young' was better than 'beautiful and damned'.

Pauline's September 1963 exhibition at the Grabowski Gallery featured an even dozen paintings, priced (according to Adam Smith) between £150 and £200, including two Marilyns, *Belmondo*, *Vitti*, *Celia*, *Colouring Book*, *Derek Marlowe* and *5-4-3-2-1* (an unfinished version of which appeared on the show's programme cover), as well as the now-lost, tantalizingly named *My Heroes*. Her bio in the programme described it as Pauline's 'first one-man show', which may have been a consequence of Mateusz Grabowski's imperfect English. A largely unheralded yet influential figure on London's art scene from the late 1950s through 1975, Grabowski, born in Poland in 1904, was a pharmacist who had fled the German onslaught to France in 1939, then continued on to England the following year. In 1948 Grabowski opened his first pharmacy in south London, relocating the following year to Draycott Avenue, in the more fashionable Chelsea district. Grabowski formalized his interest in art by launching a gallery: purchasing the building directly behind the pharmacy, at 84 Sloane Avenue, the enterprising chemist enclosed the patio between the two properties and opened a three-room venue, which could be entered directly from Sloane, or covertly through the back of his day-job establishment. 'It was around Brompton Cross as it's now called, between Chelsea and Knightsbridge,' remembers Allen Jones. 'You went in and there was this sort of counter where you could buy your medications at the front. And then you walked through the shop and it opened up into a proper little gallery. Quite mad.'

Debuting in February 1959, Grabowski initially specialized in Polish artists, but the sharp-eyed drugstore cowboy, wanting to give exposure to London's emerging *nouvelle vague*, opened his *Tomorrow's Artists* exhibition – featuring graduates from five of the city's art colleges – in August of the same year. Grabowski's instincts were exceptional. The first London venue to present Op Art, in 1962 it mounted *Images in Progress*, the all-star cast of which included Hockney, Allen Jones, R B Kitaj, Peter Phillips and Boshier, who declared it (*Blake Boty Porter Reeve* notwithstanding) London's first true Pop group show. Pauline's was one of many solo opportunities Grabowski offered a grateful generation, and the show was well reviewed – described by *The Times* as 'a confident and engaging exhibition'.

GRABOWSKI

5 4 3 2 1

PAULINE BOTY

CATALOGUE

1.	The only Blonde in the World	48 x 60 ins.
2.	With love to Jean-Paul Belmondo	60 x 48 ins.
3.	"Colour her gone"	48 x 48 ins.
4.	Portrait of Derek Marlowe with unknown ladies	48 x 48 ins.
5.	Five—Four—Three—Two—One	48 x 36 ins.
6.	Monica Vitti Heart	30 x 24 ins.
7.	Celia with some of her heroes	60 x 48 ins.
8.	My Colouring Book	48 x 60 ins.
9.	July 26th	48 x 60 ins.
10.	Tom's Dream	72 x 60 ins.
11.	Cuba Si	36 x 48 ins.
12.	My Heroes	48 x 60 ins.

As was his habit, Grabowski chose a painting, *My Colouring Book*, rather than taking a percentage of sales; the artwork can today be found at Museum Sztuki, Lodz, Poland, a part of the remarkable collection Grabowski gave the institution in 1975. Museum curator Anna Saciuk-Gasowska notes a surprising fact: 'It has to be remembered that until 1993, the only painting by Pauline Boty in the public collections was in the collection of the Lodz museum – thanks to Grabowski's donation.'

From the BBC publicity department:

A new fortnightly magazine on the Light Programme 'THE PUBLIC EAR' which will be taking a fresh look at entertainment begins on Sunday, October 6. Each hour-long programme includes news, opinion, short features and comment about current happenings and trends in entertainment. Many of the contributors will be entertainers themselves, being themselves, voicing their own opinions – sometimes serious, sometimes off-beat.

Producer John Fawcett Wilson says: 'This will not be a programme of the mutual back-slap and we won't avoid provocative subjects. We hope that the listeners themselves will be able to voice their own opinions within the programme. The conception of "The Public Ear", in terms of radio, is of the present day and aims at originality and attractive presentation for an audience of all age-groups.'

Young actor-writer Allan Scott will introduce the programme and he will be joined by two regular reporters: Pauline Boty, painter of 'pop art' and actress, and disc jockey Tony Hall. The Max Harris Group will add music in the modern idiom and there will be music on disc.

Pauline had auditioned for the programme during her *Day of the Prince* run, and the deal was sealed while her paintings were up at Grabowski. It was a significant opportunity. '*The Public Ear* was one of the great programmes that the BBC killed,' says Allan Scott. 'We had a wonderful producer called John Fawcett Wilson, he was a real innovator of radio. His idea was to do a good, intelligent magazine show, and it was fun because it was about everything in the world of the arts.'

Of Pauline, Scott says, 'Very sweet girl, very clever, very charming. Very reserved. But in a good way. I mean she wasn't reserved in the way that some people are so reserved you get nothing off of them. She just was modest. I'm actually surprised that she didn't break through as a media figure. Doing what she did, and the skill with which she did it, you would have expected it – today she would have been a celebrity.'

In fact, she was. Scott does not recall how Pauline got involved with the show – 'she was on the fringes of show biz,' he says – but it was, in a sense, inevitable. Whether or not Pauline could have imagined, short-changing the Soup Kitchen till to afford art supplies, that within two years she would become a multi-hyphenate fixture of London's cultural scene, her achievement was remarkable. With her solo exhibition, a woman who'd taken no formal painting classes, had not been part of the Brit Pop boys' club, or participated in the 1961 Young Contemporaries exhibition that set off the movement's second wave, had *made it* as a Pop artist – not tentatively, nor with a pastiche of her more established friends' work, but with personal canvases, in a distinct style, expressing a perspective so particular that the discerning Grabowski had given her a 'one-man show'. And though Blake, Carey and others had served as examples, and offered advice and encouragement, Pauline's success was largely of her own making, the outcome of what Celia Birtwell, Nicholas Garland and others identified as defiance, the force of character to go her own way. Even more remarkably, Pauline had at the same time – without training, with only the College revues as experience – created a second career as a stage and TV actress, and whatever her limitations used the 'release', as she called it, of playing a role to further personalize her art.

It was, by any measure, an extraordinary transit. Surely, Pauline's beauty and vitality helped; certainly, the anything-goes character of the times played its part. But however she found her way to Fawcett Wilson – or, more likely, he to her – Pauline must have seen the chance to fortnightly speak forthrightly on any subject, to bring the provocatrice of the easel to the airwaves and make another sort of cultural contribution, as the extension of everything she did and everything she was: the natural next step. And for the 13 weeks that *The Public Ear* endured, Pauline made the most of her moment.

'Pauline was paid 15 gns per fortnightly monologue,' notes Adam Smith. 'All were recorded at the BBC's Aeolian Hall in New Bond Street. Allan Scott introduced each programme over the scurrying theme tune *Nursery Blues* by The Shake Keane Fivetet: "60 minutes of news, comment, music and opinion" and closed with "From the people who know to the people who want to know; the news, the opinions, the sounds, and the stars – for 60 minutes every fortnight, they're all in *The Public Ear.*"'

Though the participants 'met' on air, each recorded his or her contributions separately, 'and I did the linking', says Scott. Fawcett Wilson oversaw the edit, shuffling the segments until the order flowed to his liking, adding interstitial music and effects, and co-writing Scott's intermittent commentary, which held it all together. As *Public Ear* was broadcast on the Light Programme – the BBC radio network which, from 1945 until 1967, served up suitably light entertainment – the show included regular bits by the comedy writer/performer Dick Vosburgh and the football (aka soccer) great-turned-journalist Danny Blanchflower. But unlike the celebrity fawn-fest *Movie-Go-Round*, which filled the 3–4 p.m. Sunday slot every other week, *Ear* had an edge, featuring provocative interviews, some conducted by Pauline – though not the one with 'three or four incredibly scruffy guys, who came into the studio', recalls Scott. 'That was the first time I ever saw a group called the Rolling Stones' – and even the occasional debate, including a clamorous one between pro- and anti-hunting advocates, which drew the most mail. The show succeeded almost immediately, with both critics and audiences.

... the first impression is that it has some pleasantly bright, acidulous, and off-beat ideas to fill it with.

Not all of them, I feel, quite come off yet ... Miss Pauline Boty, judging by her savage little piece on the current state of the cinema industry ('When teenagers don't like a film they tear up the seats, so it's not too hard to see how their tastes are evolving'), is much too intelligent to rest content with her present oh-so-cosy auntie-getting-hip-with-the-little-ones approach to the pop record section. But there are lots of other attractive things to make up – particularly the pace and attack and variety with which the items are presented ... As entertainment magazines go, at the moment, it registers distinctly more hits than misses, I should say.

– The Sunday Times, 6 October 1963

Yet the review hints at something that the BBC's audience research reports would, as the show moved forward, make plain – for many, Pauline grated: 'several listeners remarked on Pauline Boty's "deplorable lack of manners ... "'; 'Pauline Boty's harsh, "flat" voice considerably irritated some listeners reporting who "wondered at her gall" in criticizing what she called "ugly upper-class accents ... "'; 'Several disliked Pauline Boty, both for what she said and the way she said it – a fatuous and pointless, as well as contradictory, sneer at Englishmen, it was called, delivered in an arrogant manner in an unattractive voice ... '

Pauline's 'gall' was, of course, the point: here was a 25-year-old free-thinking woman, unafraid to state her opinions, to offend sniffy sensibilities, to kick at the received attitudes of even younger listeners – in short, to not know her place. In so doing, Pauline adroitly managed to have it both ways. A *Radio Times* review, published in March, acknowledged that 'her controversial remarks are always incisive and often pricklingly acute ... She excels at putting ginger into forgotten trifles.'

Rather than 'ginger', what one perceives most in Pauline's monologues are, on the one hand, exasperation with the old ways (those pinioning women in particular) and the sexed-up deceptions of advertising; and on the other, an impatience for the new world, as exemplified by those in her cohort, and the heroes with whom she identified, to kick into high gear. Yet there is also Pauline's pleasure in the opportunity to combine, and improve, her writing and performing abilities. On the third programme, she anatomized the adman's exploitation of the dissatisfactions and desires of the (largely female) consumer, the draping of dreary products in tantalizing veils of sin – 'sex advertising', as Pauline called it – that 'can leave us uneasy and frustrated'. Such an exposé, in 1963, wasn't absolutely new – with his Vance Packard-inspired paintings, Boshier had interrogated the idea – but Pauline's passion showed in her prose.

Do you know what you're buying when you buy your stockings, cigarettes, beer, chocolate, cars or petrol? Do you know you're buying your dream? Your secret dreams of sex? Your fantasies of promiscuity, the promise of illicit love? When you buy a pair of 7/11d nylons, you buy it with a promise of a secret tryst in a warm shady wood. You are buying smoky shades that shape and flatter. The silken highlights that shimmer and flirt. You are buying the new lovable you. Whatever the product, your life will be transformed. It may only be six pennyworth of chocolate heaven, but it's ecstatic. It's the best substitute for him that money can buy. And it's so cheap. With it and everything else comes lovely lazy promiscuous girls, tall, dark, virile men and long white sports-cars, beaches, woods, streams, sumptuous parties, gaiety, everybody loving you, and sex always just a smile away – a glimpse of future delight, a suggested violent pleasure. A life full of promise, fulfilling all those vague longing

*wanting feelings. You'll never feel lost, alone, unwanted again – if only you have the
money to buy all the things that seem to make your dreams come true.*

The exploitation of female longing remained a theme in Pauline's
commentaries, conveyed with the outrage and certainty of youth. In the fifth
programme, broadcast on 1 December, she went after romance stories, in which
tall, handsome men proved to be well-paid middle-class professionals rather than
swashbucklers: tales Pauline declared were shills for a living death, encouraging
women to trade virginity for the ultimate prize, i.e. housework and children.

*But if we follow that sort of advice, we'd properly wake up after five or six
years of marriage and have nothing, and I mean nothing except the box we live
in. The more we allow ourselves to think of marriage as the only aim in life, the
more we allow ourselves to be slaves to domesticity, the more we need these stories
to convince us that there must be something glamorous in it all and the more we
become dependent upon the visit of the gas man or anyone, after all it's someone
to talk to during the long, lonely day. You don't get this in magazine stories, it's too
real. Remember, they're the biggest commercial for marriage that exists, and when
you're advertising something, you don't have to tell the whole truth.*

Pauline's choice of the word 'box' is notable, given the artwork she created
to express loathing of her passive position in the romance with Saville. Still, in this
as in so many matters Pauline's double vision prevailed: if she protested against
the puerile scenarios purveyed to keep women in bondage, Pauline nonetheless
recognized the importance of fantasy and desire to the achievement of a heightened,
heroic sense of self – and, at that moment in time especially, its connection to
personal style. In the monologue at the beginning of this book, Pauline derided
the neutering effects of upper-class female fashion – 'the tweedy top' – and
championed a sexy iconoclasm in dress that broadcast, not just erotic freedom,
but social liberation. On the programme's eighth instalment, Pauline broadened
her manifesto from fashion to interior design, tying it to cost.

*I see a girl walking down the street and she looks so great and really elegant.
Her shoes, her bag, her suit reminiscent of Chanel, her appearance is beautiful.
Now this girl is a typist. She earns about £12 a week and yet on so little money,
she and millions like her in this country today manage to look beautiful and elegant.
And then she goes home, and somehow she looks very out of place. This elegant
creature, in a house full of badly designed furniture and hideous domestic fittings
... She can't spend a fortune on furnishings and she did her best with what was
available in a low price range. I wonder why, when it has been proved so often*

*now that a good, beautiful, cheap design sells like mad, and is what we all want.
I wonder why, oh why, all we can get cheaply are ugly, girlish domestic furnishings.
Well I for one want beautiful furniture that won't cost £150 for one chair but is
designed as well as an expensive one ...*

Pauline's essays are best appreciated, not for their elegance of expression,
but rather their prescience, and this one is a good example. Connecting aesthetic
quality to industrial success had been the idea behind Darwin's reinvention of the
RCA, and at College Pauline had been exposed to graphic, industrial, furniture
and product design's next wave. So her views were, so to speak, well-schooled,
and in fact about to enter the mainstream: that same year, her Soup Kitchen
boss, Terence Conran, transformed the world of interiors with his first Habitat
store, modelled precisely on the quality-home-furnishings-for-all ethos. On the
next programme, however, Pauline was compelled to respond to a listener's letter,
which she first read aloud.

Pauline: *'Dear Sir, At the beginning of your article on furnishings and furniture,
the speaker said "the beautiful well-dressed young girl was a typist earning £12 a
week." Would you mind telling me where there are jobs like this? Yours faithfully,
Maureen Drinkwater, Sale, Cheshire. P.S. I am not an elderly shop assistant, but a
typist earning £6.11.0d a week.'*
Voice: *Here's Pauline Boty.*
Pauline: *I'm sorry Maureen if I caused dissatisfaction in the typing pool, but
I was using the word typist comprehensively ... I agree that if you're good at your job,
£6.11.0d seems to me to be underpaid. However, the point I was making was that
you can dress beautifully nowadays very cheaply, and it doesn't require a large wage
packet any more in order to look smart.*

The tincture of impatience in her reply suggests that Pauline's sense of
humour might, in this instance, have deserted her – a not unusual occurrence
among those who, unused to being listened to, suddenly have an audience. But it
is also true that Pauline had a penchant for provocation and, on that same episode,
she indulged it with appetite: going after (and not for the first time) Elvis Presley.

*Oh, Elvis again, that old has-been. Let's hear some more of the new boys.
But no, apparently Elvis's fans are still doing a good job. They're still out there
somewhere, cheering faintly. Old El isn't quite dead yet. We've had so many letters
complaining that we always knock him, but there are some facts you just can't deny.
Remember when Elvis was king in the good old days of* Loving You *and* Jailhouse
Rock, *of* King Creole *and gold lamé suits and riots, when they broke up cinemas,*

when we fainted screamed cried, and tried to tear him apart? Elvis the king. He just raised a finger and you nearly died. And when he moved – oh how he moved – he was a real wild rocker. He was such a beautiful, beautiful boy. And in those early films his numbers were just great and we all screamed. And did you know that in the beginning his first appearance on coast-to-coast television on The Ed Sullivan Show *they apologized for only showing him in medium shot down to his waist? Now we're lucky if he even snaps his fingers ...*

You can't deny it. There's a remnant of the old magic left but you really have to dig to find it. I mean, the songs he sings now! Where does he find them? ... And all this 'Hawaiian Holiday' bit. And have you seen Fun in Acapulco? *Fun? It's like an ad paid for by Hilton Hotels. And if you really want to see our sometime rebel being a sort of singing matador with capes and Mexicanery and a square scene like that, then go along to the empty cinema and you'll know what I mean about the rise and fall of Elvis Presley, one-time King Pop, now just Sonny Boy.*

Daddy seems to be getting too old for the real nitty-gritty. All we see now is someone who looks the same as the old kickster, but there's no kick left. There's about a ton of water being poured on the fire and all we can hear is the faint hiss before it's put out completely. The spark's probably still there somewhere in that all-American boy, and with really good songs like he used to have, things could start roaring away again and he could top the hit parade. But with the kind of stuff he's been churning out lately, one of the greatest pop kings of all time seems to be saying bye-bye. And El, it's sad to see you go this way.

Woven into the essay's fabric are a trio of Pauline's passions: pop stars and their music, convention-immolating chaos, and sex. But most prominent is the pleasure she takes in rubbing the Elvis lovers' noses in their idol's perceived decline – and as a sheaf of outraged letters, still extant in the BBC Written Archives Centre, attests, they ravenously took the bait.

In an August article in the *Evening Standard*, 'Pauline, the Three-Careers Girl', published in connection with *Afternoon Men* and illustrated with a Michael Ward photo, Pauline – 'once aptly described as an ice-cream of a girl' – seemed more inclined to celebrate the moment than to look ahead: 'she thinks it's best not to have too many plans for the future.'

'There's time to do anything you want to do – plenty of it,' Pauline declares. 'I deal with things as they come up and I do what I want to do. How can one say what one wants to do in six years' time? After all one might be dead.'

12

'A VERY CONFIDENT MAN'

1963

Pauline: *I still think that people have a thing that by actually marrying someone you're saying something that you can't say in any other way. And as marriage is still very much with society, it really is, that this is the only way you can sort of say it and even if it's going to break up a year later I don't think it matters all that much because for a while you really said that thing, you know.*

'For somebody who was going the way she was going, to get married did strike me at the time as a bad move,' says Geoffrey Reeve. 'I thought she might be a lone wolf, you know. Be on her own. Have affairs. She always gave me the impression that men wouldn't be sufficient.' Reeve's point regarding male insufficiency is well-taken. On the eleventh instalment of *Public Ear*, Pauline delivered a monologue that was murderous in its contempt for the species.

Are you an Englishman? I bet you're pretty smug about it too…You know for sure that the English are the best in the world. All your life you'll be like you were at school and stick to the rules, won't put a foot out of line, think the right thoughts, do the right deeds and be a jolly good sport – the best praise an Englishman can receive. And if you went to a good public school, then you know for absolutely certain that you are better than anyone who didn't. Then you're what most people think of as a traditional Englishman.

After a few more barrages, Pauline went on to a description of marital relations that was no less withering.

Your ideal woman is a kind of faithful, adoring slave, who administers to all your physical needs without a word of complaint and certainly no payment; who speaks only when spoken to and is, in fact, a jolly good chap. When you get fat, pig-like and unscrupulously selfish, she'll just carry on allowing you to wipe your dirty feet on her.

And then, the surprise ending.

But I must say that I do like Englishmen best. I don't know if that's just because I'm most used to them. I didn't really go for all that Latin Lover bit. Who wants to be locked away and jealously guarded? There's no freedom on that scene, and I

Opposite
Pauline and Clive were wed at Chelsea Register Office on 24 June – with Natalie Gibson and her then-husband Eric in attendance.

think Englishmen are the kindest to women in their own peculiar way. After sorting through several nationalities, I married an Englishman and a jolly good chap he is too.

Pauline:*. I got married under very extraordinary circumstances, very odd. I mean – I was very heavily involved with someone who was married anyway and really I was getting rather bored with the situation because it was sort of going round in circles ... and it just got to a peak when I thought 'Well this is just incredibly boring,' and I happened to meet Clive ...*

'We were walking down the street, and I saw Ken Tynan, who I knew, and his friend Clive Goodwin was with him,' Philip Saville told Sabine Durrant. 'I could see Clive was desperate to be introduced – his eyes were popping out of his head.' Clive rang up Saville the following day, to see if the director minded his taking Pauline out. Tied up with his pursuit of the then-new practice of Scientology, consumed by a complex BBC production of *Hamlet* – to be shot on location at Elsinore Castle in Denmark, with Christopher Plummer in the title role – Saville gave Clive the go-ahead.

Pauline: *I met Clive about the time when everything was getting sort of stewed up and I just got on terribly well with him, we got stoned all the time, and I only knew him ten days before and he was the very first man I met who really liked women, for one thing – a terribly rare thing in a man.*
Nell: *It's very rare for men to like women.*
Pauline: *Yes, I mean it's extraordinary ... I mean he was the first man I could really talk very freely to but I didn't like him at all at first. But he was the first man who made me laugh sort of quite sincerely over the telephone because I'm terrible about the telephone, I don't like the telephone at all.*

'Everyone wanted to date Pauline. Then she met Clive...The next thing we knew, they were married,' Christopher Logue recalls in *Prince Charming*. '"It was a shock," Roger Smith – now down from Oxford, a script editor at the BBC television – said: "No one knew where Clive came from. He had been an officer in the RAF. Then an actor. Then he worked for Tynan."'

In truth he wasn't an unknown quantity, especially to Smith, whom Clive got into the BBC. Rather, Clive Lionel Goodwin was in many ways entirely singular, a self-created original whose character was all the more surprising for its unpromising origins. 'It's extraordinary to think of Clive and where he came from,' says Sally Alexander. 'National Service helps explain him, I think.'

Like Pauline the youngest of four children (though preceded by sisters), the 'working-class lad from Willesden', in Tony Garnett's formulation, was born

Young man in a hurry: Clive in an undated photo.

in 1932, the son of an unsalaried waiter who supported his family, as was the practice in those days, entirely on tips. A lifelong man of the left, Clive took pride in his beginnings. Nonetheless, 'He hated Willesden, where he'd been brought up,' says the author and activist Sheila Rowbotham. 'He hated it – *hated* it there.'

Clive attended Gladstone Primary School and Kilburn Grammar School, but higher education was beyond the family's means. Instead, at 16, Clive got work as a clerical assistant. 'Bowing to parental authority, I became a civil servant when I left school,' he told an interviewer in 1964 – 'an obscure clerk in a department of the Board of Trade, because it was a good, steady, reliable job with a pension.' Immortal longings, however, beckoned. '[M]eanwhile I was busy acting as an amateur with several groups, and the only night of the week I was not with one drama group or another was Saturday. Eventually one of the groups got a bit above itself. Eight of us bought a lorry for £30 and with four or five drama students we toured South Wales. To do this I took my annual leave from the department and in the end never went back.'

Conscripted into the army, Clive saw, rather than a detour, an opportunity. Instead of the usual two-year National Service commitment, he chose a short-service commission, which added a year to his stretch. 'This was his substitute for university and the passport to the professional world for which he was evidently destined,' Adam Smith observes.

Sally Alexander was not alone in viewing the military as the man's making. 'The army polished the brass a bit – he had, in his voice and his manner, that sort of presence,' believes Tony Garnett. 'We were nearly all of us working class lads who'd gone to university, which was quite novel then. Clive didn't, but that didn't seem to affect his social confidence. Maybe, having become an officer in the British army, he could see through all of that shit.'

For two of his years, Second-Lieutenant Goodwin was stationed overseas, where his theatrical interests dovetailed with an entrepreneurial impulse that, in time, would prove definitive.

'Probably I'm the only man in television who has toured a pantomime in China,' reflects Clive Goodwin, the ex-grammar-school boy who currently conducts The Celebrity Game *on ITV.*

Recalling his production of Robinson Crusoe during his national service with the Middlesex Regiment in Hong Kong, Clive, who is Master of Celebrities of the Friday programme, adds: 'I also appeared in it as Man Friday and half wrote the show. We toured the service camps with it along a 25-mile stretch of the island.'

– TV Weekly, 24 July 1964

By 1952, when he began a three-year course at London's Central School of Speech and Drama, the 'working class lad from Willesden' had transformed into what his flatmate and fellow acting student Gordon Rogoff describes as 'a Noël Coward figure'. 'He was witty, he had charm, he was well-read,' Rogoff remembers. 'Very political, very angry about Suez and all of that. But really happy to be alive. He was one of those people who didn't have a melancholy streak that I could see. At the age of 21 or so, he seemed fully formed.'

Clive saw Central's acting programme less as vocational training, more as the portal to a different sort of life. 'Clive was there with an unspecified agenda,' says Rogoff. 'Ultimately it wasn't about becoming an actor – he never thought of school as a conduit to a theatre career as such. But he did think of it as a base for developing something.' Celia Mitchell, née Hewitt, also a Central acting classmate, observed the same. 'He was ambitious to do better, so he decided on acting,' she affirms. 'He just thought it was a way forward.'

'We found a place off the Kensington High Street – very cheap but big, vast rooms, so you had your privacy,' says Rogoff. 'Clive had the worst diet of anyone I've ever seen in my life. He ate bread that he put in oil, and not olive oil, it was more like crankcase oil – that was his idea of a meal. It was a function of his poverty, he'd been terribly poor. I used to say, "What are you eating this junk for?" It's what he was used to – "this is what we have at home". I never met his family. He was climbing out of that world, and he was embarrassed by it.'

Though the training students received, as recalled by Rogoff – 'voice, speech, movement, acting, and then we were rehearsing plays' – speaks of tradition, Clive's time at Central coincided with a transformative moment in British theatre. The Royal Court, eventual home of the English Stage Company, had reopened in 1952; Joan Littlewood's Theatre Workshop appeared in London the following year; Peter Hall directed *Waiting for Godot* at the Arts Theatre Club in 1955; and John Osborne's *Look Back in Anger* (an ESC production at the Royal Court) brought it all to a head in '56. To Clive and his confrères, the shock of the new, further amped by the arrival of new-wave American plays by Arthur Miller and Tennessee Williams, contrasted violently with the presiding character of the West End's theatrical mushy peas – described by Rogoff as 'drawing rooms, maids answering phones, and young blades dashing on stage for a moment to ask "Anyone for tennis?"' And just as he had seen a three-year army stretch as a stealth finishing school, Clive perceived, in England's performing-arts sea change, another chance at self-reinvention. 'The idea was, there wasn't a good theatre magazine, certainly not one engaged with wanting to change the nature of theatre,' Rogoff explains. 'So Clive said, "Let's go to the students' union and see if they'll give us some funds to create a magazine."'

Above
Encore, which Clive created as a student at Central School of Speech and Drama with his flatmate, Gordon Rogoff, lived up to its subtitle, 'The Voice of Vital Theatre'.

The outcome, which debuted in spring 1954, was an appropriately playbill-sized bimonthly called *Encore*, subtitled 'The Voice of Vital Theatre'. Conceived as a student publication, the magazine quickly became the most influential such journal of its time, encouraging theatre's new direction via contributions from a starry cast of figures, among them Lindsay Anderson, Eric Bentley, Harold Clurman, Ian Dallas, Stephen Joseph, Michael Redgrave (whose daughter Vanessa, a Central student, served as editorial assistant) and Sam Wanamaker. Buoyed by cash from sympathetic patrons, with a subscriber roll of roughly a thousand,

Encore firmly established itself with cognoscenti in both the nose-bleed seats and the stalls. Declared Kenneth Tynan, by then an important drama critic and culture figure: 'If anyone seriously interested in the theatre is not yet a reader, he should be.'

'It was an unwitting liberation from acting as a vocation,' wrote Rogoff in his memoirs. 'We were full of ourselves, thrilled to have something resembling a mission.' For Clive, who served as editor and entrepreneurial engine, a part of the mission was clear: the magazine provided entrée into a world he was ambitious to join – through it, he met Tynan, the most important and lasting of his early professional friendships. By the time of his departure from Central in 1955, Clive was more accomplished and connected, in a diversity of ways, than most of his fellow graduates.

'It's easy to focus on his ambition,' Rogoff observes. 'But to me the most important thing was that he was very good at what he did when he did it, and he was intent upon being very good at what he decided to do. I never found him in any hesitation mode. He was a very confident man.' 'He was one of those people who *did*,' affirms Sally Alexander. 'Left-wing newspaper? We'll start it. *Encore*? We'll start it. Left-wing writers need an agency? That's what we'll do. He was extraordinary like that.'

Sheila Rowbotham, who worked with Clive in the late 1960s at *The Black Dwarf*, the broadsheet he co-founded with Tariq Ali, observed the same qualities. 'He operated like a businessman,' she says. 'I didn't come from an intellectual background. My father sold pit motors for a firm as an independent agent – the world of going around and persuading people to buy things is recognizable to me. That was an aspect of Clive that I really respected – that he knew how to go out and sell things. And in his case things that were radical and creative.'

Clive continued editing *Encore* until 1958, and remained tangentially involved with his creation until, after 11 years, its run ended. Yet for nearly a half-decade after Central, and despite Rogoff's assertion that it was more vehicle than vocation, Clive worked as an actor, in the Guildford, Folkestone and Oxford repertory companies, but most profitably for Stephen Joseph's Studio Theatre, the company that pioneered 'theatre-in-the-round' in England. 'In 1955, [Joseph] began a summer season of performances in the concert room at Scarborough's Public Library – called the Library Theatre – and in the winter, began a series of performances on Sundays in London called the Studio Theatre Club,' the archivist and author Simon Murgatroyd relates. 'From 1956, Studio Theatre began seasons of winter tours, primarily visiting towns without civic theatres with the main intention of finding a permanent home for theatre-in-the-round.'

In those first scrappy years, Joseph, who'd been one of Clive's acting tutors and an *Encore* contributor, used his former students as a talent pool (though not exclusively: Alan Ayckbourne, who would become one of postwar England's most

prolific playwrights, was working a temp job at the library when Joseph took him on). Clive joined Studio Theatre in its third season, and its director put him in six plays, including *Look Back in Anger* as Jimmy Porter, the original Angry Young Man (the cast also included Celia Hewitt, who had helped with *Encore* and, a generation later, would informally adopt Pauline and Clive's orphaned daughter with her husband, Adrian Mitchell). Clive also directed three productions (notably the season-opening *Glass Menagerie*), in one of which, *Honey in the Stone*, he also played a supporting role.

Looking back with, not anger, but hindsight, theatre-in-the-round's subsequent value to Clive – the eventual literary agent for a stable of distinguished dramatists – seems evident.

Producer Clive Goodwin points out that with a small, intimate theatre the expense is cut enormously. There is no need for a scenic artist in the productions, which saves at least £150 on a ten-week run. In addition stage hands are not required.

The only 'props' brought to Scarborough by the company for 'The Glass Menagerie' were the glass animals, a gramophone, lighting and sound equipment, and one or two odds and ends. Chairs and tables have been borrowed locally.

– Scarborough Evening News, 5 July 1957

The obvious points – the value of economy to the survival of serious theatre,

Above
Clive (standing at right) in Catherine Prynne's **The Ornamental Hermit**, at the Library Theatre in Scarborough, 1957.

the creative invention mothered by financial necessity – are significant but secondary. More important, as must surely have been evident to Clive as he watched dramas unfold on a nearly bare stage, encircled by an audience, is the absolute indispensability of an airtight script. As a review of his production of *An Inspector Calls* made clear, however well-acted and imaginatively mounted, there was no hiding from inadequate writing.

> *The present play is … a false one for its strange coincidences are beyond the bounds of credibility and in a presentation such as this we are so close that this fault becomes more clearly obvious.*
> – *The Yorkshire Post*, 12 July 1957

Of perhaps equal import to Clive – given that his clients would write, in the main, for television – was discovering the special power of an intimate medium. Desmond Pratt, *The Post*'s drama critic, evoked it in the same review.

> *The play is acted out on an open central square of floor around which the audience sits embraced by the same atmosphere that haunts the stage … Nothing is allowed to interfere between [the actors] and the audience response to the problem before them. We hover like moths around a flickering fascinating pool of light which is in our midst and of which we are part.*

For Clive the agent, every word counted, especially if it was to be spoken on the 'flickering fascinating pool of light' that was a television set. Tariq Ali recalls that he could be exceedingly tough on dramatists if he felt a script was falling short; according to Margaret Matheson, who worked as one of Clive's assistants, her then-husband David Hare quit the agency when Clive informed him that a play he'd written didn't work and he should go home and try again.

A 1958 review of a Croydon production of *Look Back in Anger* is headlined 'Clive Goodwin is an Excellent Angry Young Man', and describes him as 'acting with a natural enthusiasm and lashing out his words with a measured but not furious anger.' Ultimately, however, Clive's self-assessment, despite Central's ministrations and the subsequent years of work, called to mind Somerset Maugham's view of himself as a writer: 'I am in the very front rank of the second-raters.' He quit acting. But the lessons of Scarborough stuck.

In 1959, Clive accepted a job offer from the producer Derek Granger at Granada Television as, according to his 1964 *TV Weekly* profile, 'assistant head of drama ("Or assistant to the head of drama – I was never quite clear which")'. The work also involved nosing out new writing talent, at which Clive excelled – another harbinger of what, after Pauline's death, would be a major career. He took up residence in a basement flat in Belgravia, started throwing parties and bought a Mini Cooper, one of the first. Profiled in the style magazine *Man About Town*, 'I daren't be perfectly dressed,' Clive declared. 'Other left-wingers would think I was insincere.'

If Clive's twenties present a record of wise moves, ones that served his personality, his abilities, his circle, and his scope of knowledge and experience, perhaps the most providential was his involvement with the arts programme *Tempo*, beginning in 1961. The show's originator was Tynan, who suggested it to ABC Weekend TV as a competitor to the BBC's *Monitor* (producer of *Pop Goes the Easel*). Tynan proposed himself as editor, and asked Clive to join him in developing ideas

Above Clive (**third from left**) on the set of **Tempo** with Kenneth Tynan (**far left**). The programme's first host, the Earl of Harewood, stands between them.

for episodes. *Tempo* debuted on 1 October in the somewhat unpromising 5 p.m. Sunday time slot; the initial ten shows were broadcast fortnightly, after which five 'specials' aired in March and April 1962 (even earlier on Sunday afternoons). The Earl of Harewood, a classical music administrator and author, served as the first season's on-camera host – after which the task became, in large measure, Clive's.

The show's distinctions were many, principal among them one of its animating ideas, which was to present, not what artists of every sort made – the finished product – but how they made it. Angus Wilson, who published a book about *Tempo* in 1964 (as it happened, several years after both Clive and Tynan had moved on), cited this as one of the programme's strengths: '*Tempo* is always at its best when exploring the processes of creation, finding out exactly how a new production of a play comes into being, how a ballet is imagined and set going, how a choir is brought into unity and so on.' If *Tempo* suffered from the pretentions of the genre, it nonetheless sharpened Clive's understanding of how to transform ideas into drama and to draw on his connections (a show about Peter Blake came out of Clive's friendship with him) – and, no less usefully, made him a familiar face on TV.

> *Then in April, 1962, he took himself off to Paris for a year.*
> *'At 17 I'd gone there for three weeks and promised myself that one day when I had enough money I'd go back for a year and learn to speak French. So that's what I did when I'd saved money from Tempo. I also wanted to write.'*
> – *TV Weekly,* 24 July 1964

The city improved Clive's culinary tastes and – according to Jean-Jacques Lebel, with whom he became fast friends – enlarged his experience of, and appetite for, the avant-garde. 'There was a place in Paris where a lot of English-speaking people, expats or whatever, would meet,' Lebel relates. 'The English Bookshop, at 42 Rue de Seine in Saint-Germain. There was a 16th-century vaulted beautiful old cellar, it held about 60 people, and we used to have poetry readings. I remember meeting Clive there. He was a very, very nice fellow, I liked him a lot and we hit it off. This was smack in the middle of the Vietnam War. We figured out that we were very close politically. That's how we became friends, by going to these anti-war demonstrations together, and talking about the importance of having an anti-imperialist outlook in life. That was more than enough to found a strong friendship on – sit around and smoke a joint and change the world.'

In fact, those who knew Clive agree that his affiliations were never formalized, he didn't subscribe to one or another theory or philosophy, and had no tolerance for fine-grained political discourse. 'He didn't understand, actually, political sectarian arguments at all,' Sheila Rowbotham recalls. 'He found it just irritating. He didn't know why people got so het up over them.' Rather, she located Clive's socialism in violent emotion. 'It was almost like he had muscles that came out against the con of power – he could see the manner in which the holding of power was actually a confidence trick. That sort of class hold over people, which would make working class people feel that they couldn't express themselves, that they would stumble with words. Yes, it was class resentment, but it wasn't just that he was angry like a trade union person. He could sort of see round the corner – he understood how it was operating. Clive was absolutely determined to cut that knot in some sort of way.'

Politics aside, Clive and Lebel also bonded over one another's love of a good time. In addition to his other activities, Lebel organized some of Europe's first Happenings, several of which Clive attended while in Paris. 'He liked being part of that effervescent underground scene,' Lebel recalls. 'It was a little beyond his taste in art. But he was open-minded. In those days, there were very, very few people who understood that Happenings were a new art form. They thought it was some kind of crazy joke, but it was much more, and Clive understood that.'

Clive returned to London in the spring of 1963, and as is inevitable when memory plays a part, everyone offers a different set of particulars. The essential fact, however, is beyond dispute: ten days after they met, Pauline and Clive were wed. Saville described the denouement in his autobiography:

> My affair with pop-artist Pauline Boty was becoming strained, as she wanted a commitment of marriage. The oncoming Hamlet at Elsinore production ate up my hours as I casted and prepared the rehearsal schedule, flying back and forth to Denmark. Returning home, I went to kiss Jane [Arden, his wife]. She slapped me hard around the face, and laid a telegram on the table. She left the room, shouting, 'Read it!'
> I remember strumming my fingers on the table before I picked up the wire.
> 'BY THE TIME YOU READ THIS I WILL BE MARRIED TO CLIVE. PLEASE FORGIVE ME. PAULINE.'

'I remember her ringing me up and saying, "What are you doing on Monday?"' Natalie Gibson says. 'And I said, "Oh, nothing, do you want me to feed the cats?" And she said, "No, I want you to be a witness at my wedding." That was a complete surprise.'

Gibson wasn't the only one. 'She came down with Clive – I know they sat on the settee – and she said, "We're getting married on Monday,"' Bridget remembers. 'She was terribly excited, I mean really excited. Really bubbly, she was. And she'd never been like that the whole time she came down. I must've looked a bit aghast. And I said – it was my first words – "Have you told your mum?" And she said, "Don't you *dare* tell my parents." That was *her* first words. So I said, "Okay. Sure. Your life." Nana would have loved a big wedding. She was one of those women who would have dreamt of it, if you know what I mean. Pauline didn't want any fussing.'

'We were all a bit surprised,' admits Sally Tuffin. 'But then we all married people that nobody expected us to marry. She said, "He's the one person I can throw saucepans at and he doesn't mind."' Adds Tony Garnett: 'When asked why she'd done it, she said, "Clive made me laugh."'

Pauline and Clive married at Chelsea Register Office on 24 June, a Monday. 'But for a paparazzo called Haighton who used to hang around the registry,' Adam Smith reports, 'there wouldn't even have been photographs of the occasion.

One of the shots made it into the *Evening News* the same day, which is the first many friends and family knew of the marriage.'

'About five o'clock, the phone rang: Nana,' Bridget remembers. '"*You knew, didn't you?*" There was a photo of her in the *Evening News*. "I'm sorry," I said. "I did. She asked me not to say." And I probably didn't see Nana for six months.'

As for Saville, 'I'm not sure that Philip quite got over that,' Tony Garnett says. '*He* would leave women, women wouldn't leave him. For her to keep hold of Philip, and for him to never quite get over the fact that she left him, tells you a lot about her. Tells you more about her than it does about Philip. And fair enough, it shows he had a heart, although he didn't show it too often.'

If Saville resented the fox he'd admitted to his henhouse, he was, seemingly, the only one. 'They were an incredibly glamorous couple,' Peter Blake remembers. 'I liked Clive very much. A nice man, a really nice man. Gentle, quiet.' 'My father was very enthusiastic about her – "Clive met this girl ten days ago, and now they're married,"' Tracy Tynan recalls. 'He thought that was sort of cool and dramatic. And very happy for Clive. Clive had been a family friend, and he was always incredibly nice to me. He was very generous, always helping people, doing things for people. An incredibly simpatico, charming guy, very down-to-earth.'

That simpatico quality equally impressed Michael Lindsay-Hogg. 'I met him at Rediffusion, the television company,' he recalls. 'I was 24 or 25, and because I was much younger, I wasn't accepted like an old drama hand would be. But Clive was very, very nice, very friendly, open, approachable, funny. The other thing about Clive was that he didn't discourage affection or intimacy. I don't mean sexual. At that period in England, people tended to be a bit stand-offish. Especially older people. But Clive right from the kind of get-go was affectionate and enthusiastic. That was a great, great quality of his.'

Above all, everyone agreed, Clive proved an ideal foil for his bride. 'Pauline found a kind, clever man who loved her,' observes Christopher Logue. '[A]nd rarer – one gratified to have a wife more famous than himself, pleased to advance her career as a painter.' 'She was more high-strung, I think might be the word,' Celia Birtwell recalls. 'You needed that balance of somebody who was calm and supportive and loving. He was a proper man. Know what I mean? He could take it, because he knew himself very well. So he wasn't sort of thrown by her kind of rather eccentric behaviour. He was rather proud of her.' Says Tracy Tynan: 'I kind of had the feeling he was like, "How did I get so lucky to get her?"'

This portrait of Clive as a backward boy who stumbled into paradise is, of course, incomplete. The author Caroline Seebohm met him prior to Pauline, as her marriage to Roger Smith was deteriorating, and found herself the object of Clive's energetic flirtations. 'Roger wouldn't have known this, obviously, but he was extremely attractive to women, they flocked around him,' she recalls. 'He just looked perfect. He was very lively. He seemed very sophisticated to me, his friendship with Ken Tynan was impressive. I was a bit scared of him, because he was very confident, and aggressive in wanting to be a success. He was clearly on the make, which put me off a bit. But I was fascinated by him.'

Like the others, Seebohm saw aspects of Clive's character that would prove definitive in winning Pauline's hand. 'I remember having discussions with him about sex, and he'd ask me, very seriously, about how you pleased a woman in bed,' she says. 'He had quite the wrong impression that I knew more about it than he did at the time. I may have given a few pointers, so to speak. But I loved the encounter, I was very flattered, and it was really nice, actually, because I'd stopped being a target for him, and had now become a, an *advisor*. And I was very touched. That took some doing – it took balls! That was "good" Clive – he was on the right path.'

'They were too excited when they came down the first time,' says Bridget. 'The second time, she said, "I want to take you to the woods, it's where I've had lots of thoughts, and it's made me feel better." And they both went up the wood. And it is, it's that kind of wood. I've done it too.'

To Bridget, with whom her sister-in-law had 'talked troubles', Pauline's transformation was astonishing. 'She was a different person,' Bridget says. 'When she did get a bloke that really cared for her, the change was tremendous. She was what Pauline would have been if she wasn't always having to strive for her living. She wasn't worried what she was going to do next week. They used to chat, laugh, absolutely they were living a life. Whereas she didn't live a life before then, I suppose that's what I'm trying to say. Whereas she nearly used to get to that state when she got on the train *away* from here, she used to *come* in that state when she arrived with Clive. The Pauline I knew at the end was a totally different person than the one I knew at the beginning. She and Clive were incredibly happy. And the painting took a tenth degree down that way.'

Bridget's aside regarding Pauline's painting, the implicit linking of marital contentment to a lessening of the need to create, bears consideration. Perhaps it reflects a more traditional view, of the value of women's work versus being looked after by a husband. But if Bridget did not always understand the particular character of her sister-in-law's calling, without question she respected it. And there is this: in 1963, Pauline completed roughly a dozen paintings; the following year, the number dropped to three. Observing her absorption into Clive's milieu, Peter Blake remarked, to Derek Boshier, 'We've lost our girl.' His words may have been redolent of a would-be lover's sorrow, but they proved prescient.

13

PERSONALITY

ON

TRIAL

1964

The friend of Ken's who seemed archetypical,' Kathleen Tynan records in her biography of her husband, 'who was everything he liked best and who opened more doors to my imagination than anyone else, was Pauline Boty who lived with Clive Goodwin (then editing *Encore* and working for television). She wore eight-foot feather boas and early miniskirts. She had studied at the Royal College of Art. She acted. Under the tutelage of Peter Blake she became one of the painters of the Pop movement. She came from a suburban background, and was classless. She married Clive, and was not possessive. She liked women, and was unguilty about sex.

'She enjoyed smoking marijuana, and said so. She was committed to her work without being particularly ambitious. She had no interest in housework. In the flat she shared with Clive, we met rock musicians, drug users, writers, directors and boutique owners – long before they had begun to mix with each other. I simply had never come across anyone like her, and she shook up my view of things.'

Tynan was not alone. Author Elisabeth Luard was working for the broadsheet *Private Eye*, overseen by her future husband Nicholas, who with the satirist Peter Cook co-owned the white-hot music and comedy club The Establishment. 'Pauline was one of the few women at that time who was a person in her own right,' she says. 'Most of us were just sort of, we were addendas. Pauline stood out because she was an independent person. I would hear a lot about her from Christopher. He loved her.'

'At Aldermaston, and then on television at the Anti-Uglies demonstration, I had caught glimpses of Pauline Boty,' Logue writes. 'Now, as she and her friend and fellow artist Derek Boshier were often at [The Establishment], I got to know her. She was astonishing. A big, bright girl with a confiding laugh. Snug headband holding a toque of silver-blonde hair. Hoop earrings, jangling when she turned her head, shoes she decorated on the run – searching her handbag, out with the gold spray, whssp-whssp-whssp, then on to the dance floor.'

'She had a certain exuberance, which was very, very attractive,' says Nell Dunn. 'A sort of energy, and a boldness. She was very interested in life, in the same way that I was. How do we live, what's right and what's wrong? How do we cope with our relationships? She was just very present in a room, and not embarrassed to say what was on her mind.'

So discovered Christopher Logue. 'I think us women should demand a lot more of our men than fertilization, protection and leadership,' Logue recalls Pauline telling him. 'I don't object to giving birth to a child or two, or using a dustpan or brush occasionally, provided I can produce paintings at the same time.

Opposite Mr and Mrs Clive Goodwin, at the Oasis Sports Centre, London, August 1963.

I want to be desired but not only for what women will always be desired for. Hard to explain. It seems very big-headed to say it, but some of the things I am trying to say have never, ever, been said. There are no worked-out words for the thoughts. See? Love women who stand up for themselves. Respect and protect those who cannot. Apart from that, there is little for you men to do.'

'She was an absolutely upfront, don't-give-me-any-shit feminist, she was early in that,' Garnett recalls. 'But she wasn't grumpy. Her anger about it made her more attractive, rather than put you off. I don't know quite how she managed that. But she was very serious about it. I mean, because she was so gorgeous, and full of life, and men were in love with her – the way women are diminished is by people thinking they're not serious. And she was. I always thought she was serious.'

One wonders how many others thought the same.

After a few cramped months in Pauline's bedsit, she and Clive moved a short walk's away to 7a Addison Avenue, a Victorian terraced house owned by Roger Mayne and his wife, Ann Jellicoe. A veterinarian's office occupied the ground floor, and Pauline and Clive had the two above; the flat wasn't big, but better than Pauline's bachelorette digs, and offered the likemindedly social pair – 'they were like peas in a pod, really', says Natalie Gibson – sufficient space to entertain.

'On Sunday afternoons, a number of us, Michael and Sarah White, Roger Smith, Derek Boshier and his girlfriend Jo Cruikshank ... gathered at Clive and Pauline's flat,' Logue records. 'It was a tonic to see them together. Pauline in a pinky-blue, six-foot fake-feather boa and white, knee-high boots handing round fudge, pouring out tea. Clive, anxious that she did not take on too much.'

As Pauline left 80 Addison Road behind, so too did she grow distant from her artist friends, integrating herself into Clive's crowd, which included Tynan and his soon-to-be wife Kathleen Halton; the writer John McGrath and his wife, actress Elizabeth MacLennan; poet Adrian Mitchell and *his* wife Celia; and Tony Garnett. 'His world opened up her world; her world changed from visual artists to writers,' says Boshier. 'When she and Clive moved into that Holland Park place, I was one of the only visual artists who hung out, I think because the others weren't political – her crowd became a political crowd, and I was an activist.'

Though Gibson and Birtwell stayed in touch, and different circles overlapped – Nicola Wood, back from three years in New York, spent time with Logue and Boshier, as well as Jane Percival – it wasn't the same. 'Clive had a whole different set of friends, and that made a big difference because she was in a different milieu,' says Wood. According to Boshier, Pauline preferred the new people: 'We both acknowledged that we were lucky that we had been introduced to a new set of friends who were all writers.'

If, as Roger Smith believes, 'Clive turned her on to left-wing politics, which was where we mostly were,' Pauline teed up what would prove to be her husband's great talent. According to Logue, 'Clive had found his inspiration. "On our first evening out," he told me, "Pauline said: 'You are wasted in television – you should be an agent. For playwrights. Playwriting is all you have mentioned for two whole hours.'"' Which is what he did.'

In 2019, Roger Smith recalled that it was he and the television and film writer Troy Kennedy Martin who suggested agenting to Clive, believing that his broad network of connections, timely politics, cultivated tastes, and the supportive enthusiasm that so impressed Michael Lindsay-Hogg rendered him well suited to the profession (ultimately Clive represented both men). Yet Adam Smith's interview with Kennedy Martin, conducted in the 1990s, supports Pauline: 'Troy remembers it was Pauline who made the first approach. He took a calculated gamble signing to Clive knowing he would be a feather in Clive's cap, and would always be his first client. Troy adds this was soon after the couple returned from their honeymoon, exuding repentance at their own haste.'

Meanwhile, as Pauline embedded herself in a new life and Clive formulated his future, contemporary art departed the margins for the centre of London's cultural cavalcade, buoyed by an infusion of government support and a surge in private and institutional interest. 'By 1963 there was a new confidence in young British artists and their ability to stand comparison on the international stage,' Lisa Tickner reports in *London's New Scene*. '[Anthony] Caro, Kitaj, [Bridget] Riley, Bernard Cohen, Hockney and Richard Smith all had solo shows in 1963, Allen Jones won the Prix des Jeunes Artistes at the Paris Biennale and Alan Davie the award for Best Foreign Painter at the São Paulo Biennale. Together with a marked increase in media attention, this contributed to a newly buoyant climate for the reception of British art ... By the mid-1960s the Tate Gallery, the Gulbenkian and Peter Stuyvesant Foundations were supporting and collecting British artists, high-profile exhibitions attracted widespread publicity and contemporary art had become both an established facet of "swinging London" and a serious commercial proposition.'

The boom was not entirely Anglocentric. In October 1963, *The Popular Image*, the first major presentation of American Pop Art in Britain, opened at the ICA; this was followed, in the spring of '64, by *Painting & Sculpture of a Decade: '54–'64,* an epic exhibition at the Tate, which showcased 366 works by 170 artists, drawn from the US, UK (a total of 50), and the Continent.

But the British emphasis – on the new and the young in particular – was notable. In 1963, the Contemporary Art Society mounted the two-part *British Painting in the Sixties* (a mere three years into the decade) at the Tate and Whitechapel Galleries. And there were counter-cultural activities: Michael White brought over an abridged production of Jean-Jacques Lebel's *Festival of Free Expression*, the highlight of which was Carolee Schneemann's semi-naked, offal-covered free-for-all *Meat Joy*.

'Michael asked me to pick about 20 of the participants, and we all took the train, and he rented out a place called Denison Hall, a workers' union hall,' Lebel remembers. 'The evening was called *Collage* – we took excerpts of most of the performers and wove them into a narrative, so it was very crazy and we had a lot of fun doing it, and the audience enjoyed it a lot. It was supposed to be two nights, and it was a terrible scandal. The guy who was the caretaker of the hall called the police, and in the middle of the thing the police started arresting us! The next day there was a big denunciation in the right-wing press, the usual insults, and the second evening was cancelled.'

Of special significance for Pauline's cohort was *New Generation: 1964* at the Whitechapel. The exhibition was to be the first of five (the concept ran out of gas before the finish line), and included only a dozen artists: Boshier, Patrick Caulfield, Anthony Donaldson, Hockney, John Hoyland, Paul Huxley, Jones, Phillips, Patrick Procktor, Riley, Michael Vaughan, and Brett Whiteley. 'All except Riley were under thirty,' notes Tickner. 'All except Whiteley, an Australian, had trained at the Royal College, the Royal Academy Schools or the Slade.' Twenty-two thousand people attended.

Equally if not more influential were London's of-the-moment galleries, in particular those operated by the friendly rivals Robert Fraser, nicknamed 'Groovy Bob' by the writer Terry Southern, who opened an eponymous gallery in 1962, and John Kasmin, following a year later. 'Kasmin loved abstract painting (especially colour field painting) and Caro's sculpture,' Tickner relates. 'Among the British, he showed Bernard Cohen, Richard Smith, [Robyn] Denny, [Gillian] Ayres, Caro, William Tucker and Howard Hodgkin. Hockney was his figurative "odd man out". Fraser was associated chiefly with British and American Pop (or Pop-related) artists including Richard Lindner, Eduardo Paolozzi, Patrick Caulfield, Derek Boshier, Jim Dine, Peter Blake, Jann Haworth, Richard Hamilton and Claes Oldenburg ... Bridget Riley and Harold Cohen were the odd ones out in this company (as abstract painters), along with Jean Dubuffet.'

According to Tickner, the crowds the dealers drew were somewhat different but equally starry. 'Marlon Brando, Dennis Hopper, the Beatles and the Rolling Stones appeared at Fraser's openings; Jimi Hendrix (who lived round the corner in Brook Street), Bruce Chatwin and Antonioni at Kasmin's ... [Said Kasmin:] "We both had rather a lot of marijuana being smoked at the galleries and openings, and we both played soul and rock music. That was as near as the competition went."'

All of this was well suited to Pauline's predilections. But despite her flamboyant side, Lebel recalls, her personality was a poor fit with the moment's more outré shenanigans. 'To tell you the truth, she was extremely shy and quiet,' he says. 'I didn't have the impression that she would have done something like take her clothes off, and that's what the Happenings were about. Very outspoken politics and very outspoken sexuality. She had fun watching when she was there, but I don't think she would have been active. She was very reserved.'

Pauline did not have gallery representation – Terry Riggs, who made Pauline the subject of her 1996 master's thesis at the Courtauld Institute, notes that Grabowski handled the artist's work informally; *The Public Ear* aired its last episode on 22 March ('with George Harrison and Ringo Starr reading the credits', Smith reports, 'Harrison tripping up with "Pauline Botty ... Botty? ... Boty, sorry about that Pauline"'). Yet she stayed busy: Pauline worked twice as an actress in 1964, on productions that, for different reasons, remain of interest. *The Frantick Rebel*, a comedy set during the American Revolution, in which Samuel Johnson and James Boswell attempt (and fail) to prevent a Colonial spy from slipping a message to Benjamin Franklin, was one of three episodes of the television series *Espionage* directed by Michael Powell, creator of the classic films *The Red Shoes* and *Peeping Tom*. The other, *The Day of Ragnarok* – described by its writer/producer/director, John McGrath, as '*Lysistrata* for the Cuba missile crisis age' – was an instalment of *Six*, a half-dozen original productions created for the then-new BBC2 channel, and the first programmes made for British television to be photographed entirely on film. In the latter, in which Pauline effectively played herself, certain of her scenes were shot at Addison Avenue, in her cramped work area (the brass bed is wedged in as well) and – in addition to offering glimpses of *5-4-3-2-1*, *The Only Blonde in the World*, *July 26th*, and *It's a Man's World I* – show the painter 'at work' on the still-gestating *It's a Man's World II*.

So Pauline was painting, but she had less to show for her efforts. Surely this had somewhat to do with her changed circumstances, a necessary creative retrenching. But one suspects that there were other reasons, connected to the way Pauline was perceived and, consequently, how she perceived herself. Says Boshier, 'The art world couldn't decide whether she was an artist or an actor. All the articles that appeared in all the tabloids and the newspapers were about her as a pin-up – you know, the Brigitte Bardot of Wimbledon. They were all about her experiences in theatre rather than in the art world.' For Ray Bradley, Pauline's gender was a factor: 'I think people tended to dismiss her as a painter. Derek Boshier, David Hockney, Peter Blake were all men and serious, and she was just a pretty bird.' Boshier only partly concurs. 'What happened to Pauline, in terms of not having the recognition she deserved, also happened to male students,' he says. 'I agree with Pauline being left out partly because of being a woman. But it was also a common thing.'

The thing is, she *wasn't* being left out – 'She wasn't some little unknown lady struggling to make herself heard,' says Roger Smith. Quite apart from 1963's group and solo exhibitions, Pauline's TV, stage and radio work, the attentions of photographers, and her regular appearances in the press (for better and for worse) had surely given her a higher public profile than that of most artists, women especially. The problem was that, despite it all, Pauline's artworks were not finding a broad, dependable audience.

There are as many reasons why an artist doesn't sell as there are artists. But for an answer of sorts, let us move forward in time to 1998, thirty-two years after Pauline's death. In London, the Mayor Gallery and Whitford Fine Art presented a joint exhibition of her paintings and collages, the first time the bulk of the artist's work had been offered for sale and, in fact, her first solo show since the one at Grabowski. 'It was the wildest opening we'd ever had,' says Adrian Mibus, Whitford's director. 'The place was packed! People were out in the street. Everybody remembered her. Everybody wanted to be associated with her in some way. The fact that she was a model, a film star and an artist. Married to the right sort of fellow, in the right circles. And a great beauty – she had charm. All that. It just set her up.

'The Tate contacted us and said, "We'll let you know before the show starts. But we want to reserve four." Three months after the show I still had not sold a painting. And then the Tate finally said, "Okay, we want this one – *The Only Blonde in the World.* Not the other three." [The paintings] slowly trickled out. One here, one there. £15,000, prices like that. In the end, it took us over ten years to sell them all.

'It was her, you see,' Mibus believes. 'Not so much the art. The person, the persona behind it. She just had that natural sort of draw, and people just loved her. She was a legend before anybody knew anything about her work.' Not only did 'the legend' influence the crowd's view of Pauline – it had transformed the painter's entire *raison d'être* into an afterthought, made it virtually superfluous: you didn't need to look at, much less own, a Boty to participate in Botymania.

Returning to the 1960s, we confront, once again, the conundrum, one of the leitmotifs of Pauline's life: the difference between what she put into the world, and what the world chose to make of it. Pauline, as has been noted, embraced self-contradiction, was insistent upon being taken on her own terms, remained ruthlessly independent. She saw no reason why she couldn't paint pictures, appear on stage and screen, deliver provocative jeremiads on the radio, no reason why she couldn't celebrate her beauty, exuberance and sexuality, participate fully in the culture of her times, and be taken seriously as a painter.

But if she cultivated the character of 'Pauline Boty' to find her voice as an artist and her footing as a woman – to create a character that helped her to *build* character, as it were – the word meant something different to those on the receiving end, a world that saw 'a character' as someone whose antics made her seem less serious and more frivolous – Richard Hollis's flibbertigibbet, not the teenager who told Jennifer Carey that she wanted to transform the notion of what a woman could be. Pauline, to use a phrase that would come to stand for second-wave feminism's great expectations, wanted to have it all. But because she was ahead of her time and, indeed, ahead of the culture – because the person she was, in effect, hadn't been invented yet, and was, in Logue's recollection, saying what had yet to be said – to the world beyond her adoring circle of friends, Pauline wasn't serious about having anything.

Derek Boshier's point – that male artists were also overlooked – is a fair one. But it is hard to separate Pauline's lack of commercial success from the way that he and Ray Bradley describe her reception. As has been said by all who schooled with her, Pauline wasn't like other female art students – she was, to use Brian Newman's word, Technicolor. And if she wasn't like other female art students, Pauline most certainly didn't fit the cliché of the female artist evoked by her contemporaries, i.e. a dour, sexless wren who never told or got a joke or left her wretched studio. *Real* female artists didn't wear feather boas or spray gold paint on their shoes before Twisting at The Establishment. Pauline did, and it hurt her credibility.

Perhaps – perhaps – Pauline was not as single-mindedly committed to painting as posterity might have us believe. Unquestionably her work was evolving, rapidly. But devotion or quality were not at issue. Rather, absent the mantle of 'importance' that a Kasmin or Fraser might have bestowed, Pauline came across as a too-thinly-spread bird-about-town – famous, from a collector's standpoint, for the wrong reasons. 'In 1966 Edward Lucie-Smith, quoting an anonymous dealer, wrote in *The Times* that "the public loves artistic virgins",' Tickner writes. 'The young artist must in consequence "spread his tail, do his little dance, utter a shrill cry. Will we look, or won't we? The issue remains in doubt. But we all know well enough that it is a personality which is on trial, not a collection of works of art".'

After Clive's death in 1977, those of Pauline's paintings that had been in his possession were transferred to her parents' retirement cottage in Caterham, where they were stored in the attic, and eventually moved to an outbuilding on Arthur and Bridget's farm. When Boty Goodwin went to look at them in 1992, she found much of what had been offered for sale by Grabowski, *My Colouring Book* being a notable exception. Adam Smith reports that Saville purchased *With Love to Jean-Paul Belmondo* and *The Only Blonde in the World* but never took possession, perhaps a *beau geste* his wife would not have appreciated. But if Clive still had them, the reason was plain: the pictures hadn't sold.

'It was *her* they wanted,' Bridget says. As it was in 1998, so it was in Pauline's lifetime: the draw was not Boty, but Botymania.

It is hard to gauge the extent to which Pauline perceived a link between her public image and limited sales, the extent to which seeing her friends and recent classmates take off affected her. Nicola Wood's assertion that she 'never saw an unconfident Pauline', supported by so many, comes back to us. But we can surmise that the professional consequences of being personally misunderstood were unwelcome. And undermining: when an artist isn't catching fire, the responses tend towards the defiant 'They don't get it,' but also the uncertain 'Is it me?'

The sense of being complicit in one's own lack of success leads one to question, not only one's talent, but one's choices, and conceivably this was the case, as well, with Pauline's marriage. As with so many corners of her life, it can be considered from opposing perspectives. On the one hand, Clive represented an exceptional stroke of luck: a man who truly appreciated women and took an unmixed pleasure in playing the discreet partner to Pauline's Pop prima ballerina (plus his liberated tolerance: many of Pauline's risqué photographs were taken in the months following the marriage). At the same time, Clive was the very opposite of a Caspar Milquetoast: self-invented in his own right, attractive, energetic, ambitious, well-connected, politically aware, in every way a winner. Their sudden wedding, moreover, was piquant and unconventional; instantly, Pauline and Clive were a golden couple, a Swinging Sixties paradigm for what a 'new' marriage could be.

And yet. Pre-Clive, Pauline was hardly a shrinking violet. But her ability to be the luminous, indeed iconic, figure witnessed by Dunn, Logue and Garnett owed not a little to her husband. Penny Massot, who was among Pauline's on-the-town partners in crime, ascribed this in part to the most timeworn of reasons: security. 'Clive was a straight kind of guy, really solid,' Massot says. 'Pauline wasn't really selling paintings too much in those days. So it was like she was with a grown-up, and being looked after. He would allow her to paint – she didn't have to go out and hustle, have to bother about paying the rent or anything like that.'

Clive, inconsistently employed in television, was far from rich, and Pauline certainly didn't want a sugar daddy. But money in that moment played a role: it enabled the social and cultural participation that defined the zeitgeist, in a way that was particular to the era. 'For the first time in London's history a fair share of that money was in young hands,' Logue observes. 'Colin MacInnes had noted in 1958 that 2 million 15- to 23-year-olds each had £3 spending money per week, £312 million a year. The new mood was friendly, self-centred, improvisatory, carefree, frivolous ... ' The poet recalls a visit to the 'style store' Biba, noting its social implications. '"You must come and see it, you simply *must*," Pauline said, and Michael [White], Clive, Roger [Smith] and I went with her. And, yes, the place was full of lively young women listening – music in *shops*? – to the hits their money had made, buying democratized fashion, while as often as not the staff wore CND [Committee for Nuclear Disarmament] badges – *badges* on the staff? – pinned to designer clothes now accessible to the low-paid.'

This was not the glittering, cruel capitalism that arrived, a generation later, with Margaret Thatcher (and Ronald Reagan) but rather the braiding of a few extra quid in the kick with good causes, social change and pop chic. Not a big sum, but often beyond Pauline's reach, as became clear to Nell Dunn when she interviewed the struggling artist for *Talking to Women*. 'She was very fragile,' Dunn says. 'The fragility I saw was, how was she going to earn her living? I remember her being terribly worried about money and paying her rent. That was a huge thing. I think she asked me to take some of the things about money out. This was part of English life. You didn't really talk about money worries. It wasn't a subject you shared much. I don't think it still is.'

Pauline's sister-in-law connects the cultivation of her persona to the anxieties of which Bridget was well aware: 'I think she *became* Pauline because she was broke. She acted and modelled because the paintings weren't making the money. I think it probably became hard work to paint, because she honestly didn't think she was getting anywhere at times. And perhaps that's why she was so happy when Clive came along, and she could be the person she wanted to be. A girl. A mother. Look what she gave up for motherhood.'

Surely Pauline, like the sillies she scorned at Wimbledon, wasn't killing time at the easel until a husband materialized. Yet Bridget's blunt manner masks an acute sensitivity to character. Nor was the view uniquely hers: though perhaps not the most reliable witness, Saville in his memoir recalls Pauline pushing for a marriage commitment. Lebel goes further. 'In the subconscious of many people, including today, art is not for women,' he observes. 'And I think Pauline was a victim of that ideology. I felt she wanted to be normal. She wanted to have a husband, she wanted to have a house, she wanted to have kids. You know? Painting came afterwards, not instead of. I had that impression, definitely.' It does not fit the narrative of Pauline as uncompromising feminist. Yet for all of its positives – and they were absolutely genuine – the Boty/Goodwin union could be seen as a modern bourgeois contract: the chance for Pauline to have the support enjoyed by Veronica absent the restrictions imposed by Albert.

Possibly Pauline, handing round the fudge and pouring tea even as she rued her haste to Troy Kennedy Martin, came to see it that way herself. For Clive, for all his irrefutable positives, was generationally a man on a cusp. 'In the early days of Women's Lib, he was really a supporter,' recalls Lynn Horsford, for a time a Goodwin Associates assistant and his on-and-off girlfriend in the 1970s. 'Genuinely he liked women, he wanted women to do well. But he was misogynistic in other ways, the way men were at the time.' In her memoir *Promise of a Dream*, Sheila Rowbotham suggests what Horsford might have meant: 'Within a few days of knowing Clive I was conscious of being handled. Despite his charm, he was far more overtly autocratic than was customary in the left I knew ... Democracy never entered Clive's head where women were concerned; he simply assumed it was the men's job to talk politics.'

'He was quite sort of bossy with me and Sally [Alexander],' Rowbotham recalls of the time the two friends worked at *The Black Dwarf*, allowing that 'neither of us really totally resented it, because it was always for a good purpose that he was bossy. He wanted to get something done efficiently, and I wasn't used to having to do things efficiently'. Yet the low smoke of gender imbalance never entirely dissipated. 'He would accept you to the extent to which you behaved as a man,' Rowbotham explains. 'He didn't expect you to get sort of emotional or anything. He thought you ought to be like a bloke. Or like the front a bloke could put on.'

Among those interviewed for this book, Sally Alexander comes closest to illuminating the divide in Clive's view of women. The two shared a special intimacy. They met at a dinner, and upon hearing her story, Clive quickly encouraged Alexander, the mother of an infant daughter, to meet his pregnant, ailing wife – believing that Pauline would appreciate the friendship and gain a sense of optimism regarding motherhood and, indeed, life. Alexander recognized that this was both a loving and an astute thing for a man to do, and the two single parents (she divorced the actor John Thaw in 1968) remained close after Pauline's death, helping one another out with their nearly same-age daughters, who themselves remained friends into adulthood.

For Clive, Alexander stands as an unmatched character witness – with a caveat. 'He was surrounded by women who were very capable, very good at what they did, and he respected and loved us all,' she relates. 'He really, really liked women. And you felt that. A lot of these guys, they might fancy you, but whether they *liked* you, I don't know that that was true. Clive knew that women had to emerge, and he wanted to hear what you had to say. And yet it was a man's world, very much a man's world, in his front room – building *Black Dwarf*, and running the agency.

'I remember when I told Clive that I wanted to go to university. He said, "Oh, Sally. You don't need to go to university. *Why?*" "Because I don't know anything, Clive." "You *do!* You just don't think you do, darling. You're just one of those people who thinks everyone knows more than you do, darling. If you want to go to university, go to university. You don't need to."'

It is hard to imagine Clive speaking this way to, for example, Tariq Ali. In even the most enlightened marriage, this mentality would have been hard to entirely expunge.

An exchange with Nell Dunn points to another issue.

Nell: *And do you feel more secure now you're married?*

Pauline: *Well, Clive has made me feel much more secure in the way that now I don't mind telling more people about what I think. Because he's given me confidence in the fact that, well, perhaps people are interested in the things I want to say, you know.*

Nell: *Does passion mean anything to you?*

Pauline: *Well passion always sounds to me like something without any humour in it at all, and I always find humour terribly interesting, and very much a part of life.*

Her response is a bit of a dodge. Roger Smith offers his interpretation. 'I don't think she was that excited, let's put it that way,' he says. 'She decided to marry him so quickly, she only knew him for ten days before they got married. We were good friends, and she'd come round to my place a lot, and everything like that. But I think she wanted rather more than I was prepared to give – more than a kiss and a cuddle. I would have liked to have done it. But it was really being a bit disloyal to Clive, and I'd known Clive for quite a long time.'

In separate conversations in 2018 and 2019, Smith first admitted to, then denied, a fling with Pauline, raising his guilt about Clive on both occasions. Either way, the takeaway is Smith's sense that Pauline wanted not just fleeting erotic gratification but a different kind of life. It will come as no surprise, given her undisguised appetites and the tenor of the times, that the married Pauline had lovers (Saville among them, Pauline 'making a secret trip to his Ibiza retreat', according to her first biographer). But Smith's recollections, however contradictory, suggest that Pauline was more deeply dissatisfied: that for all the positives adorning Clive, she'd acted too hastily and – if to escape Saville, to embrace stability – for reasons of which she might not have been terribly proud.

Whatever the case, as 1964 progressed, the previous year's creative torrent slowed, and Pauline produced notably less work. Kathleen Tynan's observation that she wasn't 'particularly ambitious' may have been meant as a compliment – i.e. that ambition for its own sake was, given the times, uncool – but it is more likely that Pauline's diminished output owed itself, at least in part, to depression. In *Talking to Women*, Pauline speaks at length about the malady, which she dates from the onset of her mother's tuberculosis, when Pauline was 11. The conversation with Nell Dunn suggests episodes of increasing severity.

Pauline: *I've been going through a terrible period of depression and when you get very depressed everything goes along somewhere down there, on a sort of horrible level …*

Nell: *Do things happen to you or do you make them happen?*

Pauline: *I'd like to think that I made them happen to me, but I think it's both* *you know ... Clive's always telling me I must stop being like an orphan tossed in the storm. And I do get moments like that when I feel completely dominated with emotional feelings that I just can't control especially with depressions, which is a very worrying thing.*

Nell: *It's an enormous thing. What is one to do about it?*

Pauline: *I find it one of the most difficult things to control, or to find out ways of stopping. I think that one must do and I must start a plan, I think, and I'll have to because I can get so depressed that it's ridiculous. I've stayed down there far too long and it's got worse as I've got older instead of better.*

Nell: *I think it does.*

Pauline: *And I think one must fight – instead of sitting there with your depression or lying there crying with your depression, is to really force yourself – and this goes against it – to say get up and do something, even if it's washing up or sweeping the carpet or something like that ...*

Nell: *When I was young I got depressed but for a very definite reason, whereas now I wake up depressed for no reason at all sometimes.*

Pauline: *Well I think you see there probably is a reason which one doesn't really admit to oneself because it's too big a reason somehow.*

Depression lives by its own laws. But it is difficult to believe that – off her game, acting intermittently, unable to establish a sustainable footing in the art world – Pauline's decline in creativity owed nothing to a malaise motivated by 'a reason which one doesn't really admit to because it's too big a reason'.

'I think that, at the age of 25, 26, a woman intellectual, living in the misogynistic soup, suddenly realizes what she's up against,' Caroline Coon suggests. 'When you're very young, you look out into the world and you feel the same as everybody else. I feel like being a painter, I feel like being an astronaut. Why can't I? And you suddenly begin to be conscious of, it's not *my* thought that I'm not allowed to do this, hold on a second, there's a structure here, a culture, which is telling me no.'

'This is obviously an issue that many women feel,' observes Leslie Dick, who was Boty Goodwin's principal tutor at the California Institute of the Arts. 'Am I allowed to be an artist? Am I allowed to express myself? It's not going too far to say that the dominant culture, such as it is, is constantly telling women to shut the fuck up. You're a silly young girl with blonde hair, be quiet. We don't want to hear any more from you. And you're always complaining! And for a woman to step outside of that injunction – to please just be beautiful and be quiet, *please?* – is to move into a space where you ask yourself, "Is what I have to say or what I have to offer worthwhile?"'

Roger Smith believes that Pauline's identification with Marilyn Monroe was not their shared beauty, talent and glamour, but rather the star's frustration at not being understood. 'I think Pauline just always wanted more, really,' Smith says. 'I think she somehow expected more out of life than she was getting.'

In September, Pauline gave *Epitaph to Something's Gotta Give* to her friend Penny's husband, the filmmaker Joe Massot, by way of apology for having withdrawn, at the last moment, from a commercial Massot planned to direct. 'I'm sorry to have let you down, after all this time you spent pushing me,' she wrote to him. 'You see, these last fourteen months I feel I've got too far away from my painting, and I seem to be getting more and more miserable. I have to find out if not-painting is the cause of my depressions.'

It was a good instinct. Pauline was an artist. Painting was, as Bridget put it with simple eloquence, the thing she had left home to do, and any home without it would be compromised. Yet if 1964 saw the finish of only three new canvases (actually two and a half, as *Man's World II* was concluded the following year), two were among her very best. Pauline's life to date had been instructive. However slowed her output may have been by circumstances within and without, those life lessons saturated her work.

Countdown to Violence might have been the outcome of Clive's encouragement of a left-wing agenda in Pauline's pictures, though whether or not she needed a push is questionable. Either way, the painting is a *cri de coeur* against political, racial and imperialist violence within, or sanctioned by, the US, and takes as its focus three representative incidents from 1963. In the upper half, beneath the starkly rendered legend 3-2-1-ZERO, portraits of the murdered presidents Lincoln and Kennedy hang above the latter's flag-draped coffin, resting atop his funeral caisson. Below, at left, a rendering of Malcolm Browne's *Associated Press* photo of Thich Quang Duc, the monk who set himself ablaze on a Saigon street in May 1963, in protest against the persecution of Buddhists by the American-backed South Vietnam government. Pauline's interpretation exaggerates the flames, in vivid orange, spewing from Thich's gasoline-soaked body, they flail across the canvas towards the black-and-white image at right: based on a press photo of the Birmingham, Alabama, riots of May, in which civil-rights demonstrators were attacked by police using clubs, dogs and fire hoses.

Countdown is awkwardly organized and in places clumsily executed (the presidential portraits are notably unpersuasive), which suggests that Pauline's principal concern was making a point. In fact, the picture's true interest derives from its subtext, expressed in three references to the artist's earlier work. There is of course the countdown, which appeared in 1963's *5-4-3-2-1*: then it was a fairground-style banner advertising the moments leading up to orgasm; here it is a fatal descent to ZERO, indicative of the depicted horrors. To the left of the

funeral caisson, partially obscured as though muscled into the background, is a multicoloured abstraction excerpted from one of Pauline's Hollywood musical-inspired pictures of a few years previous. And Pauline sampled the big hand holding secateurs, which appeared in one of her most effective collages, the comic-horrific Victorian nightmare in which the clippers airlift two girls over a lush botanical garden. In *Countdown*, the down-pointing hand is laid over the flames, the blades snipping the stem of a red rose.

Pauline's point is unmissable. The countdown, previously to an erotic climax, is now to death; the colourful abstractions, inspired by joyful music and dance, are obscured by a coffin-bearing wagon; and the big hand is amputating Pauline's symbolic sexual organ. The artist has drawn on her own iconography to express not only anti-American political outrage, but an intimate anger at a culture that destroys pleasure, hers especially.

Pauline's other two 1964 paintings – *It's a Man's World I* and *II*, the former begun late the previous year, the latter finished in early '65 – are arguably her most fully realized, deeply personal and lucid. Neither is enigmatic, true of much of her mature painting: unlike the collages, pungent stews of ambiguity, Pauline's canvases are as straightforward as the woman herself. But both come at the idea of a man's world – a subject ever more on the artist's mind – from different directions, and both turn that world on its head.

Most of *I*'s four-by-five-foot, mixed media surface celebrates what Minioudaki calls 'male geniuses of high and popular culture', in three rows evocative of Pauline's collage wall. At the top, the artist offers a traditional treatment of an enormous country house – identified by Christopher Skelton-Davies as the Palazzina di caccia of Stupinigi in northern Italy – stretching nearly the full width of the canvas and set in a formal landscape decorated with stands of cypress. Laid over the centre of this composition are a portrait of Muhammad Ali wearing an 'I'm the Greatest' badge, head tilted back and eyes closed, somnolent and regal; and a photo of a sculpted classical Greek head, captioned 'Beginning a new series – The Creative Adventure,' which served as a cover of *Life* magazine in July 1962. The pleasures of this composition, at once academic and Pop, derive in no small measure from its unexpectedness: architecture, antiquity ... and Ali? But of course – who more completely embodies the ethos of timeless masculine authority than The Greatest?

Having set the tone, Pauline next offers, below, two rows highlighting the best of the male species à la Boty. In the first, Elvis in his sultry heartthrob days, painted from a studio portrait; a detail from what appears to be one of Irving Penn's iconic 1957 Picasso photos; a Native American chief with an extravagant feathered headdress, inexplicable unless it's a playful if naïve comment on the trope of the male peacock; and in a famous pose, the literary Elvis, Proust. In the next row, a matador (presumably the legendary El Cordobés), as resplendent in his colourful costume as the chief; an interregnum in the form of a red rose, Pauline's sexual signature, which seems to gaze at us with a distinctly clitoral eye; then two examples of male artistic camaraderie: Fellini and Mastroianni, the great collaborators of European cinema; and Ringo and John in a collaged photo, the two Beatles holding flowers of their own.

And then Pauline palls our pleasure. Into the wild blue yonder above the landscape, an American B-52 with an X-15 manned rocket-plane under its wing (taken from a NASA photo published in a 1962 *Sunday Times* supplement) zooms in from the left, with a portrait of the helmeted pilot in the upper right, a hero with the wrong sort of right stuff. And at the picture's very bottom, between images of Vladimir Lenin and Albert Einstein, Pauline has painted, in an impressionistic, colourful blur, the penultimate frame from Abraham Zapruder's 8mm movie of the Kennedy assassination: an instant before the explosive head shot, JFK hunched, clutching his throat – Texas governor John Connally, mouth agape like an agonized fish, in the seat in front of him – as pink-clad Jackie turns towards her husband, pillbox hat agleam in the sunshine. Interestingly, Pauline has amplified and enlarged a detail that generally escapes notice: the bouquet of

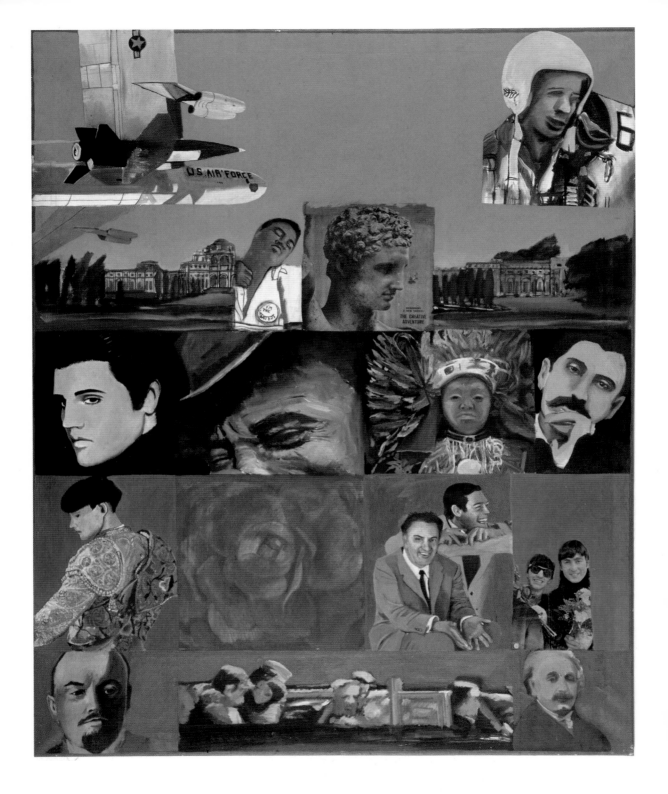

yellow roses held by Connally's wife.

My encounter with *Man's World I* in 2013, the first of Pauline's paintings I had seen and the first I'd heard of her, inspired this book: not only its qualities as an artwork, but the force of the painter's personality, that penetrating point of view, both celebration and condemnation. A man's world might be glamorous, powerful, artistic and sexy, Pauline tells us – indeed, enviable. But it's also a trap, a will not to triumph but oblivion. Better the lush red petals of *l'origine du monde* than the long-stemmed yellow rose of death. Who could disagree?

Man's World I is Pauline, artist and individual, in sublime synchronicity, the painter and the woman at peak. The same might be said of its companion piece. But if the confident mood of the first reflected the successes of the year previous, *Man's World II*, finished a year later, presents a different Pauline: no less critical but, rather than defiant, resigned.

The concept is simple: a vertical rectangle, layered with nudes drawn from *Playboy*-style men's magazines – a kind of soft-core mood board – set against an elegant country landscape. In *Ragnarok*, filmed in the summer of 1964, the in-progress painting seems about halfway there. The pin-ups along the right-hand side have found their final placement, but on the left only the uppermost image is in the finished work. The major change Pauline made to the figurative zone, post-*Ragnarok*, involved the nude at its centre, who appears in the film to be standing in front of the board, and is revealed from head to toe; in the final version the figure's head and lower legs are covered by pin-ups, amping the paste-up effect, and suggesting that even a 3-D woman will ultimately be flattened. Another difference: Pauline parted the figure's thighs to reveal a diminutive grisaille nude peeking out from between them.

There is also no background on view in the film – Pauline has painted in some amorphous place-holder shapes – and this is the most significant difference. The landscape she ultimately inserted is what is typically described as brooding: mostly a deep blue, darkening sky and, towards the very bottom, distant hills and a lake; the architecture, so imposing in *Man's World I,* is here reduced to a tiny neoclassical temple on the lake's far shore (identified, by Skelton-Davies, as the Pantheon at Stourhead).

Though it is the collage of nudes that dominates, the background contextualizes Pauline's point. Adam Smith describes it as 'a Palladian landscape typical of settled masculine authority'; to Minioudaki it 'exposes conventional associations of femininity with nature'. Either interpretation suggests that the enervated eroticism of the cheesecake pix, with their predictable come-hither poses – supine models exposing their breasts as they loll on rumpled beds, posteriors presented submissively – is merely part of the eternal male landscape, both internal and al fresco.

Notable is the painting's similarity to *Sunflower Woman*. In each, a central dominating femininity is set against an expanse of sky, above a natural landscape in the picture's lower register. The difference is that *Sunflower* is La Godzilla, a Pop avenging angel under assault from industrial capitalism; there is wit, and bite, and for our heroine, mighty as the mountains at her feet, conquest seems inevitable. In *Man's World II*, however, the mood is muted, neutered; the landscape could be the view from a sanatorium, the mighty woman has been torn up and returned, in pieces, to the passive pages of a stroke book. *Why fight it?* Pauline seems to ask. There may be no men on view, but it's their world after all.

We may surmise that the differences between *It's a Man's World I* and *II* reflect the trajectory, over some two years, of Pauline's life: from a personal and creative peak to disillusionment and depression. By the end of 1964, more the Pop cognoscenti's mascot than Marilyn or Bardot, lost in the weeds of TV as the Aquarian Age blazed into view, Pauline was ready for her rose to bloom again. It did, but the thorn proved fatal.

It's a Man's World II,
1964–65, oil and
collage on canvas,
125 × 125 cm

211

14

PAULINE'S CHOICE

1965

In the latter part of 1965, Pauline and Clive moved again, to 79 Cromwell Road in South Kensington, a short stroll from the Stained Glass department in which the artist had earned her Royal College degree. 'It was a grand first-floor apartment at the western end of a five-storey Victorian terrace with a balcony overlooking Stanhope Gardens to the rear,' Adam Smith relates, noting that the couple kept Addison Avenue as Pauline's painting studio and remained on the electoral register in the Labour-leaning district: 'their votes would have been wasted in the Tory stronghold of South Ken'.

Clive Goodwin Associates was formalized as a literary agency in 1966, after Pauline's death, and one of his early assistants was Margaret Matheson, who remained through November 1969. Clive worked from home, and Matheson remembers the Cromwell Road flat well. 'You came up the stairs, up to the first-floor level, you came in through a hallway, and you turned right into the office, two big tables, one for him, one for me,' she relates. 'It was on the road side. Or you turned left into the living room. A very big room, with his bed in one corner, and sofas and a huge long table covered in books he never read, with enough chairs around it that you could have a meeting there. A lot of open space, in which you could have a party. And the walls are covered in Pauline's paintings. As is the office, as is the hallway. As is the upstairs, [where] there was a bathroom and a little bedroom. They're absolutely glorious, so there's a massive sense of fun, and light, and positivity.'

The couple needed more space, for a happy reason: sometime in the spring, Pauline got pregnant. Bridget remembers hearing the news. '"We weren't planning it, but we're not at all upset,"' Pauline told her sister-in-law. 'It was all plus. She never said a minus thing about it. We were absolutely amazed – we thought, "Gonna be the modern girl,"' by which Bridget means 'childless'. She had good reason to believe so.

> **Nell:** *Would you like to have children eventually?*
> **Pauline:** *Well I suppose so eventually.*
> **Nell:** *. But you don't feel the urge now? It interests me because I've wanted to have children since I was about fourteen ...*
> **Pauline:** *Well I like children you know, but I don't know the sort of feeling that you're describing at all ...*
> *At one time I used to get fed up when I went home, this wasn't when I was*

married or anything, and my father used to be playing with his grandson or something and if I held it he'd say 'That's what I want to see' and I'd think 'You silly old fool.' I used to drop it like a hot brick ...

Nell: *You never have a kind of yearning, when you're in the middle of a film or something that you could – that you were just an ordinary housewife with ten children?*

Pauline: *Never.*

Nell: *You just don't see yourself at all in that role?*

Pauline: *I'd be so bored, I really would. I couldn't stand it.*

Nell: *You don't think you'll ever become that?*

Pauline: *I hope not. But if I did it would be because I wanted to. At the moment I can't conceive of wanting to. But if I did do it, if it happened to me, I would have wanted it to happen.*

'I talked to Pauline twice,' Dunn remembers. 'You can kind of tell. There's a sort of jump where she isn't pregnant when I talked to her. And then she is pregnant. I think she came over to my place. She wanted to put that in. That visit, when she told me she was pregnant, it was a very happy visit. I don't remember exactly what she said, but something like, "I never thought I wanted children, I'm so happy."'

Nell: *Now you are pregnant what do you feel?**

Pauline: *At first I was terrified because I was going to produce something that was part of another person – because you have to accept the fact that you're creating something that is part of them and you're more married to them than you were – and the other big thing – the fear of losing my freedom. But although mentally I didn't like the idea, everything in you works towards you wanting it – I've started becoming obsessive about it – it's taken up a whole great section of my thinking. Also this vanity thing – I'm a very vain person. Before I was pregnant, I didn't want a baby, thinking perhaps my tits would sag but now it seems unimportant, all those fears are sliding away. And although it was an accident, I'm secretly more pleased about it than I could ever admit.*

*June 1965

'You have several prenatal visits,' Dunn explains. 'Probably every month in those days. So she didn't know then that she was sick. It's so sad. It makes me sad now.' 'She got pregnant, and that was kind of wonderful and celebratory,' says Tracy Tynan. 'And it was kind of funny, because Clive's not exactly a family man, and it was like, "How's Clive going to deal with being a father?" And then all too quickly it went to shit.'

Logue was with Clive when he got the news. 'Pauline was pregnant. In hospital for tests. Clive and I were going to the Tynans. Nothing special. Drinks. He had visited Pauline at lunch time.

'"Do you mind if we call at the hospital?" he said. "I'll just say hello."

Logue offered to join him, but Clive declined. 'After half an hour I thought: "What does he mean – just saying hello?" Then it was an hour. Then well over an hour. Then he came out, crying. "She has lymphatic cancer. She's going to die," he said.'

The Royal Marsden Hospital's medical records retention period for deceased patients is 30 years. As Pauline's history is absent, exactly what sort of malady she suffered from is difficult to ascertain; different sources name lymphatic cancer, leukaemia and malignant thymoma. Also unknown are possible precipitating factors of Pauline's illness, though multiple childhood X-rays related to Veronica's tuberculosis and exposure to toxic fumes and glass dust in the RCA Stained Glass studio are possible suspects. What is not in dispute is that, in response to her doctors' explanation that, to receive the best possible treatment – with the most likely survival outcome – she would have to terminate her pregnancy (which, under the circumstances, would have been legally permissible), Pauline refused. Instead, she opted for a more limited regimen until after giving birth.

'We were the first to know,' Bridget says. 'They came down that weekend. She was going into hospital, she said she'd got a lump and they were going to have it out. She wasn't having the radiography – it wasn't chemo in those days. She'd decided against it. When they said the baby won't survive, she said, "I want the baby, I'll take the consequences." And she did.

'What a terrible pull that must have been. To put that before your life. Takes a lot of pluck. I'm sure there's an awful lot of people who started to say that and then had the abortion. She must have been strong to fight the doctors on that, Pauline. Very, very brave. That was the last time she came down. I never saw her again.'

'Back then, cancer wasn't really discussed,' Tracy Tynan observes. 'Who was she going to go to, really? To talk to, or get advice. And maybe feeling that if she had the treatment, she'd never be able to have children – there was no saving of eggs. I don't know how powerful her urge was to have a child.'

'But any sensible person wouldn't make that choice, right?' asks Leslie Dick. 'They'd say, "Okay, I'll terminate this pregnancy, and I'll live, and then I'll have six children." As opposed to, "I won't terminate this pregnancy, I'll give birth, then I'll start treatment and then I'll die and this motherless child will be in the world." Won't *that* be a good thing!'

'What seemed more important to her was a baby that could end up without her,' says Roger Smith. 'She shouldn't – she *shouldn't* – have had a child. And she just absolutely refused to go through that process, which would mean killing the unborn baby. She insisted on having that. I don't know why anyone would have made the decision that she made. She might have thought, "Oh well, I've got a chance of recovering." But once she'd given birth, she only lasted, what? Another four months? She was determined not to lose the baby, it was going to be her child and that was it. I never really understood that, I really didn't.'

'Maybe I'm reading too much into it,' says Dick. 'But just as I feel [Pauline's daughter] Boty had a leaning towards death, I see her mother having a leaning towards death as well.'

'There may have been part of her that felt she'd had enough of it all,' Smith believes. 'The kind of tragic way she opted for death, really. It's what it was.'

'It's interesting Roger said that,' Sally Alexander says. 'I think that's very moving, because Roger's a man of great passion. But as a woman, I don't remember being so utterly shocked by the decision. Terribly upset! But I don't remember feeling outraged or angry. It was a tragic decision, and I wasn't sure that I'd've made it. But when you're pregnant, if you have a child growing inside you ... '

'I think there's some instinctual element there, of wanting to protect this thing inside you,' Tracy Tynan says. 'I'm not sure she could understand, in some weird way, the reality of not doing that. That it would be some fundamental problem, some crime that she committed, by saying, "I'm more important than my child." I don't think, until you're in those shoes, you know how you'll respond. I mean, I can sit here and say I would have had the abortion. But I don't know.'

'Somebody gives you the choice of life or death, and you have a living being in you, and to me, of course, that's the only choice you can make,' says the American Pop artist Rosalyn Drexler. 'You're not going to kill the life force that you brought into life, living in you, so that you can be experimented upon. They give you no choice, there was no choice whatsoever. Either you abort and then we can treat you, and if you don't abort, you'll be sure to die of what you're sick with. She chose to give life, and that's grand – you could say, the grandest gesture. I would do the same, and I understand that, very much so.'

'If in fact she definitely knew she was going to die, maybe the idea of having the baby was a way of perpetuating herself,' says Allen Jones.

'I don't remember how many times I talked to Clive about it, while Pauline was alive,' Alexander says. 'But I know what he'd told me, which was that Pauline made the decision, and Clive went along with it. He didn't say *we* made the decision. "Pauline has decided, Sally."'

'He was unhappy about that,' remembers Tariq Ali. 'I said, "You could have put your foot down." And he said, "It was her choice, really, Tariq. I couldn't put my foot down. It was her decision, she had to make it." And then he said to me once, when we returned to the subject, as we did at various times, he said, "You know, the other thing is this. Suppose she'd aborted the baby, and they still hadn't been able to treat her?" It was quite primitive, in those days, treatment of leukaemia. Not too many people survived. And Clive said that that's why Pauline took the decision. That she felt, "At least there will be something left of me, for you and others to remember when I'm gone." She was adamant.'

'That's typical of her,' believes Jean-Jacques Lebel. 'Not thinking that her painting would do that, not being strong enough, faithful to her own art. It's very strange because artists often think that posterity will be their art, not their children. That's the difference between artists and normal people. They think their real children are their books or paintings or music. She didn't have faith enough in her own art. That's what it means, don't you think?'

'David Hockney becomes pregnant,' declares Caroline Coon. 'And in the first three months he's told he's got a very serious cancer. Would they have allowed David Hockney, this brilliant, talented artist, not to have treatment? I am aghast, that none of her friends, none of her social circle, had validated her enough not to think that she'd live to paint some more. That her husband didn't say, "That's rubbish, you are going to have an abortion." But it wasn't a feminine thing to do, she would have been called selfish – the whole patriarchy was on her shoulders at that point. She just missed the seventies feminism. I'm used to quite a few of that generation of man saying, "Oh, she wasn't a feminist, she didn't need feminism." My God, she needed feminism. She *died* because she wasn't able to be feminist. This is my outrage as a woman artist, this example of what happened to a woman I just thought was superb, whose painting was superb, whose activism was superb, whose engagement in life and politics was superb.'

Of all the positions taken, none was more poignant than Veronica's. 'Nana would have agreed with Pauline – in front of Pauline,' Bridget says. 'Nana was never confrontational. Brought up as a Catholic, knowing Pauline was doing the right thing, but fighting the urge to say she'd done the right thing 'cause she wanted her to stay alive. That came out ever so clear. Didn't say very much. Just the heartbreak on her face. Mostly afterwards.

'That was a real hang-up of Nana's. She couldn't kind of come to terms with whether she'd done the right thing.'

15

JOURNEY'S
END

Pauline. Clive. & Boty.

1965–1966

'The last time I saw Pauline, she said she was hoping to become a filmmaker rather than a painter,' Charles Carey recalls. 'I happened to be walking down Bond Street, and I bumped into her, and she said, "I'm going to show you how to be rich." We wandered into a shop – Fenwick, I think. And she started looking at things. In the end, she had the whole shop serving her, as if she was very rich. And taking a tremendous amount of trouble over her. Clothes littered everywhere. And then she said, "I *don't* think there's anything in here for us, Charles." And she marched out.

'She said, "I'm dying, you know." When I saw her in Bond Street. She knew she hadn't got a long time to live.'

In her September 1964 letter to Joe Massot, Pauline allowed that too much acting and not enough painting might be the cause of her depression. Yet the following year she continued her television work, before and after her pregnancy was discovered and cancer diagnosed. 'She played female lead opposite Jeremy Kemp in Victor Canning's six-part BBC2 thriller *Contract to Kill*, filmed in London and Paris between March and May, for which she got herself a new [Vidal] Sassoon bob,' Adam Smith relates. 'Pauline netted £470, topped up with 10 gns for an appearance on BBC2's *Late Night Line-Up* following transmission of the first episode ... After *Contract*, Pauline was immediately engaged for a small part in *Day Out for Lucy*, a single BBC2 play starring Frances White and Ronald Lacey. Pauline changed agents and netted £123, a big improvement on her *Contract* rate.'

This was followed by a silent bit, as the randy 'manageress' of a dry-cleaning establishment, in *Alfie* ('an' I was gettin' a suit cleaned in the bargain,' says Michael Caine in voice-over as he and Pauline embrace amidst the racks), her only theatrical film appearance; and, in October, her last role, a substantive turn as 'Nell Pretty', a sharp-tongued nightclub owner – looking neither pregnant nor ill – in *Strangler's Web*, an instalment of *The Edgar Wallace Mystery Theatre*.

(Though ostensibly developing his talent agency, Clive too remained active in television. Having hosted *The Celebrity Game*, a quiz show modelled on the American programme *Hollywood Squares*, for three months in 1964 – and appeared once on another such show, *Don't Say a Word*, alongside Pauline – Clive served as producer of Rediffusion's nine-episode *That's for Me*, conceived by *RSG!* mastermind Elkan Allan. A review in *Punch* called it 'the brightest request programme on television these days. Viewers are invited to ask for film clips as well as recordings

Oh! Calcutta! Calcutta!

Top
Pauline with
Michael Caine
during the
filming of **Alfie**,
her sole
appearance on
the big screen.

Above right
Clovis Trouille,
**Oh! Calcutta!
Calcutta!**, 1946,
paint and collage
on canvas

of their favourite stars, and the resultant textural variety saves the show from the monotony of some of its pop rivals.' The programme ran through March 1965.)

Despite the emphasis on acting – presumably motivated by finance, especially once a baby was on the way – Pauline's artworks remained on view: in 1965, she participated in *Contemporary Art*, a group show at Grabowski, and the Bradford City Art Gallery spring exhibition (in which Pauline was also featured in 1966, the show closing on 5 June, a month before her death).

And there was a final painting. Entitled *Bum* (and preceded by a preparatory study, in watercolour and ink, on paper), it was commissioned by Kenneth Tynan as a set design for his 'erotic' theatrical revue *Oh! Calcutta!*, which opened off-Broadway in 1969 and in London the following year. A wildly successful enterprise – the initial West End run surpassed 3,900 performances, and subsequent revivals did even better – the show was comprised of sex-themed sketches by noted writers, including Samuel Beckett, Sam Shepard, Edna O'Brien and Jules Feiffer, and featured full nudity by both women and men. 'Writing excitedly about his plans to the impresario, William Donaldson,' Sue Tate reports, 'Tynan listed a gamut of ideas including dance numbers, one of which was "a pop art ballet designed by Pauline Boty based on paintings that focus on the principal erogenous zones".'

'Casting about for a possible poster for *Carte Blanche* [a planned *Calcutta* sequel] I think of Pauline Boty's *Bum* which hangs in the dining room,' Tynan wrote in his journal. 'In the Mount Street flat I covered one wall of my study with wallpaper I had made up of a huge enlargement of a detail from a nude photo of La Goulue – the detail being the cleft of her bottom. Multiplied thousands of times, it was of course unrecognisable, and I used to challenge guests to guess what it was. Nobody got near it till one day I showed the wall to Pauline. "That," she said instantly, "is a girl's bum" (which gave me the idea of commissioning the painting).'

As it happens, *Oh! Calcutta!* took its title from an artwork: the 1946 *Oh! Calcutta! Calcutta!* by Clovis Trouille (1889–1975), a Frenchman whose many anti-clerical, pro-sex paintings suggest an unlikely, appealing blend of Vargas, Dali and Bosch. A mixed-media canvas (painting and collage), tinted a lurid purple and bearing a subversive resemblance to Ingres's *Grande Odalisque, Oh! Calcutta! Calcutta!* (the title references the French 'Oh! Quel cul t'as,' roughly 'Oh! What an arse you have') features a reclining, fabric-draped woman, her back to the viewer, presenting a round bare derrière, each cheek gracefully adorned with a three-leafed stem, its declivities giving it the appearance of a large pepper (though according to the website Weimarart, Trouille felt that 'the ass forms a perfect circle designed to suggest the conquest of the moon').

The painting eloquently reflects the spirit of the revue (and vice-versa), and one can imagine its appeal to Pauline, as well as that of Trouille's particular blend of proto-Pop and Surrealism. Indeed, *Bum* – which features a woman's posterior (modelled, according to Tracy Tynan, on her stepmother's) beneath an elaborately designed and decorated upper proscenium, flanked by curtains and Corinthian columns, and looming above the word BUM in huge red block letters set off by elongated Pop Art chevrons – echoes a similar classical/theatrical motif in Trouille's contemporaneous *La morte en beauté* (1963).

It is hard to know what to make of *Bum*. It is impeccably designed, detailed and executed – nothing slapdash, as though Pauline wished to answer those who questioned her abilities – and the eponymous object itself deserves Caroline

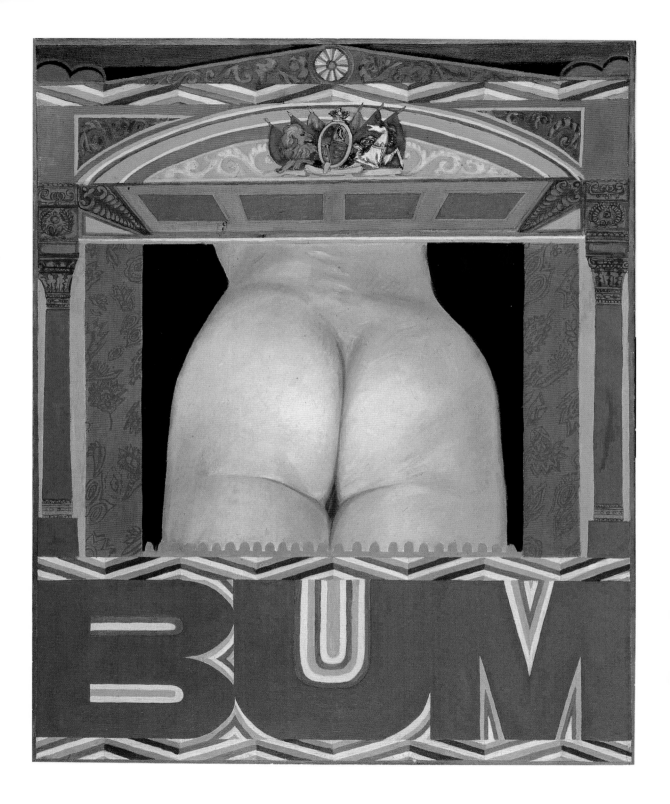

JOURNEY'S END

Coon's stated admiration: 'The painterly quality of the bum is exquisite.' Yet the picture lacks Pauline's usual pungent presence; though it was not ultimately used as such, *Bum* really does feel like a set design. Perhaps this is the point: something was asked, and something was given. Still, it is as though the artist chose to sign off with an enigma: a perfectly, even brilliantly rendered female arse, boxed in an elaborate Greco-Roman sarcophagus, the statement of its name – BUM – at once loud and dumb. Either the joke is light-hearted or macabre, the artistry engaged or efficient; whether Pauline is fully present or has begun to wave goodbye – to leave, as it were, the stage – one cannot entirely say. Perhaps it is all of these, and *Bum* is Pauline Boty at her most clinical, and heartbreaking.

In 2017, the painting was offered for sale by Kenneth and Kathleen's two children, Roxana and Matthew (Tracy is the offspring of Tynan's first marriage). Pauline's previous auction record, set in 2014, was £40,000. The price for *Bum*, realized at Christie's, was £632,750. Fifty-four years after Grabowski, a generation after the paintings went begging at the Mayor and Whitford galleries, Pauline Boty at last hit the big time.

Sally Alexander remembers her first encounter, following Clive's request that she come to visit, with Pauline. 'She was lying on the sofa, at the Cromwell Road flat, and she was being looked after. You felt you had to care about her. She was very warm and friendly. And also very weak, and not very well.'

On subsequent visits, Alexander says, 'People came in all the time, it was very, very sociable. There was a tremendous buzz. Derek Boshier kept his eye on her – gosh, what a nice man he was. Christopher Logue was the other person who was there all the time. Christopher, Derek, Troy Kennedy Martin, Adrian and Celia. They were always there, always good friends. There was also a woman in the middle of it who was very ill.'

One senses why Pauline's fate might not have seemed, to some, to be sealed. 'She was very, very beautiful, she really was,' says Alexander. 'Pauline was more beautiful in real life, to me, than she was in pictures. And you know, with women, you either look great when you're pregnant or you don't. She looked great. She was very long-limbed, and when she did develop a bump, it was beautiful. And sort of easy to talk to, and curious about me – I was a friend of Clive's, Clive liked me. I remember them lying on the sofa, watching nature programmes. They loved nature programmes.

'I somehow don't think I took this in, initially. How severe it was. Clive and she did know. And, you know, they didn't dwell on that. I mean all these guys, who were all frightfully kind of cool and jokey and witty and funny and smoking dope and going to parties and all that, all around Pauline all the time. And that's how she wanted it.'

Inevitably, the illness became manifest. 'I would go round, and over the weeks and months you would see this big-boned, gorgeous sort of English robust, big-personality young woman gradually disappear,' Tony Garnett remembers. 'She was never down or anything like that, she was always good company. But of course that was put on for visitors.' 'They know in the back of their minds they're going to die, but they want to put on a good show for everyone else,' Bridget says. 'She'd've talked sense. She wouldn't have said, "Poor me."'

Pauline's rather startling good humour was broadly noted. 'She was cheerful,' says Boshier. 'I mean, she was herself. I saw a lot of her when she was sick. I was free, I didn't have deadlines and stuff. I used to go down the road and talk to her. It was amazing. She joked, she'd be almost herself. She lived with it.' 'She had an outside swing seat in her sitting room, and she'd be sitting on that, swinging away,' Roddy Maude-Roxby remembers. 'And that was very photogenic.'

At times, there was laughter. 'I remember the big French windows, and her on this daybed,' says Birtwell. 'Lying on the daybed, talking about her hair falling out. We were talking about getting a wig, and it was jolly-ish. All I remember was trying to be jolly while she was on this daybed looking thin.' 'It's nice being thin,' she told Roger Smith. 'I've never been thin before.'

The mood proved unsustainable. 'When Arthur went to visit Pauline, he came back very upset,' Bridget remembers. 'She wasn't "Pauline". Very, very ill. I should think she'd've been quite striking, being very ill. Her eyes'd still have been big, wouldn't they?' According to Logue, 'Clive moved their bed into the sitting room. Ken Russell brought his projector round and showed her films. She weighed less and less. Sarah White told me: "I visited her on a sunny day. 'Shall I move you into the sun?' I suggested. 'No,' she said. 'I don't want to be in the sun anymore.'"'

'I remember her going back home to Cromwell Road, and not being able to sit in the sun,' Natalie Gibson says. 'I suppose it was just bits in between hospitals and things. But it just didn't occur to me that she was going to die. I had this teacher at the Royal College. I was going to see Pauline, and he said to me, "Well she's dying." You know, because his wife had died of the same thing. And I was going, "No, no – I wouldn't have it. She's not dying!"'

Dying, Pauline, as Rosalyn Drexler puts it, gave life: On 12 February 1966, she and Clive welcomed their daughter, Boty Goodwin, at Queen Charlotte's Hospital. 'I do remember that she seemed so happy with this baby,' says Alexander. 'Just being thrilled, absolutely thrilled, that there was a little baby.' 'She was completely overjoyed,' Nell Dunn recalls. 'I remember taking baby clothes as a present, which is what one did in those days. Pauline was completely charmed and thrilled and delighted and happy. I remember that Boty was beautiful, too. Delicate and lovely. Tiny little crib beside her bed with the baby in it. I think I was allowed to hold the baby, actually. She let me. She knew I had babies.'

'After she died, I had this crazy idea of adopting her daughter,' Nicola Wood admits. 'Because I thought, she hasn't got a mother anymore.'

'Pauline kept Boty only a few days before placing her in her grandparents' care,' notes Adam Smith. 'The rest of Pauline's life was divided between Cromwell Road, the Royal Marsden in Chelsea, and the Marsden's specialist Belmont Hospital near her family in Carshalton, where she underwent radium treatment.'

Owing perhaps to having achieved her objective, Pauline projected beatitude. 'My first husband, knowing he was going to die, he was just lying there saying, "Why me? Why me?" And really upset,' Wood says. 'Pauline was quite normal and happy. She was probably tranquillized, of course. But she seemed very relaxed and calm. She still had her own sense of presence, oddly enough. I had a nice visit with her. I only went once.'

'She was always starving, and wanting veal and ham pie,' Gibson says. 'That's the funny pie with the hard-boiled egg in the middle of it. And she had a pile of books by her bed, and she was reading about her illness, voraciously. And telling me whatever it was she had was going to take ten years off her life, probably.'

'I must have seen her, it felt like a week or two before she passed away,' says Allen Jones. 'She was sitting up in bed, looking of course a little wan, because she was ill, but she was still Pauline. You know, if there was any difference, it was the kind of difference to do with make-up or hair or something. It never crossed my mind that she was about to die. She most likely knew it, but that wasn't apparent, it wasn't a part of the conversation. It was, "Hey, get well soon, see you," and all that kind of stuff.'

In reality, Pauline's suffering was next to intolerable. In 1967, Clive, who advocated strongly, and with remarkable public candour, for the legalization of cannabis, gave testimony to the Wootton Committee, created by England's Home Office Advisory Committee on Drug Dependence to consider the good and the bad of pot and LSD. 'My wife died of cancer,' he told the members. 'For six months I knew she was dying and she guessed. We smoked marijuana, which we had smoked often before, but during this period we smoked it almost every night. It was an enormous help in allowing us to get through that particular period. No doctor offered us any other drug.'

Whatever relief Pauline derived was insufficient. 'At one point she asked me to bring her some pills, because she couldn't stand it any longer,' Penny Massot told Sabine Durrant. 'But I told Clive and he said no.'

'Clive took me to the Royal Marsden Hospital, and she was in bed, and she had a little black spot on her chest,' Birtwell remembers. 'That clearly was the mark where they were giving her chemo, but I didn't realize that. And when I asked him afterwards, you know, what's going wrong, he couldn't talk about it. He just couldn't talk about it.'

Boty Goodwin. Living with her grandparents, she was called Katy, as Veronica and Albert found her given name a painful reminder of their loss.

'Clive was so upset,' Boshier says. 'The last two or three days, he didn't go in so much, he was devastated. So I went in – I used to sit in the hospital garden with her. I think it was two days before she died, and I don't know if I'm dramatizing, Ken Tynan wrote a piece in the *Evening Standard* to say, "Great news! Pauline's in hospital but getting better." Just to show her.'

Tynan's squib, published on the *Standard*'s 'Diary' page, appeared on 1 July, Pauline's final day: 'She is suffering from a glandular disease. But her husband Clive Goodwin says she is beginning to recover.' It is unlikely that Pauline lived to see it. 'After she returned to hospital Roger and I visited her only once,' Logue writes. 'She lay back, two pillows under her head, shivering, her face covered in sweat. A day later she died.'

'The friendship stopped when I married Jann Haworth,' says Peter Blake. 'Very similar to Pauline. Jann was American, but they were the leading women Pop artists. And it was strange that I was in love with Pauline and a very good friend of hers. And married Jann. It's an odd sequence of events. I think there was an element of jealousy from Jann about Pauline. So the friendship stopped. ('Oh, no, not at all,' Haworth says. 'I never said a word to him about that. It was in the past. There's no "there" there.') So I knew she had leukaemia, and we were in the Royal College one day, and I met Natalie Gibson. She said, "Pauline's really ill, she's in a hospital very near the Royal College, I know she'd love to see you." So we drove straight round to the hospital, and she'd died ten minutes earlier. It would have been a last goodbye.'

'My studio was like a minstrel gallery, twenty feet high and then you walk down,' says Wood. 'Jane burst into my room at the top and said, "Pauline's died! Pauline's died! Pauline's died!" And we just cried. It was an impossible thing to happen.'

'People say they remember where they were when Kennedy died,' Charles Carey says. 'I remember when somebody told me Pauline had died. It gave me a type of shock that you get usually when a relative dies.'

'I had left the theatre completely, I was a cartoonist at a newspaper,' says Nicholas Garland. 'I'd changed everything, and a great chunk of my life fell away. I was in the picture library doing a bit of research for something. And some pictures of Pauline were out on someone's desk. I said, "Why have you got them out?" And he said, "They're for obits." I remember a terrible feeling of shock. It was like a blow.'

'I remember Ossie [Clark] coming into the College and saying he had just made a dressing gown for Pauline,' Stella Penrose recalls. 'He didn't tell me she was actually dying. But I got the feeling from what he was saying that she was. It was terrible. But I didn't feel I could visit or take her something. I didn't feel close enough to do that.'

Fate had been kind to Pauline's first fan. From Wimbledon, Penrose had gone, at 19, to study Fashion – Dress, as it was called – at Kingston School of Art, which she hated and quit; unemployable as a 'half-trained art student', newly married, she moved from Sutton to London and took a dead-end job as a telephone operator. Then her luck improved: after two years of evening classes at Saint Martins – '*the* fashion school in London' – Penrose won a place in the Royal College's Fashion department. In spring of 1966, as Pauline lay dying, Penrose graduated. 'Julie Christie came to our fashion show, and she got me my first job in New York. Because Paul Young, who'd had the first boutique in New York – Paraphernalia, on Madison Avenue – she'd done some modelling for him. So she gave me his name, and I met him at Claridge's the day after my convocation. And he offered me a job. I went out to New York, and worked as a designer, at Paraphernalia.'

'It was wonderful,' Penrose says. 'I've had the most marvellous life.'

Pauline: *... I like growing older.*

Nell: *You never look with dread at the idea of being forty or fifty?*

Pauline: *I don't look upon fifty, funnily enough between forty and fifty I think must be hell. No, I have a kind of vague – I can imagine myself being thirty and all through the thirties up to thirty-nine sounds great. What's so extraordinary is that when one was younger one had an idea that say at twenty-one, when one was very young you were an adult therefore you were in command of situations, you never had all this faltering feeling and in fact it seems that the areas of non-confidence just change, or new ones develop as more demands are made on you. I wouldn't like to think, 'I think this' and think it forever, things always change, I hope.*

16

FOR
PAULINE
BOTY
Gone Ladies

Where in the world is Helen gone,
Whose loveliness demolished Troy,
Sheba, Salome, and the wan
Licentious Queen of Avalon,
And where is she who could enjoy
Caesar — and Anthony enthral,
And she who bore God's only boy?
Where is the snow we watched last Fall?

And tell me anyone who can
The whereabouts of Helois
Whose so by love enchanted man
Sooner would risk castration than
Leave her; and was. Does Beatrice
Still cross the bridge at evencall?
And who is waiting for Lucrece?
Where is the snow we watched last Fall?

And where is Marilyn who crept
Into an endless reverie
Where death her comforted and kept
Safe in his arms until she wept?
Where is Sheherazade and she
On whom some people blame it all,
Delicious Eve, oh, answer me!
Where is the snow we watched last Fall?

Bird, do not seek to know from me
Who was the fairest of them all;
What would you say if I asked thee,
Where is the snow we watched last Fall?

CHRISTOPHER LOGUE

GONE

1966

Her death was a lesson to me: stay alive. Don't succumb to your agonized feelings, your suicidal feelings. Stay alive. Stay alive.

– Caroline Coon

Pauline's funeral, presided over by Father Albert Tomei, took place at St Margaret's, Carshalton's Catholic church, followed by cremation at Reigate, 11 miles away. 'I didn't go,' Bridget admits. 'It was in the afternoon. It was milking again. This is why I didn't see Pauline when she was ill. Arthur wouldn't have gone on his own, but I said he had to go. So he went.'

Clive did not. Instead, he held a memorial the following day at the Cromwell Road flat, attended by none of the Botys. 'It was incredible,' Penny Massot recalls. 'Everybody was there that was in the arts. We were all told, "Do not come in black." So we all went in bright colours. It wasn't a sad affair, it was a celebration of Pauline's life. We were all looking like we were going to some sort of party.'

'Clive wanted to give me their big brass bed, and it had one of Pauline's bras hanging on it,' Nicola Wood remembers. 'I love brass beds but there was no way I could accept it. It was slightly haunted, I suppose.' 'I remember Clive asking did I want anything,' says Natalie Gibson. 'I felt I couldn't. I've got one thing, actually. It's a little tin horse-and-cart thing. A little tin toy. I don't know when she found it. It's in quite a lot of my husband's paintings.'

'Eulogies from Troy [Kennedy Martin] and John McGrath and poetry from Adrian Mitchell lent a spiritual flavour to the firmly secular gathering,' notes Adam Smith. 'Elkan Allan remembers the event was "in a sense very moving and should have been embarrassing"; Clive read extracts from love letters so intimate "it transcended bad taste ... you felt that you were intruding, but as he had offered the intrusion, it was very touching".' Clive also delivered Pauline's farewell words, now lost, a message to her friends set down as she neared the end. Surprisingly, it was more political than personal. 'Her testament,' wrote McGrath, 'was a message of undying hope, of solidarity with the oppressed, and of certainty about the future that gave all of us more than courage.'

'Pauline wrote what she wanted to happen,' says Boshier. 'Clive played music – she did have some very particular pop music. And she wanted everyone to dance. People found it very hard to do that. People were crying. We couldn't do it.'

'Imagine if Rosenquist had died in '64 and had only done those wonderful pictures from '61,' says David Alan Mellor. 'Or any of those people. There is a special poignancy about a career cut short, and works that never see the light of day.'

'We were all in the act of becoming,' Jann Haworth recalls. 'We were not formed, we were all chrysalises. I think of my own work at that time and the distance that I've traveled. It's hard to say what she would have become. She was so young.'

'She was just getting started,' Rosalyn Drexler says. 'We don't know that she would stay on the obvious subjects. But I know that she took great pleasure in her work, and in her life. She danced, she went out and she enjoyed everything that you're supposed to enjoy. Sex and relationships and all that stuff. But she was a great, great person inside of herself, something that I really sympathize with.'

'You just felt, actually, she'd done so much more than most people in her lifetime,' Natalie Gibson concludes. 'She'd sort of done everything.'

Of London in the summer of 1966, Sheila Rowbotham wrote, 'Freedom and movement sang to you everywhere. The search for pure authenticity gave way to a delight in free expression. Something original, energetic and confident was coming out of Britain.' Then and now, the view was not hers alone. *You Say You Want a Revolution? Records and Rebels 1966–1970*, a monumental 2016 exhibition at the Victoria and Albert Museum, cited 1966 as the year the decade came into its own, a notion affirmed, in its time, by the 15 April edition of *Time* magazine – published ten weeks before Pauline's death – the cover of which featured a Pop-influenced painted collage beneath the headline 'London: The Swinging City'. Artist and activist, dolly bird and social critic, fan and feminist, libertine and housewife, glamorous bombshell and one of the boys: Pauline was in every way a founding participant in the new world that achieved lift-off virtually in the moment of her death. London was swinging, and Pauline was gone.

We know what Pauline accomplished – it has filled a book. Yet hers was an unfinished life, and the circumstances surrounding its premature conclusion sit uncomfortably in the mind. At the particular moment in which Pauline was presented with the twin possibilities of a new life and her own death, she was vulnerable: struggling against depression, pursuing a trivial avocation at the expense of her passion, misunderstood by the culture and doubting of herself. Had she not simultaneously gotten pregnant and gotten cancer, Pauline's existential crisis – her bad patch – would surely have passed. The future might have led anywhere.

Over and again, those who knew Pauline speak of her defiance, her determination to do things her own way, her signature embrace of self-contradiction. Yet it is a hard truth that, while the defining characteristic of one's nature may remain indestructible, its direction can be warped or perverted by the stress of circumstances. As a teenager, Pauline was determined to be a creator, to reinvent the idea of womanhood, to subvert expectation and convention. A decade later, she seemingly felt so discouraged regarding her accomplishments – regarding even the purpose of her existence – that she was prepared to die to give birth, seeing the baby as the only means by which she might endure, all of value that she'd accomplished. That signature defiance, her impregnable narcissism – for what is creating a motherless child if not the acme of self-centeredness? – remained intact. But its objective had changed utterly. If we interpret Pauline's story as the transit from defiant self-assertion to defiant self-negation, then it is, alas, a man's world.

Yet if a fundamental of feminism – of freedom – is the right to choose, then what seems like a failure of self-belief can equally be seen as the opposite. Perhaps Pauline's youthful optimism hadn't curdled into a deathbed embrace of Victorian values and female insignificance, but rather transformed into something radical and infused with power. For Pauline was, and was not, her parents' child. The inheritor of Albert's iron will and Veronica's sensitivity, to be sure. But committed to her own prerogatives – her right to choose – as neither could have been. In that respect, Pauline was the child of no one but herself, which perhaps accounts for her much remarked-upon serenity, her pleasure in her friends' company and Boty's arrival. If we do not negatively judge Pauline for wanting to be a mother – if we see her choice as the throwing off of the moment's wrong-footedness and the seizing of possibility – then her story ends, not in surrender and desperation, but with independence, hope and love.

As with so many aspects of this woman's life, its conclusion can be read in contrasting ways. How it is interpreted – what the takeaway might be, how the lessons might be applied – Pauline Boty, like all true artists, has left to her audience.

EPILOGUE

NOTHING LEFT IN THE WORLD

This is, to be sure, a biography of Pauline Boty. Yet it is important to relate what became of her husband and child after the artist's death. Partly this has to do with the fact that both were distinctive individuals in their own right. But it derives as well from something else: time and again in conversation, the saga of this family was described to me as a 'Greek tragedy'. This was, I believe, meant in a symbolic rather than literal way, and arose from the terrible events that, one after another, befell each of them. And yet, considering the lives of Clive and Boty, one is reminded of two themes of this particular dramatic form: the ineluctability of fate, and the ineradicable flaw.

Clive was, in Sheila Rowbotham's words, 'a creative power pack': a man of action who entertained no self-doubts, and believed no obstacle was insurmountable. Nothing could stop Clive, and the tragedy of his death lies in the knowledge that *only* what happened could have stopped him: an occurrence that deprived him of his essential strengths, and left Clive at the mercy of precisely the sort of people he detested: frauds, hiding behind the presumptive arrogance of 'authority'. Clive's end recalls the ancient Greeks' belief in a preordained fate: an outcome that lies beyond even the most strenuous mortal efforts to outrun it.

Boty's story is more complicated. While both father and daughter had to push forward in the face of personal loss, they were responding to very different conditions, at different points in their development. Boty was 11 when she was orphaned. And though her father's contemporaries, observing her courage in that awful moment, believed that she would endure, Boty proved unequal to the task. Thus does the life of this twice-cursed child more closely resemble the classical definition of Greek tragedy: a drama in which an individual, possessed of exceptional qualities, is undone by a fatal combination of circumstance and character.

At least there will be something left of me, for you and the others to remember when I'm gone.

Pauline could hardly have imagined that, within three decades, there would be nothing left in the world of any of them, not even the daughter for whom she'd given her life. Yet her wish, in a way, did come true: if this is tragedy, there is a note of triumph in it, one that arises, not only from an essential component of the artist's nature, but the presence of the same impulse within her husband and child. We are all, by and by, forgotten. But as these three lives demonstrate, how we choose to live can leave a legacy.

'There is a memory of Pauline beginning to take shape,' Sally Alexander observes. 'But Clive, there's nothing. He wasn't a creative artist, there isn't a body of work. But he did represent all of these extraordinary playwrights, and he was behind so many things. He was friends to lots of people, he made things happen. God help him.'

Following Pauline's passing, Clive found his métier, as one of the most influential literary agents of the time. Like his wife, who'd been instrumental in the formulation of British Pop Art, he participated in a transformative cultural moment: the flowering of left-wing British drama, in theatre, cinema and, especially, television. The writers who passed through Clive Goodwin Associates included Tariq Ali, Howard Barker, Brian Clark, Simon Gray, Trevor Griffiths, Pam Gems, David Hare, Dennis Potter, Sam Shepard, Fay Weldon and Colin Welland, as well as the directors Stephen Frears, Roland Joffé and Ken Loach – a cavalcade of talent that continued to prosper, creatively and otherwise, long after the agency's demise, and some to the present day.

Clive's energetic, can-do personality, too, came ever more to the fore. 'He just kind of ran his life, and knew all these great people, and was kind and open,' says Margaret Matheson, one of his many assistants. This was apparent in the manner in which Goodwin Associates did business: work and play were conducted out of the Cromwell Road flat, Clive's life in all its untidy parts fully on display. The dining room, off the kitchen, served as the office – Clive's of-the-moment employee sat by the window, he worked at the dinner table – and, other than occasional visits from the bookkeeper, the two handled everything. Clive's client relations were comparably informal, and shot through with mischief, as Ken Loach discovered on a trip to France. 'Clive was responsible for my smoking a cannabis cigarette in the back of a car in Cannes,' he says. 'I didn't do anything like that, and he was very insistent. So I took it, drew on it, coughed and passed it back. That was my only experience of the Swinging Sixties.'

By all accounts, Clive was a good negotiator: matter-of-fact, not a shouter, with a sense of how hard he could push and a willingness to walk away. But his most profitable ability, one and all agree, came from his enthusiasm, Clive's unequivocal (though not uncritical) belief in his roster's talent. 'He was very nurturing, very good at explaining to clients what he could do for them and how he could raise their profile,' says Lynn Horsford, an assistant and sometime girlfriend. He also put financial muscle behind his instincts: Clive invested in his client Simon Gray's hit play *Butley*, and his friend Michael White's production *The Rocky Horror Show*. And he poured his considerable energies into political action, most notably via the creation of the short-lived but influential left-wing broadsheet *The Black Dwarf*. Principally associated with Tariq Ali, its co-founder and editor, *Black Dwarf* in fact 'was a collective idea', Ali states. 'It's Clive who brought us all together.'

And in a time, and a town, in which kicking out the jams was at a premium, Clive's parties stood apart. The Cromwell Road flat provided him a stage on which to set forth his personality and his way of life, each a reflection of the other. 'He had a glass that he hardly drank from, and he'd stroll around among the most amazingly disparate group of people,' Tony Garnett says. 'All the movers and shakers of London were there,' says Caroline Coon – 'there was the world.' 'They were all talking about ideas and writing and films, and what they'd seen the night before and what they were going to do that morning,' Sally Alexander recalls. 'And they were all political,' says the interior designer Melissa North, a close friend. 'They all wanted to start a revolution.'

It is an exceptional legacy. Yet the most notable of Clive's accomplishments was the least heralded, and the least likely: his success as a parent.

Shortly after her birth, Pauline and Clive's daughter was placed in the care of her grandparents, who were, at the time, 59 and 55 years of age. 'Your daughter's husband, my father, was too inexperienced in child rearing and too incapacitated by grief,' wrote Boty Goodwin. 'He gave me to you, even though your politics, principles and beliefs were diametrically opposed.' So traumatized were Albert and Veronica by Pauline's death that they re-named their granddaughter: in suburban Caterham, to which they'd retired, Boty was known as Katy Goodwin.

Despite his in-laws' disapproval of him, Clive visited Boty regularly, and as she got older brought her on outings; Celia Mitchell remembers Clive and three-year-old Boty spending Easter at the family's Yorkshire farmhouse. 'The grandparents would have preferred for her to be brought up in Caterham,' says Horsford. 'Clive fought hard to make sure that Boty kept in touch with the world her mother had chosen to live in.'

Those familiar with Boty's early days in London describe an evolving father/daughter relationship affecting in its tenderness. 'He was very good with her – took her out, introduced her to his friends,' Tariq Ali says. 'She became a part of his world.' 'Any woman who worked for him became a kind of surrogate mother or auntie,' recalls Suki Dimpfl, who served at Goodwin Associates from 1972 until the following year. 'She knew how to hold a conversation, and she was also a feminist at that age too. She felt that Clive could be oppressive. She had a thing on her door saying "Men By Appointment", when she was six or seven.'

As Boty's educational needs became more serious, her schedule reversed: weekdays were spent in London, Saturdays and Sundays in Caterham. Dimpfl remembers her attending Bousfield, a primary school near Clive's flat, and then Holland Park, the comprehensive favoured by the city's lefties. 'When she came back from school, she had to come through the office, to get to the kitchen to make a snack,' Horsford says. 'She'd very often sit with us, sit down at one of the desks and do her homework. I remember her reading out essays or short stories that she'd done. It was just part of her natural life to be there.'

In the aftermath of Pauline's death, Clive's anguish was overwhelming, the more so for his unwillingness or inability to share his pain. 'I knew him probably better than anyone,' says Tony Garnett. 'But he was a closed book.' And though he endured, and prospered, and became in time a figure of consequence, all of his friends wondered how Clive would cope with caring for a child. Indeed, Clive wondered about it himself. But the confidence he so profitably applied to all aspects of his life saw him through – that, and Clive's affectionate, enthusiastic and supportive character, so well-remembered and vividly evoked, nearly half a century after his death, by all who knew him.

'Clive threw a fancy-dress party for Boty's birthday, and I had to go,' recalls Boty's friend Abigail Thaw, Sally Alexander's daughter. 'My mother was not very good at things like that. So at the last minute, she wrapped a sheet around me, put a pillow down my front, and then took me out in the garden, broke off a twig, stuck it in my ponytail, and I was a turnip. And everybody went, including [Adrian and Celia's daughter] Sasha Mitchell, who went as an *apple tart*. Of course, so witty. She was done up as a tart, in make-up, but also an apple. And I was a turnip. It was awful, it was one of the most humiliating experiences of my life. But Clive loved it, of course – told my mother mine was his absolute favourite costume, and gave me a prize for the best.'

By 1977, 'The agency had really taken off,' says Horsford. 'It was actually a full-time job.' In fact, Clive was putting together the highest-profile deal in Goodwin Associates' 11-year history: his client Trevor Griffiths would co-write the screenplay of *Reds*, a Hollywood epic about the American Communist John Reed, in collaboration with Warren Beatty, also the film's star and director. To solidify the arrangement, Clive planned a trip to Los Angeles and had booked a room at the Beverly Wilshire Hotel, Beatty's residence, where Griffiths was also a guest. He checked in on 7 November, then transferred to the (hipper, cheaper) Chateau Marmont, at the east end of the Sunset Strip, six days later.

Shortly before 5 p.m. on 14 November, following a meeting with his client at which he complained, according to Griffiths, 'that he had the most terrible headache that he had ever had', Clive became violently ill in the lobby of the Beverly Wilshire, vomiting uncontrollably and crying out that he was 'sick, sick, oh so sick' before lapsing into semi-consciousness. As Clive was no longer a registered guest, rather than seeking medical assistance, hotel security called the Beverly Hills police, who – finding Clive unresponsive – unquestioningly accepted the security man's assertion that he was drunk. After handcuffing

235

their prisoner, the two responding officers dragged Clive through the lobby and took him to headquarters, where – following a thorough examination – Clive's drunkenness was confirmed by two paramedics (who, like the officers, claimed that he reeked of alcohol). He was then deposited, face down, on the concrete floor of the drunk tank, and left to sleep it off. Clive was discovered there the following morning, dead of a massive brain haemorrhage. Neither alcohol nor drugs were found in his system. He was 45.

Clive's death – in effect, criminally negligent homicide, all the more shocking for its pointlessness – comprised a perfect storm of malign conditions: bureaucracy, stupidity, groupthink, indifference and astonishing ineptitude, all of it crowned by the inability of Clive, that most articulate of men, to speak on his own behalf. 'I just couldn't believe that Clive, who was so good at dealing with people, that such an unlikely thing would happen to him,' says Melissa North. 'I kept saying, "It can't be Clive, it can't be Clive." Because he would have told him who he was.'

It is, one observes, the stuff of drama – a slow-rolling catastrophe that a left-wing literary agent would surely have appreciated, as a savage work of moral and social indictment. But it was also the end, the end of a man who was, in many respects, irreplaceable.

As Sally Alexander put it: God help him.

On 3 December, Michael White presented a memorial for Clive at Kings Road Theatre, home to *The Rocky Horror Show*. 'I remember thinking, "I wonder if Boty will come to this,"' says Natalie Gibson. 'Not only did she come, she'd written a little act. That she was at home, being told off for not doing her homework, by a nanny. Then there was a phone call, and it was Clive, ringing up from Harrods because he was having people for supper. And he couldn't remember the recipe for spaghetti Bolognese. And her saying, "You have to have pine nuts," and this and that.' 'She blew us away with this extraordinary skit,' says Suki Dimpfl. 'So we realized then that she would be all right.'

Some years before, watching their young daughters at play together, Clive had told Adrian and Celia Mitchell that, if anything happened to him, he wanted them to take Boty. Phil Kelvin, one of Clive's assistants, recalls that she did spend a few nights with the Mitchells following the news from LA. But within a week, Boty was again the de facto child of her grandparents. Living with Clive, Boty returned to her given name. Now, she was Katy again.

Initially, she attended Eothen, a local Catholic school, but after two years transferred to the Convent of the Sacred Heart (today the Woldingham School), four miles from home. Though predominately a boarding institution, Boty began as a day girl, in September 1979. She was 13.

'I remember saying to her, "Why, why, have you decided to place yourself in a Catholic boarding school, as a day girl?"' says her schoolmate Kate Terence. 'She very much indicated it was her choice. I wondered if it was true, or was she feeling her mind into coping with it.'

If Boty wished to knit herself into a reassuringly conventional fabric, to be one stitch among many, it was too late. 'She was,' says Terence, 'a very hot oddity.' Boty 'had a way of looking at things that was very different from the sort of horse-and-hound type that most of the girls at the convent aspired to being', says her friend Kate Poyner. 'She was verbally very adept, very witty. She had this veneer of sophistication, from being in Clive's world.' Pip Rampling, another classmate, also noted Boty's singularity. 'She was an incredible op shop dresser,' she recalls. 'Fifties, sixties clothes, you know, polka-dot dresses and things like that. Even to wearing a little bow in her hair.'

Fitting in was no less fraught in that nest of convention, her grandparents' suburban retirement bungalow – 'a tidy small house with net curtains', recalls classmate Kitty Beamish. Despite Veronica's conservatism, Boty's attachment to her was evident to another Sacred Heart friend, Stephanie Duncan, who overnighted in Caterham, sharing Boty's room. 'Her grandmother used to bring tea and an orange in the morning into the bedroom, which I found extraordinary. She used to, in a lovely way, spoil her.' Boty's ambivalence, however, remained ever-present. 'She blamed her grandmother for not supporting Pauline,' Poyner says. 'There was always a massive tension between those two areas of Boty's life.'

If Veronica and Albert seldom spoke of Pauline, Boty's friends discovered, neither had Clive. 'He couldn't have her name mentioned, he broke down, apparently,' Terence says. 'Boty said it was painful, because all she wanted to do was talk about her, which she did, all the time.' Boty's longing for Pauline's presence found poignant expression in the Caterham attic. 'We used to go up, and she would show me her mum's paintings,' Duncan remembers. 'They were in the eaves of this bungalow – you could flip through them, as if you were in a poster shop.'

Clive, too, was on Boty's mind. 'She used to talk about how she'd come back from school and open the royalty cheques,' says Duncan. 'It came across as being a really fun time in her life, and I guess that's what she was mourning as well.' 'She had to grow up incredibly fast,' Beamish observes. 'And possibly little sections of her hadn't. And, literally, just an absolute desperation to be loved and understood, I think, was always there with her.'

On occasion, Boty's need to belong produced extreme behaviour. 'There was one time when we were at a birthday party,' Beamish says. 'There was a bowl, and everyone spat in it, and then we dared her to eat it, and she ate it. It freaked everyone out. I felt quite close to her, and then I pulled away,' she admits. 'Boty was really miserable, and I wasn't very good at supporting her.'

'I would see her in the common room, and I would sit with her,' Rampling remembers. 'The way she laughed, which was wholeheartedly, was also the way she cried.' 'I have memories of her sitting in a beanbag, weeping uncontrollably, you know, when you're weeping so much you've got snot running down your face,' Duncan says. 'You know when certain things get seared on your soul? That was one of them.'

While the anguish, the neediness, her life's irreconcilable poles might have made Boty remote, she was, instead, empathic. 'She was the person that you would tell things to, because she'd been to a place that we, I, had never been to,' Poyner says. 'She pushed conversations into places that no other of my women friends ever did. And she was such a gentle and witty person – I cannot tell you how funny she was. That may have been how she learnt to navigate her life.'

In the summer of 1982, at 16, Boty, who'd been spending weekends and holidays with the Mitchells and their daughters, Sasha and Beattie, took them up on their promise to Clive and moved in. 'She called herself our "extra daughter",' Celia recalls. Boty was happy to be in what Poyner calls 'a North London, artistic household, with that left-wing, *Guardian*-reader stuff going on', and to enrol at Haverstock Comprehensive, and Camden School for Girls, where she took art classes, as Boty rather than Katy.

The pleasures of London life, however, were marbled with strain. The Mitchells treated Boty, Terence believes, 'with a lot of love and patience'. But for Poyner, the situation, following upon Woldingham and her 'day girl' status, sharpened the point of a fact. 'It always felt like she was camping in the spare room,' she says. 'As much as they welcomed her, it was very apparent that it wasn't her family.' Under the circumstances, it is not surprising that the 'extra daughter' would want to be on her own. Says Terence, 'She was by this time quite ready to live her life.' Thanks to Tony Garnett, Boty would be able to do so – and in a manner she could never have imagined.

In 1978, Garnett undertook a wrongful death complaint, on Boty's behalf, against both the city of Beverly Hills and the hotel. 'People said, "You cannot take on the Beverly Wilshire, and you certainly can't take on the Beverly Hills Police Department,"' Garnett remembers. 'But I had a good lawyer.'

The latter came from Warren Beatty. 'He came over to London, he said, "I want to do whatever I can to right the injustice Clive suffered,"' Lynn Horsford recalls. Beatty insisted that his own representatives, the Century City-based Mitchell Silberberg & Knupp, take on the work, and in his deposition testified that Clive was on the cusp of becoming far more successful than he'd ever been, thus entitling Boty to substantial damages.

The action commenced in September 1978, and a good faith settlement with Beverly Hills (in which the hotel refused to participate) was signed by

Garnett in October 1983. 'The clincher was to be the appearance of Boty herself, defending her father's reputation,' Garnett wrote in his autobiography. 'At this point, when we were at the door of the court, both parties – or rather their insurance companies – caved in.'

The size of the settlement has proven difficult to ascertain. Per Beverly Hills, the result is clear: Boty and the city reached a sliding-scale recovery agreement, which guaranteed her $1 million, with the possibility of obtaining more from the hotel for a maximum of $1.5 million. What is missing from the record is the outcome of the Beverly Wilshire's efforts to avoid liability. Garnett's door-to-the-courtroom story may pertain to the hotel; he was, regrettably, unclear about the particulars, in his book and in conversation. Mitchell Silberberg & Knupp took the case on a contingency basis, in exchange for 40 per cent of the winnings; John Furse, Suki Dimpfl's husband, served as Boty's informal financial advisor, and remembers her receiving 'about £400,000', which suggests a million-dollar settlement. But using the payment schedule outlined by Beverly Hills, and depending on how it went with the hotel, on 12 February 1984 – her eighteenth birthday – Boty received between $600,000 and $900,000, to do with as she pleased.

At the Mitchells' urging, Boty bought a flat, from Jasper Conran – the son of Pauline's Soup Kitchen employer – at 5 Chalcot Road in Primrose Hill. (A two-bedroom triplex within a townhouse, the place was, in Abigail Thaw's formulation, 'very swish'.) 'We thought it was the best way to keep the money safe, and give her somewhere to be,' Celia explains. Boty's radical change in circumstances 'was quite unreal', Duncan says. 'A typical day was waking up late, meeting someone for lunch, maybe going shopping in the afternoon.' 'All of us were darting around, trying to see what we could do, how we are going to make our living,' says the art director Poppy Luard, then an assistant milliner. 'Whereas Boty didn't have any of that conflict. Financial independence and no parents – top combo, isn't it?'

To Thaw, her friend's sudden wealth 'was the ruin of her', the more so as 'she didn't know how to be a grown-up'. Yet Boty had inherited her parents' indispensable talent for self-invention; and, despite a beginning scarred by trauma, grief and dislocation, she used her legacy (and her windfall) to fashion a distinct, compelling character. 'I was surprised,' admits Luard, 'that she wasn't as much of a mess as you might have expected. It felt to me like she lived with confidence and relish.'

Boty cultivated a glamorous style – 'Rita Hayworth as Gilda,' the writer Tim Adler says, 'luscious red hair, a moon face, lovely full lips.' 'Incredibly well dressed, all designer clothes,' Thaw remembers. 'But also incredibly intelligent and well-informed. Very politically aware, much more than I was, and I was brought up in a very political household.' This was not quite as it sounds. As one of what John Furse calls 'Thatcher's Children', Boty participated in a paradigmatic irony of the 1980s. 'On the one hand, she would go to meetings with her accountant, trying to pay as little tax as possible,' Poyner says. 'And in the next breath she'd be railing against Thatcher and her de-nationalizing everything, while embracing the ideas of socialism.'

Boty was not without ambition, though it had yet to take form. At once intellectually and aesthetically restless, she was a woman of words and images both, uncertain as to which would, or should, prevail. 'She was torn between being a writer or an artist,' Duncan believes. 'She was brilliant at both, and so quite rightly didn't know which way to go.' Like her mother, who had a talent for verisimilitude, 'Boty was a very good fine-art painter,' remembers Chris Baylis, for a time her boyfriend. Also like Pauline, 'She was very humble about her art. I'd have to cajole her to tell me what she'd been doing.'

The 'constant need to find a way to express herself', in Poyner's formulation, drew her into a new group, one which shared Boty's interest in creativity. 'It was a circle of friends,' Adler remembers, which included himself, the production designer Gideon Ponte, and Ponte's girlfriend, illustrator/author Polly Horner, then both at Chelsea School of Art. 'We were all wanting to have careers in the arts,' Adler says, 'whether it was writing, acting or painting.'

It was also 'a great fun circle, quite wild', Baylis says. Boty has been described, not always charitably, as a party girl. Yet it might be fairer to say that she had inherited Clive's knack for scene-making. 'She would throw these champagne parties – Boty's Bollinger Binges – which would be fun for all of us,' says Luard. What everyone remembers about the Boty of Chalcot Road is joy. 'We did a lot of laughing together – masses and masses of laughter,' Terence recalls.

If Boty remained wary of being exploited, 'her most distinctive trait, once she trusted you, was generosity', says Adler. Boty's penchant for partying and open-handedness combined, in Luard's case, into a version of patronage. 'I used to make clothes for people with money,' she says. 'There'd be an endless kind of, "Oh, can you take it in a bit here, is that flattering enough right about there?" Whereas Boty just got into the fun of it. We'd come up with some sort of silly eighties big-shouldered velvet embroidered monstrosity, the more embellishment the merrier. She was glamorous in a way that was quite daring, just really leaning into what the night or the world might offer.'

And there was another inheritance: Boty shared her mother's healthy carnal appetite. 'She was very sexual, Boty, very, very sexual,' according to Thaw. 'I remember going round for dinner, and she was passing around these Polaroids of her having a threesome,' Adler says. 'Yes! Photographs and everything,' Thaw affirms. 'She loved doing that to me, so I could become this kind of prudish – "Oh, God, Boty, I *really* don't want to see that, I *don't* want to know."'

Despite her libertinism, her love of laughter and cultivation of a swinging style, 'there was a part of Boty you couldn't quite reach', says Baylis. This was manifest in one of her most remarked-upon impulses. 'She was quite compartmentalized. She would definitely hide things from different groups. It was just her way of coping, I suppose, her way of dealing with people. It goes back to that search for love and trust, which I'm not sure she ever found, really. There was that sense of searching for the mother who'd sacrificed herself. She'd sort of tried to find her, in her own way – she wanted to be bohemian. But there was a sadness to it.

'Her parents,' says Baylis, 'were at the centre of her character. Obviously they were dead. But they were still there, with her.'

Part of the lost world Boty sought to replicate involved drugs. Pauline and Clive were great consumers of marijuana, and Clive, according to one of his assistants, toyed with psychedelics. Both reflected the consciousness-raising ethos of the 1960s – as opposed to cocaine, the conscience-erasing drug of choice in Thatcher's arrogant, eat-the-poor 1980s. Boty embraced coke – a peerless killer of emotional pain, it offered, as Freud put it, 'exhilaration and lasting euphoria' – to the dismay of her straight friends, who were 'appalled', according to Adler, by what they were seeing. None objected more than Rampling. 'These kinds of drugs, it's not just harmful to you,' she says. 'There was some bank, some organization, that was making money out of people. I hated the idea of it, and I would tell Boty off frequently. She didn't seem to mind.'

Eventually, however, she did. Boty's friends – Rampling in particular – learned that questioning her drug use would earn them a brutal freezing out. Presumably this began after Boty began using heroin. 'She did, but not that much,' Baylis believes; such dabbling as there was largely involved smoking and snorting rather than needles.

And then there was California. 'When she got to LA, she took a lot more heroin than she ever did in England,' Baylis says. A likely contributing factor was the loss, in December 1987, of the last person in her life who represented stability, love and family: Veronica.

'It was nine thirty on a Saturday morning,' Boty wrote. 'I had had a party the night before in my apartment. I hadn't slept yet. I picked up the receiver and sat down in my kitchen still wearing my tight fitting dress, my black fishnet tights and black suede thigh boots. My lipstick had long worn away and my eye makeup was halfway down my cheeks. [Uncle] John told me you had died in the night, as I sat among the wine stains, the empty beer cans, cigarette butts, roaches and snorted envelopes. Among all those things that my mother had flaunted in your face and that now I would have to keep hidden from you forever.'

'She had said to me she was never going to LA,' Kate Terence relates. 'Because it killed her dad. She said, "LA will kill me." And then she decided she was going. She said, "I think it would be good for me. This is what I need."'

Boty had, by 1988, begun visiting Los Angeles, moving between London and California (with excursions to New York) before settling in LA and beginning what would prove to be her life's last act. It is surprising that she chose the city, given what Boty told Terence. But just as Pauline at Wimbledon sensed that, despite her ambition to paint, studying stained glass with Charles Carey would serve her better, so did Boty know instinctively that, foreboding aside, LA was the right choice. 'Her parents led exceptional lives, and that was a lot to live up to,' Lynn Horsford observes. 'I'm sure that was one of the reasons she went to California: to get out from under their shadow.'

She succeeded. 'When I first met her, Boty was living in some weirdly pre-old state,' Gideon Ponte remembers. 'She had the flat done up like a grown-up's, her style was kind of retro Victorian.' But in the seven-odd years between Boty's initial LA sojourn and her death, he believes, 'There was this transformation. She became much more liberated, by the drugs, by sex – I remember being excited because she'd found writing, it just felt like she was onto something.' For all of Boty's *joie de vivre*, 'her identity, when I first met her, was quite damaged', Ponte observes – 'It's all about identity, in the end, with Boty. It's just really sad that she didn't have longer to be this new version of herself. Because it was great.'

When Boty connected with the avant-garde Los Angeles gallerist Roscoe Johnson is difficult to pinpoint, but the link, surely, was Maynard Monrow. Today an artist and assistant to the noted American collector Beth Rudin DeWoody, Monrow in 1986 was living in Notting Hill and go-go dancing for the lunch crowd at a club catering to, he says, 'married men getting their jollies'. Monrow fell in with Boty's friends and was introduced to her, he recalls, sometime in 1987. Shortly thereafter, Monrow invited Johnson, whom he'd known in high school in LA's San Fernando Valley, to visit London – and when he, in turn, met Boty, says Monrow, 'the fire was lit, the kindling started to burn'.

Johnson was, by all accounts, an original. Freed from necessary work by an inheritance, 'he was easy-going in ways that not many people were', says the costume designer Nancy Steiner, who met Johnson in her late teens. 'He wasn't ambitious, he wasn't a climber, he didn't care about fame or money or any of that phony shit. He lived in the moment.'

Certainly, he was ahead of his time. When Johnson began Abstraction Gallery in 1986, in an 8,000-square-foot loft at the corner of Sixth and San Pedro streets, 'he was one of the first to run a gallery in downtown LA', says Cathy Metcalf, who helped Johnson craft the live/work space out of drywall and reclaimed plumbing fixtures. Abstraction showed off-the-radar local artists, hosted bacchanalian openings with then-unknown bands like Jane's Addiction and Red Hot Chili Peppers providing entertainment, and played host to a floating collection of subletters and arts-minded individuals who'd flop for weeks or months, Adler, Baylis and Ponte among them.

Boty, as it happened, missed the action: when she arrived in California, the gallery had folded, and Johnson was living in a house in Echo Park. But by then, she'd fallen deeply in love with him. That – as well as Monrow's suggestion that CalArts, in nearby Valencia, would be a good match for her creative ambitions and unconventional temperament, and Boty's own need to break away – conspired to shift the intercontinental back-and-forth decisively to LA.

Though she was initially more restrained observer than rowdy participant (not unlike Jean-Jacques Lebel's memory of Pauline), Johnson facilitated Boty's immersion in the city's dynamic art, music and cultural scenes. He also shared his IV heroin habit; and as their dependence deepened, it rendered the couple less social, increasingly isolated in the Echo Park house. 'They would just sort of hole up and get high,' Metcalf says. 'Heroin unchains you, the shackles come off,' Monrow believes. But he acknowledges a pattern noticed by others in Boty's crowd: she would become hooked in LA, then return to London to detox, a seesaw that continued after September 1990, when Boty began at CalArts.

The institute, then in its twentieth year, had been designed by Walt Disney and his brother, Roy, as a laboratory, one that might inspire interdisciplinary exchanges between creators of every type, overseen by faculty who encouraged the production of new ideas, forms and artistic practices. The CalArts that Boty joined was not unsimilar to the lively, experimental Royal College of Pauline's day, a significant difference being that the transformations wrought by the 1960s had embedded themselves in campus life. 'Teachers would be smoking joints in the hallway with their students,' recalls Stavros, an aspiring conceptual artist who became Boty's boyfriend (and asked that his last name not be used). 'They had these art studios in the main building, and people lived in them. Everyone was trying to do something, fix something, feel something – it was a bunch of 20-year-olds set free to do whatever they wanted.'

Boty, who gained admission as a painting student, was older than her classmates and less certain of her path. Whatever her intentions, one factor remained consistent: though she and Johnson parted ways, Boty continued to use heroin, notably with Stavros, whom she introduced to the drug. By the time Pip Rampling arrived for an extended visit in spring 1992, Boty, then living off Venice Beach, had a longstanding, intractable habit.

Among Boty's relationships, the complicated interdependence with Rampling stands out. At Sacred Heart, Rampling was head girl – 'the mother of the school', says Kitty Beamish – who stood watch over the ostracized orphan who drank spit on a dare and blubbered in a beanbag; on Chalcot Road, amidst the revels, Rampling played the unwelcome role of moralizing scold, calling Boty out on her drug use and condemning her less savoury hangers-on, even as the friendship deepened.

Venice shattered the connection. Rampling was forbidden to enter Boty's bedroom, 'which was strange, because we used to share a bed, chat through the night'; in her absence, Rampling broke the injunction, and found vomit on the floor. Boty would lock herself in the bathroom for hours at a time, unresponsive to entreaties; one afternoon, walking on the beach, she nodded out for several hours, her fearful friend seated beside her in the sand. 'I didn't know how to deal with it,' Rampling admits. 'I was actually desperate to leave, but she didn't want me to.'

After a month, Rampling could bear it no longer, and caught a flight to New Zealand to visit family. Days before, she had loaned Boty a hoodie, which she was wearing on the plane; putting her hand in the pocket, Rampling felt what she assumed was a pen and proved to be a syringe. In the course of a Honolulu stopover, she gathered her gumption (and her pocket change) and called a London friend from a pay phone.

'I said, "She needs help, we have to figure something out." And this person told someone else, who then rang Boty.' The two friends spoke, for what proved to be a final time, by phone. Claiming that Stavros was a self-injecting diabetic and the syringe was his (untrue), Boty said 'that I was misunderstanding everything – she said I didn't see what I saw', Rampling remembers. 'She was very disappointed, and upset with me.'

When Rampling returned to London, six months later, 'I was left out of everything. The general idea was that I was over-paranoid about drugs, I'd read more into it than was there.' It was an excruciating example of shooting the messenger. 'I lost the people that I was closest to,' she says, 'the Woldingham crew.' Traumatized, Rampling 'ran away to India'; apart from several brief visits, years apart, she never returned to England.

It is conceivable that, given their history, Boty had invited her friend to Venice because she knew she needed saving. And despite Boty's denials (and their outcome), Rampling's public alarm seemingly registered: that same spring, she broke, mutually, with Stavros and flew to London. This coincided with a serendipitous bit of luck: grandfather Albert's relocation to Bridget and Arthur's farm.

Following his wife's death, Albert soldiered on in Caterham until Bridget brought the ailing old man to Kent, installing him in a trailer and restoring his vigour with an unending series of Horlicks malted milk drinks. Feeling 'happy as Larry', says Bridget, Albert informed her that he was selling his house and staying on.

It fell to Albert's son John to put the Caterham bungalow on the market, distribute things of value and dispose of what was left. 'When we got there, John was taking all the accounts to the tip,' Bridget says. 'And he said, "The next few things will be Pauline's paintings"' – that is, the work that had been stored in the attic since Clive's death in 1977. 'We didn't know at the time they were worth what they were, mind you,' Bridget says. 'But John wanted to get rid of them because they were a nuisance to him. And I said, "If Katy's in America, and her mother's stuff's there, you've got to wait 'til she comes back."'

Bridget and her family loaded the paintings into a horsebox – 'a little lorry we used to carry cows around in' – and took them to the farm, storing the canvases in an unused shower room. Thus was nearly the entirety of Pauline Boty's major *oeuvre* saved from the ash heap by a farmer with a horsebox (and a conscience). 'Wonder what Pauline would think of *that* one,' Bridget says.

On a visit to see her grandfather, Boty was informed of the paintings' presence and went to have a look. When she returned, says Bridget, 'She was flummoxed – she wasn't expecting to have anything flung at her like that.' The visit coincided with David Alan Mellor's preparation for his exhibition *The Sixties Art Scene in London,* to open at the Barbican Centre the following year. Mellor's obsession with Pauline began with *Pop Goes the Easel,* and he was determined to include her work in the show – if he could find it. It was Adrian Mitchell, Mellor remembers, who tipped him off about the farm. 'And then I contacted Boty,' he says, 'because she was the key to it.'

With his colleague Barry Curtis behind the wheel, Mellor and Boty drove to the farm on what Curtis describes as an atmospherically gloomy Sunday. Opening the door to the shower room, seeing the paintings – some 15 in all – for the first time, Mellor likens to the discovery of Tutankhamun's tomb: 'That was just an overwhelming thing, seeing these treasures. I was very moved indeed.' Though Boty had encountered the pictures previously, the realization that her mother's work – and, thus, her mother – would re-enter the world affected her deeply. 'Barry and her went to the car and sat in it for a long while,' Mellor remembers. It was, Curtis says, 'very poignant'.

The paintings were transported to the Barbican, and a selection included in the exhibition – Mellor remains unclear about the precise number, but remembers the two *Man's World* canvases and *The Only Blonde in the World.* Boty attended the March 1993 opening. She was, Abigail Thaw remembers, 'very, very, very proud. She was very excited that her mother's paintings were going to have some kind of recognition. And that was part of the healing process. You know, not just this fantasy figure, but someone concrete, and *there.*'

When she returned to CalArts in autumn 1992, Boty had turned a corner. Having become friends with photography student Darcy Hemley, she asked if they might live together, in Hemley's apartment in Glendale. 'I said to her, "I'm nervous about your heroin use,"' Hemley recalls. 'And she was like, "Stav and I broke up, I'm not doing that anymore." And I trusted her, and it turned out that she wasn't [using].'

After completing a CalArts writer-in-residence fellowship, the novelist Leslie Dick had become a full-time faculty member, and Boty sought her out. 'She wanted to do an independent study with me because she was writing,' Dick says. 'She sat in my office and said, "I'd like to read you this piece." And it's very upsetting to remember, but what she wrote was the story of her father's death.' Remarkably, Dick had heard it before: her husband, the theorist and filmmaker Peter Wollen, had known Clive in London. 'She was completely taken aback, because nobody had any idea who Clive Goodwin was. So there was this immediate move out of the ordinary teacher/student relationship.

'She had this air of like, "I'm not serious about anything," but I knew that was not the whole story,' says Dick. 'What one felt was this sensitive person inside, and her trying to make the different parts of her match up.'

In 1994, Boty and Hemley moved to a house on Electric Avenue in Venice, taking Denise Prince, a CalArts alumnus, as a roommate. If Glendale was 'a depressing time, she had just broken up, just quit drugs,' says Hemley, in Venice, 'she seemed brighter, happier, more positive. Once she started writing, she got a spark, because she could see the progress. Also she started kind of exercising. She'd be like, "Yeah, I had a salad and a smoothie and took a walk, and now I'm like all California." I think she loved the beauty of Los Angeles. I never got the sense that she missed England.'

Boty's writing, Leslie Dick recalls, grew from strength to strength. 'I felt she was struggling with the problem of there being an ideal she couldn't live up to,' Dick says. 'Her mom, her grandmother, her dad – each one was dead, and each represented a standard of fulfilment.'

The effort paid off: the CalArts Critical Studies department had recently added an MFA in Creative Writing, and Boty was accepted into the programme, to begin in January 1996. Despite her not inconsiderable means, she received a full scholarship – an acceptance, based entirely on her abilities, which was especially sweet. All that remained was the completion of her undergraduate degree, an event for which Boty had big plans.

To graduate, CalArts requires that each student present an exhibition in one of the institute's galleries, located in the same building as the individual studios. As a writer, Boty's offering would differ from those of the visual artists: she proposed to read a piece about her childhood, focused on her grandmother – Veronica's frustration and grief about Pauline, and her desire to transform her granddaughter into the perfect child of her fantasies. Boty decided to 'set-design' her gallery, using screen-printed wallpaper featuring significant images from her personal history; to execute the work, she enlisted two English friends, decorative artists then working in LA. One was Olivia Raeburn, whom she'd met while at the Mitchells'. The other, surprisingly, was Kitty Beamish, who'd rejected Boty's best-friend overtures at Woldingham.

However difficult their relationship, like everyone present for the occasion – Thursday, 10 November 1995 – Beamish found herself captivated. Boty, who'd cut her hair short and gone platinum blonde in recent months, returned it to a deep red for the reading, augmented with dark nail varnish and lipstick. The 40-odd people squeezed into the gallery – students, faculty, friends – were struck by Boty's confidence and clarity, her presentation's dark power, most of all by the bravery of what she'd written. Boty Goodwin – who had concealed much behind her frivolity, her secrecy, her profound sadness and impenetrable solitude – surprised them all. Afterwards, many remarked upon something she read towards the end. As was the entire piece, it was addressed to Veronica:

I used to fantasize about dying. I wanted you at my funeral. I wanted everyone there, in pain and confusion, devastated with grief. I liked that idea. That was revenge. Nobody knew why or how I'd died. There was no note. That would have been too easy.

The building's six galleries held concurrent presentations, and the evening ended in celebration, with half a dozen overlapping after-parties. Boty catered her own with good food and drink, happy to lift a glass to a job well done, a life transformed. Darcy Huebler, a teacher with whom Boty had become friends, remembers them chatting about her acceptance into the MFA programme. 'She was incredibly excited,' Huebler says. 'Going on as a graduate student was really important to her, so she was thrilled to have passed that hurdle.'

Boty Goodwin's is not the story of an addict – addiction is never the whole story of anyone's life, and especially not this one – yet drugs, inescapably, lie at its heart. Having been clean for months, it was with drugs that Boty chose, that night, to reward herself: doing coke, smoking a bit of heroin, as the hour grew late. Though Boty encouraged her friends to stay, gradually they peeled off, with congratulations, regrets and, in one case, ambivalence. 'I kissed her goodbye, but I got this kind of betrayal feeling that I always had with her,' Beamish says. 'She looked at me like, "Why are you leaving me?"'

It is a long drive from Valencia to Venice, and her friends cautioned her to sleep in her studio: the wine was flowing, and Boty was a notoriously bad driver. She could party on and go home the next day. And so she did: at some point, Boty excused herself, returned to her studio, and locked the door.

Her body was discovered on Sunday morning, almost 18 years to the day after Clive's death. According to the autopsy report, 'drug paraphernalia was found next to the decedent'. Darcy Hemley and Denise Prince were not at first concerned when Boty failed to return, but after another day and a night, they reached out. Campus security broke into the studio; the sheriff was called. Darcy Huebler identified the body from a Polaroid. The Mitchells flew over to collect Boty's belongings – Adrian anguished, Celia stoic. Such was Boty's ability to compartmentalize that they had no idea she'd ever used drugs. Leslie Dick saw to Boty's cremation at Forest Lawn, and shipped her ashes to England.

'She loved to laugh, she loved intellectual challenges, she loved expressing herself,' Kate Terence reflects. 'But I never got the feeling, ever, really, that Boty absolutely adored life. Which is why none of us will ever quite work out whether she fancied a fabulous time on heroin for having done so well. Or she thought, "Right – it can't get any better than this."'

Leslie Dick remains a strong proponent of the latter. 'What I felt was that the death of her mother, and then her father, had been a cliff that hung over her life and cast this incredible shadow,' she says. 'It was as if some part of her said, "You're not allowed to have your show, and an audience of people clapping for you, knowing you're going to go on and have a life." And that's tragic.'

Most of Boty's friends, however, posit a less dramatic, more likely explanation: that after an extended period of abstinence, she was unused to a hard drug, and her system couldn't handle it. She rolled the dice, and came up snake eyes.

'She called me that night, because she'd done so well,' Abigail Thaw recalls. 'That's what was so awful about it. I'd never known her so in herself, so proud, for the first time, really proud of the work she had done. I just thought, "You stupid girl. You stupid, stupid, stupid girl."'

Boty's CalArts friends planted a sapling on campus as a living memorial. No plaque explains it, but there is a sly connection, one that, surely, she would have appreciated. It is the traditional 'tree of awakening' – the Bodhi tree.

The Boty/Goodwin family story, which began in the 1930s, came to its conclusion six decades later, with the burial of Boty's ashes at Redstone Cemetery in Redhill, a short distance from Croydon, Pauline's birthplace. 'That was an awful day, an awful, snowy day,' says Tim Adler. 'They had this headstone, and it said KATY GOODWIN. I never knew that her name was Katy. And out stepped these perfectly normal people, saying they were Boty's uncle and aunt. She had never spoken of them, never spoken about her living family. So for them to step forward now and take possession – it felt like the end of *The Great Gatsby*, when the father steps forward. Boty had been this fabulous, larger-than-life, vivacious character, and for it all to end here was so wrong.'

Like many of Boty's friends, Adler still feels the loss. 'I miss her terribly,' he says. 'I miss growing old with her. I miss her thoughts about what the world is like now. That's what I miss. I think she would have made a fabulous mother, I think she would have been a great old lady. She was so full of life.'

At least there will be something left of me, for you and the others to remember when I'm gone.

Of Pauline, Natalie Gibson said, 'You just felt she'd done so much more than most people in her lifetime. She'd sort of done everything.' A half-century after Pauline's death, Gideon Ponte made a similar observation about Boty: 'Even though she lost her life doing it, she became closer to the person she wanted to be than if she'd stayed in London and never risked it all. Maybe that makes it not for nothing.'

Pondering what makes a life 'not for nothing', one is reminded of another of Ponte's observations: that it was, for Boty, all about identity. This was, of course, no less true of Pauline and Clive – who, roaring forward, refused to accept their assigned roles, the dreary lives decreed by class and circumstance, and claimed the selves they desired. Considering the accomplishments of Pauline, Clive and Boty, one is most struck, not by what they did, but rather that it was the self-determination of identity that enabled them to do it. For the note of triumph in this 'Greek tragedy', let us paraphrase another tragic figure, Macbeth: upon their bank and shoal of time, they jumped the life to come.

To have the courage to claim oneself, no matter the cost: that legacy remains in the world.

Boty Goodwin,
1990.

INDEX

ACKNOWLEDGEMENTS

I worked on this book for eight and a half years before I found a publisher. In that time, I received a number of rejections, in the US and UK, mostly on the grounds that Pauline Boty was too obscure a subject to merit a biography. (A few felt that she didn't deserve one.) In fact, Philip Cooper himself turned the book down in 2019, because he wasn't in a position to publish it; but when we met again in 2022, his circumstances had changed, and he accepted the manuscript wholeheartedly. Thank you, Philip. I shall always be grateful to you for believing in the value and importance of Pauline's life and art.

As the representative of the Boty estate, Adrian Mibus, director of Whitford Fine Art – who in 1993, in collaboration with James Mayor of The Mayor Gallery, presented the first comprehensive offering of the artist's work – generously granted permission to publish Pauline's artworks and essays (and Boty Goodwin's writings as well) and provided Frances Lincoln with many of the images found herein. Adrian is an art patron of great passion and conviction, and has for decades been Pauline's unshakable champion. My gratitude to Adrian, and to his gracious and able associates, cannot be overstated.

Emily Nemens, who edited the manuscript, encouraged me to go further in certain places and to hold back in others; she challenged the lucidity of my thinking, the accuracy of my language, my ways and means of expression, my punctuation and my syntax; and, from the first word to the last, she kept me honest. In a half-century of writing, no editor has made so indispensable a contribution to my work, and I hope someday to repeat the adventure.

At the centre of this book lie the conversations and communications I had with those who knew Pauline, Clive and Boty, or took an interest in their stories, and who were exceptionally forthcoming with their memories, observations, emotions and advice: Charlotte Adler, Timothy Adler, Sally Alexander, Tariq Ali, Philippe Axell, Richard Bawden, Chris Baylis, Ken Baynes, Kitty Beamish, Warren Beatty, Gwyneth Berman, Celia Birtwell, Peter Blake, Derek Boshier, Bridget Boty, Fiona Boty, Ray Bradley, Patricia Britton, Charles Carey, Caroline Coon, Tom Courtenay, Barry Curtis, Leslie Dick, Suki Dimpfl, Rosalyn Drexler, Stephanie Duncan, Nell Dunn, Robert Fox, Stephen Frears, John Furse, Nicholas Garland, Natalie Gibson, Tom Glover, Tony Garnett, Christopher Gregory, Philip Harrison, Jann Haworth, Warwick Hembry, Darcy Hemley, Rosemary Hill, Ben Hilton, Richard Hollis, Lynn Horsford, Darcy Huebler, Allen Jones, Phil Kelvin, George Keskeny, Jean-Jacques Lebel, Hal Lieberman, Michael Lindsay-Hogg, Marco Livingstone, Ken Loach, Elizabeth Luard, Poppy Luard, Charles Mapleston, Penny Massot, Margaret Matheson, Roddy Maude-Roxby, Nancy Meckler, David Alan Mellor, Cathy Metcalf, Adrian Mibus, Kalliopi Minioudaki, Celia Mitchell, Maynard Monrow, Simon Murgatroyd, Gerald Nason, Andy Neill, Brian Newman, Paula Nightingale, Melissa North, Neil Parkinson, Stella Penrose, Michelle Plochere, Gideon Ponte, Kate Poyner, Olivia Raeburn, Pip Rampling, Frederic Raphael, Geoffrey Reeve, Lane Relyea, Terry Riggs, Gordon Rogoff, Sheila Rowbotham, Philip Saville, Sebastian Saville, Caroline Seebohm, Eileen Shaw, Allan Scott, Adam Smith, Roger Smith, Nancy Steiner, Rochelle Stevens, Kate Terence, Abigail Thaw, Kenith Trodd, Sally Tuffin, Matthew Tynan, Roxana Tynan, Tracy Tynan, Fay Weldon, William Wilkins and Nicola Wood.

Various institutions and collections opened their doors to me, immeasurably enriching my knowledge of Pauline and her world. I am indebted to the Women's Art Library at Goldsmiths, University of London, and its director, Althea Greenan; the Royal College of Art, and Neil Parkinson, the RCA's Archives & Collections Manager; the Wolverhampton Art Gallery, and Collections Assistant Clare Marlow; the National Arts Education Archive at The Yorkshire Sculpture Park, and archivists Roger Standen and Anita Cormac OBE (Anti-Ugly Action material used with the permission of Krysia Brochoka-Baynes); the BBC Written Archive Centre; and the British Library.

It is my pleasure to acknowledge the generosity of Philippe Axell; Peter and Chrissy Blake, and the artist's gallery, Waddington Custot; Bridget Boty; Mila Askarova, George Lionel Barker and Anastasia Shapovalova, of Gazelli Art House; Natalie Gibson; Roddy Maude-Roxby; Geoffrey Reeve; Gordon Rogoff; Tom Thompson, of ETT Imprint; and Andrzej Wroblewski, all of whom supplied me with essential visual materials and granted permission to include them.

I have quoted at length from previously published materials, and wish to express my thanks to the authors, editors and executors who permitted me to do so: Nell Dunn, *Talking to Women;* Christopher Frayling, *The Royal College of Art*; Rosemary Hill, on behalf of Christopher Logue, *Prince Charming*, and Gavin Stamp, *Anti-Ugly Action: An Episode in the History of British Modernism* (article, included in *AA Files 70*); Emily Lees, of the Paul Mellon Centre, on behalf of Lisa Tickner, *London's New Scene*; Marco Livingstone, *Pop Art: A Continuing History*; Anne Massey, *The Independent Group*; Kalliopi Minioudaki, *Pop Proto-Feminism: Beyond the Paradox of the Woman Pop Artist* (essay, included in *Seductive Subversion: Women Pop Artists, 1958-1968)*; Sheila Rowbotham, *Promise of a Dream;* Sue Tate, *Pauline Boty: Pop Artist and Woman;* and Matthew, Roxana and Tracy Tynan, for *The Life of Kenneth Tynan*, by Kathleen Tynan, and *The Diaries of Kenneth Tynan*.

I owe a very special debt of gratitude to Maria Smith, for permitting me to quote from her late husband Adam's unpublished biography of Pauline, *Now You See Her,* which preceded this volume by several decades. A lively and meticulously researched exploration of the artist's life and the worlds in which she lived, the book is both an irreplaceable resource and, for anyone interested in Pauline, Clive and Boty, essential reading.

I was helped in my research by Christopher Gregory, whose website, paulineboty.org, amounts to an online catalogue raisonné of the artist's works; the writer Tom Glover, who shared with me contacts and information derived from his own research into Pauline's lost painting *Scandal '63;* and my dear friend of many decades, Marjorie Ornston, for her research into the legal actions arising from Clive Goodwin's death in Los Angeles.

At Frances Lincoln, I benefitted from the patience, sensitivity, good humor and hard work of my editor, Charlotte Frost, and the sharp eye of my copy editor, Daniela Nava, who uncovered many shocking errors of fact.

Finally, I wish to acknowledge Michael Lindsay-Hogg, Norman Mailer and Gay Talese for their generosity, support and encouragement, and for their example, which remains, every day, an inspiration.

PICTURE CREDITS

Quarto

First published in 2023 by Frances Lincoln Publishing
an imprint of The Quarto Group.
One Triptych Place, London, SE1 9SH
United Kingdom
T (0)20 7700 6700
www.Quarto.com

A catalogue record for this book is available from the British Library.

ISBN 978-0-7112-8754-9
EBOOK ISBN 978-0-7112-8755-6

10 9 8 7 6 5 4 3 2 1

Design by Clare Newsam

Printed in China